# Learn
# Microsoft
# Visual Basic 6.0
# Now

**Michael Halvorson**

PUBLISHED BY
Microsoft Press
A Division of Microsoft Corporation
One Microsoft Way
Redmond, Washington 98052-6399

Library of Congress Cataloging-in-Publication Data
Halvorson, Michael.
    Learn Microsoft Visual Basic 6.0 Now / Michael Halvorson.
       p.  cm.
    ISBN 0-7356-0729-X
    1. Microsoft Visual Basic   2.  BASIC (Computer program language).
    I. Microsoft press.   II.  Title.
    QA76.73.B3H3355   1999
    005.26'8--dc21                    99-21357
                                    CIP

Printed and bound in the United States of America.

1 2 3 4 5 6 7 8 9   QMQM    4 3 2 1 0 9

Distributed in Canada by ITP Nelson, a division of Thomson Canada Limited.

A CIP catalogue record for this book is available from the British Library.

Microsoft Press books are available through booksellers and distributors worldwide. For further information about international editions, contact your local Microsoft Corporation office or contact Microsoft Press International directly at fax (425) 936-7329. Visit our Web site at mspress.microsoft.com.

**Acquisitions Editor:** Eric Stroo
**Project Editor:** John Pierce
**Technical Editor:** Don Lesser for Pioneer Training, Inc.
**Project Manager:** Peter Whitmer for nSight, Inc.

# CONTENTS *at a glance*

PART **5** ## Advanced Techniques

# TABLE OF CONTENTS

# Introduction

Microsoft Visual Basic is one of the hottest programming languages in the
world. As of early 1999, the Visual Basic software development community is over 3.5 million members strong, and the chorus grows daily. Students, managers, and technical employees use Visual Basic to learn how
to write practical, Windows-based programs; business professionals use
Visual Basic to write macros in their Microsoft Office applications; and
experienced software developers use Visual Basic to build powerful, commercial applications and corporate productivity tools.

Whether you fit into one of these categories or you're just curious about
Visual Basic programming, this self-paced book-and-software package is
the learning system for you. *Learn Visual Basic Now* contains a real,
working version of Microsoft Visual Basic 6, which you can use to write
useful and interesting applications for the Microsoft Windows operating
system.

This course introduces programming concepts one at a time—starting at
the *beginning*—and reinforces them with step-by-step exercises, practice
files, and in-depth explanations. A specially prepared compact disc containing a working model of the Visual Basic 6 Development System plus
all the sample applications and practice files in the book is included to
jump-start your programming efforts. In the "Installing the Software"

section of this Introduction you'll find instructions for copying the software and practice files to your computer's hard disk.

---

**OTE**  This book includes 19 lessons from the popular book *Microsoft Visual Basic Professional 6.0 Step by Step* (Microsoft Press, 1998) and a CD-ROM featuring a special working model of the Visual Basic 6.0 Professional Edition software. You don't need to buy Visual Basic to use this book.

---

# Have You Written Programs Before?

This book is designed both for new programmers who are learning Visual Basic and for experienced programmers who are moving to Visual Basic from another programming environment, such as an earlier version of BASIC, Visual Basic for Applications, Microsoft Visual C++, or Microsoft Visual Java++. The readers who will benefit most from this book are application and database users who have had previous experience with Microsoft Windows and Windows-based applications, such as Microsoft Word, Microsoft Excel, and Microsoft Access. The graphics applications you'll create in this book will look similar to those available with these products. If you want to create applications and utilities that make Windows 98 and Windows-based applications easier to use, you're in the right place.

As you work through this book, you'll learn the features of Visual Basic by using the Visual Basic 6 Working Model, a product that is identical to Visual Basic 6 Professional Edition except that you cannot create executable (.exe) files and a few features are disabled. (A few ActiveX controls are not included, and you cannot use the DHTML Page Designer, the Data Environment Designer, or online Help.) The Visual Basic product team hopes that you will like Visual Basic programming enough to upgrade to one of the full retail editions of Visual Basic (see the sidebar below). So please do buy Visual Basic if you read this book and then want to create programs that you can distribute to your friends, coworkers, or business customers. But don't run off with your checkbook until you see what this impressive working model can do. You'll find it has enough power to handle many useful tasks for you right now, as the sample programs demonstrate.

> ### Different Versions of Visual Basic
>
> Visual Basic 6 is sold in three versions: Learning Edition, Professional Edition, and Enterprise Edition. All three versions of Visual Basic have the same base set of features, so the exercises in this book apply equally to all three products. Visual Basic Learning Edition is the foundation product. It has full support for 32-bit programming under Windows 98 and Windows NT. Visual Basic Professional Edition includes additional features related to creating IIS and DHTML applications, database programming, creating OLE Automation servers, and enhanced data binding. It also includes a larger collection of Windows metafiles and bit maps, which you can use to add colorful artwork to your programs. Visual Basic Enterprise Edition is the high-end, client-server version of Visual Basic. It includes all the features of Professional Edition plus special components that support team development, remote automation, and Visual Database tools integration.
>
> Visual Basic also appears in several Microsoft applications, including Word, Excel, Access, Microsoft PowerPoint, and Microsoft Project. So if you plan to write macros in your Microsoft Office applications, the training you receive here will help you do productive work now and in the future.

## How This Book Is Organized

This book is divided into five major parts, each containing several related lessons. Part 1 introduces you to the Visual Basic programming environment and teaches you how to create a functional user interface by creating objects, setting properties, and writing program code. Part 2 discusses how to build Visual Basic program statements, with an emphasis on variables and operators, decision structures, and debugging. Part 3 covers how to add printer support, error handling, artwork, and animation to a user interface. Part 4 discusses different ways to manage data in a diverse workgroup or corporation, including reusing code with modules and procedures, managing data with collections and arrays, processing text files with string processing techniques and encryption, working with Access databases, and using Automation to call the commands in Microsoft Office applications. Finally, Part 5 covers advanced programming techniques and tools, including "professional" ActiveX controls, Internet programming fundamentals, and advanced database management.

Start by reading "Installing the Software," the next major section in the Introduction, and follow the instructions for installing Visual Basic and the practice files. Then find where you fit in the following table to determine where to start in the main body of the book.

| If you are | Follow these steps |
| --- | --- |
| New to Visual Basic and new to programming | Be sure to read "How to Think Like a Programmer," later in the Introduction. Then work through the lessons in order, starting with Lesson 1. |
| Experienced with Visual Basic for Applications | Work through the lessons in Part 1, skim the lessons in Part 2, and work through the lessons in Parts 3-5. |
| Experienced with QuickBasic or MS-DOS Qbasic | Work through the lessons in Part 1, skim the lessons in Part 2, and work through the lessons in Parts 3-5. |
| Experienced with Visual C++ or Visual J++ | Skim through the lessons in Parts 1 and 2, and then work through the lessons in Parts 3-5. For specific information about creating a user interface by using Visual Basic, read Lessons 2-4, 8-9, and 16. |

Before you start the lessons, you should take a look at the terms and conventions I'll use throughout the book.

## Typographic Conventions

- Characters for you to type appear in **boldface**.
- New terms and the titles of books appear in *italic*.

- Names of keyboard keys for you to press appear in Initial Capitals.

- Program code appears in monospace type:

  ```
  Label1.Caption = "Welcome!"
  ```

- In syntax statements, which are generic program statements that show you the structure of program code, placeholders appear in monospace italic type:

  ```
  Print expression
  ```

- Here, when you created a real program, you would replace *expression* with a real expression.

- Optional parts of syntax statements appear inside square brackets:

  ```
  Dim variable [As type]
  ```

## Procedural Conventions

- Numbered lists (1, 2, 3, and so on) indicate steps you should follow.

- A arrow bullet (→) indicates a single task for you to do.

## Other Features of This Book

*Open Project*

- You can perform many operations in Visual Basic by clicking a button on the toolbar or a control in the toolbox. When the instructions in this book tell you to click a toolbar button or a toolbox control, a picture of the button or control will usually be shown in the left margin of the book, next to the instructions. The Open Project button in the margin next to this paragraph is an example.

- Screen capture illustrations show sample user interfaces and the results of your completed steps.

- Notes labeled "TIP", "NOTE", and "IMPORTANT" alert you to additional information or alternative methods for a step that you should consider before continuing with the lesson.

■ Sidebars introduce special programming techniques, background information, or features related to the information being discussed.

■ You can continue exploring the techniques you have learned by following the instructions in special sections entitled "If You Want To Boost Your Productivity," near the end of select lessons. These programs give you a chance to experiment with the new skills you've explored in the context of more sophisticated utilities. (See the C:\LearnVb6\Extras folder on your hard disk for a list of these projects.)

## Installing the Software Using the Practice Files Disk

The CD attached to the inside of the back cover of this book contains the Visual Basic Working Model software and the practice files that you'll use as you work through the lessons in this book. Some of the practice files on the disk are partially completed programming projects that you'll work on to learn programming techniques. Other files are the finished results of the projects in the book, for your reference.

In the following exercise, you'll install the Working Model software and practice files on your hard disk. Install the practice files in the default installation folder (C:\LearnVb6), if possible, so that your installation matches that shown in the lessons in this book. Your Visual Basic software will be installed in a folder on your hard disk named C:\Program Files\Microsoft Visual Studio\Vb98.

**NOTE** In the instructions and exercises in this book, it is assumed that your Step by Step practice files are installed in the default C:\LearnVb6 folder on your hard disk. If your practice files are not in this folder, adjust the pathnames for the practice files as necessary when you work through the exercises in the book.

## Installing the Visual Basic Software and Practice Files

Follow these steps to copy the Working Model software and practice files to your computer's hard disk so that you can complete the lessons.

1. Start Microsoft Windows.

2. Remove the CD-ROM from the package inside the back cover of this book.

3. Insert the CD-ROM into your CD-ROM drive.

4. On the taskbar at the bottom of your screen, click the Start button, and then click Run. The Run dialog box appears.

5. In the Run box, type **d:\vb\setup.exe** and then click OK. Don't add spaces as you type. (If your CD-ROM is associated with a different drive letter, such as e, type it instead.)

6. Follow the instructions on screen.

   The Visual Basic Setup program appears with recommended options preselected for you. Specify a Custom installation and select all options if you want to copy all of the Visual Basic program features to your hard disk. The Working Model requires a minimum of 50 MB of disk space.

> **TIP** Specify the Graphics option if you want to install approximately 3MB of icons, cursors, metafiles, bitmaps, and video clips in the \Program Files \Microsoft Visual Studio\Common\Graphics folder. These extra graphics files are fun to work with and you'll have plenty of opportunity to use them in this book.

When the Visual Basic Setup program is finished, you should install the Learn Visual Basic Now practice files. Follow these steps:

7. Click the Start button, and then click Run.

8. In the Run box, type **d:\setup**, and then click OK.

9. Follow the instructions on the screen. (Be sure to accept the installation defaults to place your practice files in the proper location.)

10. When both installation programs have finished, remove the CD-ROM from your computer and replace it in the package inside the back cover of the book.

If you run one or both installation programs in the future, Setup will enter Maintenance Mode, which allows you to add or remove individual components (or the entire installation) from your system.

---

**IMPORTANT** In addition to installing the practice files, the Learn Visual Basic Now Setup program created a shortcut to the Microsoft Press World Wide Web site on your desktop. If your computer is set up to connect to the Internet, you can double-click the shortcut to visit the Microsoft Press Web site. You can also connect to the Web site directly at *http://mspress.microsoft.com/*.

---

# Thinking Like a Programmer

If you haven't written a program before, you might be wondering just what a program is and how you go about creating one in Visual Basic. This section provides an overview of the programming process.

A *program* is a set of instructions that collectively cause a computer to perform a useful task, such as processing electronic artwork or managing files on a network. A program can be a tiny utility, such as a program that calculates a home mortgage, or it can be a large application program, such as Microsoft Excel or an Internet browser. A *Visual Basic program* is an application written specifically for Windows or Windows NT using the Visual Basic Development System. To write a Visual Basic program, you determine what you want your program to do, design the screen—or *user interface*—for the program, and then build the program by using Visual Basic. Let's examine each of these steps in detail.

## Planning the Program

The first step in programming is determining exactly what you want your program to accomplish. This sounds simple (isn't it obvious?), but without a mission statement even the best programmer can have trouble building an application he or she is happy with. Planning a program is a little like planning a barbecue. For a barbecue to go off smoothly, you need to prepare for it ahead of time. You need to organize the menu, invite your friends, buy the food, and (most likely) clean your house. Although a barbecue can be entertaining if friends just happen to drop by and bring stuff, programs usually don't turn out the best if they're built with the "stone soup" mentality.

When you're learning to program, you should spend some time thinking about the programming problem you are trying to solve well before you sit down in front of your computer. Up-front planning will save you development time down the road, and you'll probably be much happier with the result. One part of planning might be creating an ordered list of programming steps called an *algorithm*. An algorithm for a barbecue might look like this:

> **Mission:** Barbecue next Saturday!
>
> **Planning:**
> - Decide on menu (burgers!)
> - Send invitations
> - Clean house
> - Mow lawn
>
> **Day of barbecue:**
> - Buy food
> - Light grill
> - Prepare food
> - Volleyball?
>
> **Afterward:**
> - Clean up

## Designing the User Interface

After you have established a clear goal for your program, it's important to think generally about how your program will look and how it will process information. The complete set of screens and images used in a program is called the program's *user interface*. The user interface includes all the menus, dialog boxes, buttons, objects, and pictures that users see while they operate the application. The Visual Basic Programming System lets you create all the components of a professional Windows-based application quickly and efficiently. Several of these elements are visible in the following Windows program, which I created by using Visual Basic:

If you're familiar with Windows-based applications, you'll recognize most of the user interface elements. *Menus* contain many of the *commands* available in a Windows-based application; *dialog boxes, buttons,* and the *mouse pointer* help the user supply information to the program; and *windows* and *scroll bars* allow the user to view and navigate information displayed on the screen. To maximize the usability of your Visual Basic program, it is important that you use the Windows user interface elements in a standard and predictable way. Microsoft has published a set of design guidelines for Windows-based applications, and you'll learn about the most important interface guidelines as you read this book. Because most Windows-based applications are used by people other than the original programmer, it is important that you design them so that they have as many familiar features as possible.

### Ask yourself questions

When you plan Visual Basic programming projects, you might find it useful to draw a rough sketch of the user interface you'd like to present to your users. Doing this will not only help you design the interface, it will also help you think about how your program should work. It might be useful to ask yourself the following questions about your program:

- What is the goal, or mission, of the program I am writing?

- Who will use the program?

- What will the program look like when it starts?

- What information will the user enter in the program?

- How will the program process the input?

- What information (output) will the program produce?

Even before you know *how* the program will do what you want it to, you should have a good idea of *what* it should do and how it should look. After you have finished this preliminary work, you're ready to start building the program by using Visual Basic.

 **TIP** Lessons 2 and 3 discuss how to build an effective user interface.

## Building a Program by Using Visual Basic

Building a Visual Basic program involves three programming steps:

1. Creating the user interface by using Visual Basic controls.

2. Setting the characteristics, or *properties,* of elements in the user interface, as needed.

3. Writing the program code for one or more user interface elements, as needed.

Creating a Visual Basic program for Windows is surprisingly easy, as you'll see in Lesson 2. If you've used a drawing program such as Microsoft Paint, you have many of the skills you need to create an effective user interface. To build the interface elements, you click an interface control in the Visual Basic toolbox, and then you "draw" the user interface element by dragging and clicking with the mouse. This is usually a simple matter of clicking to position one corner of the element and then dragging to create a rectangle that's the size you want. After you create the element—a text box, for example—you can refine it by setting properties for the element. For a text box, you can set properties to make text in the text box boldface, italic, or underlined, for example.

You complete your program by typing code for one or more user interface elements in a special window called the Code window. Writing program code gives you more control over how your program works than you can get by using the design controls alone. By using program code, you completely express your thoughts about how your application will process data, input, and output. The Visual Basic programming language contains several hundred statements, functions, and special characters, but most of your programming tasks will be handled by a few dozen easy-to-remember keywords. The Visual Basic programming language is not unique to the Visual Basic software you're using; Visual Basic for Applications is included in Word, Excel, Access, PowerPoint, Project, and other applications for Windows. If you've used the most recent version of one of these applications, or if you've had some experience with Basic in the past, you'll recognize most of the keywords, statements, and functions in Visual Basic 6.

> **NOTE**  The rules governing the structure and content of the Visual Basic programming language are called its *syntax*. The word *syntax* comes from the Greek verb *syntattein*, which means to draw up an army in an orderly way. When you write Visual Basic program code, you will be marshaling keywords for the compiler.

## The Origins of Basic

The original Basic language was created by John G. Kemeny and Thomas E. Kurtz in 1963 at Dartmouth College. It quickly became popular as a teaching language in universities and schools and was adapted for use on personal computers by Bill Gates in the mid-1970s. Since those early days there have been several updated versions of Basic created for personal computers, including Microsoft QuickBasic and MS-DOS QBasic. Although Visual Basic's fully graphical development environment and programming language are a far cry from the early Basic interpreters, the elegance and simplicity of the original Basic has, to a great extent, remained in the language. Visual Basic's power and ease of use are the primary reasons it was chosen as the programming language for Windows applications such as Excel.

## Testing, Compiling, and Distributing the Program

 **TIP** The complete programming process is often called the software development life cycle.

After you create a working version of your program, you need to test it carefully to verify that it is working correctly. If you wish to distribute your program, you also need to compile it into an executable program (that is, a stand-alone Windows program), and give it to your users. This isn't a step you can complete with the Visual Basic Working Model (you can only compile with the Learning, Professional, or Enterprise Editions), but I include this final step now to give you the complete picture of the process. If you decide to revise the program later, you repeat each of these steps, beginning with planning and an analysis of any new goals. These steps complete the software development life cycle, which is illustrated in the diagram at the top of the next page.

### Testing the program

Testing a program involves checking it against a variety of real-life operating conditions to determine whether it's working correctly. A problem that stops the program from running or from producing the expected results is called a software defect, or *bug*. If you've used software for any length of time, you've probably run into your share of computer glitches caused by faulty software. Now that *you* are the programmer, it's your job to stamp out these problems *before* they reach the end user. Fortunately for all of us, Visual Basic provides some excellent debugging tools to catch bugs. You'll learn how to find and correct bugs in Lesson 6.

### Compiling the program

When you've finished creating and testing your program, you can compile it into an executable (.exe) file that will run under Windows 98 or Windows NT. Creating an executable file with a retail version of Visual Basic is as simple as clicking the Make Project1.exe command on the File menu. The Visual Basic Working Model included with this book also lets you run Visual Basic programs, but you must run them from within the Visual Basic programming environment, not as stand-alone application programs. If creating executable (.exe) programs is important to you, you must purchase one of the retail versions of Visual Basic.

### Distributing the program

If you want to share a Visual Basic executable file with friends or colleagues, or if you want to sell your program, you'll need to put the program and a few necessary support files on a disk (or the network), where your users or customers can get at them. All Visual Basic programs require one or more dynamic-link library (DLL) files in order to run, so you'll need to copy the necessary files from your hard disk to a distribution disk to get your users up and running. The exact DLL files needed depend on the operating system your users are running and the Visual Basic features used by your program. (The Package & Deployment Wizard, included in the Microsoft Visual Basic 6.0 Tools folder, manages this process.)

If you plan to distribute software commercially, you'll need to upgrade to a retail version of Visual Basic. The documentation and Help files that come with the retail products describes how to build your distribution disks and create a custom setup program that will install your software. For now, be assured that when you create Visual Basic programs, you and your users will immediately be able to enjoy the benefits of the new software.

Let's get started!

PART 1

# Getting Started with Visual Basic

# Opening and Running a Visual Basic Program

Microsoft Visual Basic's ability to perform some impressive tasks rests on key fundamentals we'll cover carefully in the first part of this book. After a few lessons, you'll see that it's easy to use Visual Basic to write powerful Microsoft Windows–based programs. Even if you haven't written a program before, you'll find that programming uses many of the same reasoning abilities and computer skills you use every day. In this lesson, you'll learn how to start Visual Basic and how to use the Visual Basic Programming System to open and run a simple program. You'll learn the essential Visual Basic menu commands and programming procedures; you'll open and run a simple Visual Basic program called StepUp; and you'll get your feet wet by changing a programming setting called a property. You'll also learn how to exit Visual Basic.

# The Visual Basic Programming Environment

The Visual Basic programming environment contains all the tools you need to build powerful programs for Windows quickly and efficiently. Use the following procedures to start Visual Basic now.

---

 **IMPORTANT** If you haven't yet installed the Visual Basic Working Model and the book's practice files, follow the instructions in the Introduction to this book. Then return to this lesson.

---

## Start Visual Basic

1. In Microsoft Windows, click the Start button, point to Programs, and point to the Microsoft Visual Basic 6.0 folder. The icons in the Microsoft Visual Basic 6.0 folder (a folder and an application icon) appear in a list.

---

**TIP** The exercises in this book are specifically designed to be completed with the Visual Basic Working model, but you can also use a retail copy of the Visual Basic 6.0 Development System (Learning Edition, Professional Edition, or Enterprise Edition). If your copy of Visual Basic is part of the Microsoft Visual Studio suite of development tools, point to the Microsoft Visual Studio folder to display the Visual Basic program icon.

---

2. Click the Microsoft Visual Basic program icon.

   The New Project dialog box appears. This dialog box prompts you for the type of programming project you want to create. (The exact contents of the dialog box depend on the edition of Visual Basic that you're using.)

3. Click Open to accept the default new project.

   A new project opens in the Visual Basic programming environment, along with some of the windows and tools shown in the illustration on the following page.

The Visual Basic programming environment contains programming tools to help you construct your Visual Basic programs. The *menu bar* provides access to most of the commands that control the programming environment. Menus and commands work as they do in all Windows-based programs, and you can access them by using the keyboard or the mouse. Located below the menu bar is the *toolbar,* a collection of buttons that serve as shortcuts for executing commands and controlling the Visual Basic programming environment. If you've used Microsoft Excel or Microsoft Word, the toolbar should be a familiar concept. To activate a button on the toolbar, click the button using the mouse. Along the bottom of the screen is the Windows *taskbar.* You can use the taskbar to switch between various Visual Basic components and to activate other Windows-based programs. You may also see a taskbar icon for Microsoft Internet Explorer or another Internet browser program.

Other available features that you may see are the toolbox, the Project Container window, the Form window, the Project window, the Immediate window, the Properties window, and the Form Layout window. The exact size and shape of these windows depends on how your system has been configured. In Visual Basic, you can align and attach, or *dock,* windows to make all the elements of the programming system visible and accessible. You'll learn how to use these features to customize your programming environment in this way later in the lesson.

In the following exercise, you'll practice using the menu bar and toolbar to load and run a sample Visual Basic program called StepUp.

## Use the Menu Bar To Open an Existing Programming Project

1. On the File menu, click the Open Project command.

   The Open Project dialog box appears. This dialog box allows you to open any existing Visual Basic program on your hard disk, Internet connection, or network drive, CD-ROM, or floppy disk. Visual Basic project files are distinguished by the .vbp, the .mak, or the .vbg filename extension.

*Up One Level button*

2. Browse to the C:\LearnVb6\Less01 folder by clicking the Up One Level button three times, double-clicking the LearnVb6 folder in the root directory, and then double-clicking the Less01 folder.

   The \LearnVb6 folder (the default folder created by the Learn Visual Basic Now installation program) contains all the practice files for the book. You'll use the Less*xx* folder corresponding to each lesson as you work your way through this book.

3. In the Less01 folder, click the StepUp.vbp project, and then click Open.

   The StepUp project file loads the user interface form, the properties, the program code, and the standard module of the StepUp program.

4. If the StepUp form is not visible, double-click the Forms folder in the Project window, and then click Form1 (StepUp.frm).

   Before you can work with a component in a project, you must select it in the Project window.

*View Object button*

5. Click the View Object button in the Project window to take a look at the program's user interface.

   The program form appears, as shown in the following illustration:

If you don't see the project container around the form, it is maximized and you need to click the Restore Window button on the toolbar to view the project as shown.

StepUp is just a simple Visual Basic program designed to get you in the swing of things. Because StepUp contains several of the elements found in a typical Visual Basic program, you can use it to explore some of the fundamentals of the programming environment. When you run StepUp, it displays some animation and a message welcoming you to this book.

*Start button*

6. Click the Start button on the Visual Basic toolbar to run the StepUp program in the Visual Basic environment.

   The toolbox and the Properties window disappear, and the StepUp program starts to run.

7. Click the Begin button to see some simple animation. Your screen will look like the following illustration.

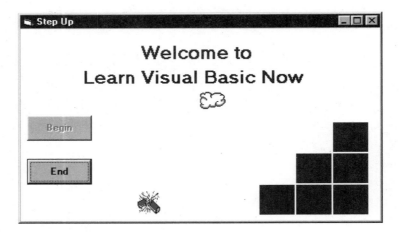

8. Click the End button to quit the program and return to the programming environment. That's all there is to it—you've just run your first program in Visual Basic!

## Moving, Docking, and Resizing Tools

With seven programming tools to contend with on the screen, the Visual Basic development environment can become a pretty busy place. To give you complete control over the shape and size of the elements in the development environment, Visual Basic lets you move, dock, and resize each of the programming tools.

To move a window, the toolbox, or the toolbar, simply click the title bar and drag the object to a new location. If you align one window along the edge of another window, it will attach itself, or *dock*, to that window. Dockable windows are advantageous because they always remain visible. (They won't become hidden behind other windows.)

If you want to see more of a docked window, simply drag one of its borders to view more content. If you get tired of docking and want your tools to overlap each other, click the Options command on the Tools menu, click the Docking tab, and then remove the check mark from each tool you want to stand on its own (that is, make an overlapping window).

As you work through the following sections, practice moving, docking, and resizing the different tools in the Visual Basic programming environment until you feel comfortable arranging them to suit you.

# The User Interface Form

In Visual Basic, a *form* is a window you customize to create the user interface of your program. In the StepUp program, the form is the window you saw while the program was running. A form can contain menus, buttons, list boxes, scroll bars, and any of the other items you've seen in a typical Windows-based program. When you start the Visual Basic programming environment, a default form called Form1 appears. On this form is a standard grid (a group of regularly spaced dots) that you can use to create and line up the elements of your program's user interface. You can adjust the size of the form by using the mouse; the form can take up part or all of the screen. You can add additional forms by clicking the Add Form command on the Project menu.

If part of the form is covered by the programming tools, you can either close or resize the programming tools so that they take up less space, or you can click the form's title bar and drag the form until you can see the hidden parts. Moving the form around the screen in the development environment has no effect on the form's location on the screen when the program actually runs. This run-time characteristic is controlled by the Form Layout window. To set the starting place for a new form, simply drag the tiny preview form in the Form Layout window to the location you want.

# The Toolbox

*Toolbox button*

You add the elements of a program's user interface to a form by using the tools, or *controls,* in the toolbox. To open the toolbox, click the Toolbox button on the toolbar. The toolbox is typically located along the left side of the screen. It contains controls that you can use to add artwork, labels, buttons, list boxes, scroll bars, menus, and geometric shapes to a user interface. Each control you add to a form becomes an *object,* or programmable user interface element, in your program. These elements will be visible to the user of your program when the program runs and will operate like the standard objects in any Windows-based application.

The toolbox also contains controls that you can use to create objects that perform special "behind the scenes" operations in a Visual Basic program. These powerful objects do useful work but are not visible to the user when the program is running; they include objects for manipulating information in databases, working with Windows-based applications, and tracking the passage of time in your programs.

You can display the name of a control in the toolbox by placing the mouse pointer over the control for a few moments. You'll start using the controls in the toolbox later on in Lesson 2.

# The Properties Window

The Properties window lets you change the characteristics, or *property settings,* of the user interface elements on a form. A property setting is a quality of one of the objects in your user interface. For example, the welcome message the StepUp program displayed can be modified to appear in a different font or font size or with a different alignment. (With Visual Basic, you can display text in any font installed on your system, just as you would in Excel or Word.) You can change property settings by using the Properties window while you are creating your user interface or you can add program code by using the Code window to change one or more property settings while your program is running.

The Properties window contains an object drop-down list box that itemizes all the user interface elements (objects) on the form; the Properties window also lists the property settings that can be changed for each object. (You can click one of two convenient tabs to view properties alphabetically or by category.) You'll practice changing the Caption property of the End button in the StepUp program now.

## Change a Property

1. Verify that the StepUp program has stopped running. (You'll see the word *design* in the title bar when the program has stopped.) Then click the End object on the form.

   When the End object (a command button) appears surrounded by rectangles, it is *selected*. To work with an object on a Visual Basic form, you must select the object first.

*Properties Window button*

2. Click the Properties Window button on the toolbar.

   The Properties window is activated in the programming environment. (If the Properties window was not open, it will appear now.)

3. Double-click the Properties window title bar to display it as a floating (nondocked) window.

   You'll see a window similar to the following illustration:

Caption — property

## Thinking About Properties

In Visual Basic, each user interface element in a program (including the form itself) has a set of definable properties. You can set properties at design time by using the Properties window. Properties also can be referenced in code as the program runs to do meaningful work. (User interface elements that receive input often use properties to convey information to the program.) At first, you may find properties a difficult concept to grasp. Viewing them in terms of something from everyday life can help.

Consider this bicycle analogy: a bicycle is an object you use to ride from one place to another. Because a bicycle is a physical object, it has several inherent characteristics. It has a brand name, a color, gears, brakes, and wheels, and it is built in a particular style. (It may be a touring bike, a mountain bike, or a bicycle built for two.) In Visual Basic terminology, these characteristics are *properties* of the bicycle object. The mold that created the bicycle frame would be called the bicycle control. Most of the bicycle's properties would be defined while the bicycle was being built. But others (tires, travel speed, age, and options such as reflectors and mirrors) could be properties that change as the bicycle is used. As you work with Visual Basic, you'll find object properties of both types.

The Properties window lists all the property settings for the second command button on the form. (In all, 33 properties are available to the command buttons.) Property names are listed in the left column of the window, and the current setting for each property is listed in the right column. On the Alphabetic tab, the properties are listed in alphabetical order.

4. Scroll in the list box until the Caption property is visible.

   The Properties window scrolls like a regular list box.

5. Double-click the Caption property (in the left column).

The current caption ("End") is highlighted in the right column, and a cursor blinks to the right of it.

6. Press Del, type **Quit**, and then press Enter.

   The setting of the Caption property is changed from "End" to "Quit." The caption changes on the form, and the next time you run the program, *Quit* will appear inside the command button.

7. Return the Properties window to a docked position above the Project window.

This is a good time to practice your docking technique. Double-clicking the title bar is the quickest method, or you can fine-tune the window's position by dragging it above the edge of the Project window. Because there are so many windows close together, "manual docking" takes some practice and can be a little frustrating at first. But when you use these programming tools later, you'll benefit greatly from a well-organized workspace and your experimentation time will pay off.

## The Project Window

A Visual Basic program is made up of several files that are assembled together, or *compiled,* when a program is complete. As you work on a project you will need to switch back and forth between these components. To help you, the designers of Visual Basic have included a *Project window* in the programming environment. (This tool is also known as the *Project Explorer* in some circles.) The Project window lists all the files used in the programming process and provides access to them with two special buttons: View Code and View Object. When you add and save individual files to and remove files from a project by using commands on the File and Project menus, these changes are reflected in the Project window.

The project file that maintains the list of all the supporting files in a programming project is called the *Visual Basic project (.vbp)* file. Beneath the project name, the Project window displays the components of each project in a tree structure similar to the outline view presented by Windows Explorer. You can expand and collapse its "branches," including Forms,

Modules, and other categories, by clicking the plus and minus signs next to the folders.

In the next exercise, you'll examine the Project window for the StepUp program.

## Display the Project Window

*Project Explorer button*

1. Click the Project Explorer button on the toolbar.

   The Project window (also known as the Project Explorer) is activated in the programming environment. (If the window was not open, it will appear now.)

2. Double-click the Project window's title bar to display it as a floating (nondocked) window.

   You'll see a Project window that looks like this:

Click this button to see the program code in the active form.
Click this button to see the active form.

— Active form

3. Click the plus signs next to the Forms and Modules folders (if you haven't already) to view all the project's components.

   The project file in this programming project is named StepUp.vbp. In the StepUp.vbp project, the files StepUp.frm and StepUp.bas are listed. StepUp.frm contains the user interface form and any program code associated with the objects on the form. StepUp.bas contains code shared by all parts of the program. Later on, when the program is compiled into an executable file (or prepared so that it can run under Windows), these files will be combined to form a single .exe file.

4. Double-click the Project window's title bar to return it to its docked position.

# Exiting Visual Basic

When you're finished using Visual Basic for the day, save any projects that are open and close the programming system. Give it a try.

## Exit Visual Basic

1. Save any changes you have made to your program by clicking the Save button on the toolbar. (If you are prompted for the name and location of your project's components, specify them as directed.)

2. On the File menu, click the Exit command.

   The Visual Basic program exits. Nothing to it!

# Writing Your First Program

As you learned in Lesson 1, the Microsoft Visual Basic programming environment contains several powerful tools to help you run and manage your programs. Visual Basic also contains everything you need to build your own applications for Microsoft Windows from the ground up. In this lesson, you'll learn how to create a simple but attractive user interface with the controls in the Visual Basic toolbox. Next, you'll learn how to customize the operation of these controls with special characteristics called property settings. Then, you'll see how to identify just what your program should do with text-based program code. Finally, you'll learn how to save and run your new program—a Las Vegas–style slot machine.

# Lucky Seven: Your First Visual Basic Program

The Windows-based application you're going to construct is Lucky Seven, a game program that simulates a lucky number slot machine. Lucky Seven has a simple user interface and can be created and compiled in just a few minutes using Visual Basic. Here's what your program will look like when it's finished:

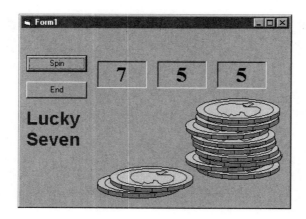

# Programming Steps

The Lucky Seven user interface contains two command buttons, three lucky number windows, a graphic of a stack of coins, and the label Lucky Seven. These elements were produced in the program by creating seven objects on the Lucky Seven form and then changing several properties for each object. After the interface was designed, program code for the Spin and End command buttons was added to the program to process the user's button clicks and produce the random numbers. To re-create Lucky Seven, you'll follow three essential programming steps in Visual Basic: creating the user interface, setting the properties, and writing the program code. The process for Lucky Seven is summarized in the following table.

| Programming step | Number of items |
| --- | --- |
| 1. Create the user interface. | 7 objects |
| 2. Set the properties. | 10 properties |
| 3. Write the program code. | 2 objects |

Another way to think about the Lucky Seven program is to use the following *algorithm*, or list of programming steps. Creating an algorithm can be a useful starting point when developing a program.

Mission—The Lucky Seven program should
        perform the following actions:

• Provide a user interface that has
  Spin and End buttons, 3 spinner
  windows, a descriptive label, and
  a winner display window.

• Pick three random numbers and
  display them when the user clicks Spin.

• Display a stack of coins and beep
  if the number 7 appears in one
  of the spinner windows.

• Terminate when the End button
  is clicked.

# Creating the User Interface

In this exercise you'll start building Lucky Seven by creating a new project and then using controls in the toolbox to construct the user interface.

### Create the User Interface

1. On the File menu, click the New Project command.

   Click No if you are asked whether you want to save any changes to the StepUp program from Lesson 1. This removes the StepUp program from memory.

2. Click OK to create a standard Visual Basic application.

   Visual Basic cleans the slate for a new programming project and displays in the center of the screen a blank form you can use to build your user interface.

   Now you'll enlarge this form, and then you'll create the two buttons in the interface.

3. Position the mouse pointer over the lower-right corner of the Form window (not the Project Container window) until the mouse changes into a sizing pointer, and then increase the size of the form to make room for the objects in your program.

   As you resize the form, scroll bars appear in the Project window, as shown in the following illustration:

Drag to resize the form

To see the entire form without obstruction, resize the Project Container window to remove the scroll bars and move or close the Properties window, the Project window, and the Form Layout window.

Now you'll practice placing a command button object on the form.

IP   Confused by all this resizing? Don't sweat it. You're working with two windows here: the Project Container window and the Form window (which fits inside the Project Container window). The troublesome part is that you resize each window by using the resizing pointer in the lower-right corner of the frame, and these two corners tend to overlap a bit. To get more real estate to design your projects, you may want to run Windows in 800 x 600 mode, which you can do by clicking the Windows desktop with the right mouse button, clicking Properties, clicking the Settings tab, and then moving the Screen Area slider to 800 x 600.

*CommandButton control*

4. Click the CommandButton control in the toolbox, and then place the mouse pointer over the form.

   The CommandButton control is selected, and the mouse pointer changes to cross hairs when it rests on the form. The cross hairs are designed to help you draw the rectangular shape of a command button. When you hold down the left mouse button and drag, the command button object takes shape and snaps to the grid formed by the intersection of dots on the form.

   Try creating your first command button now.

5. Move the mouse pointer close to the upper-left corner of the form, hold down the left mouse button, and then drag down and to the right. Stop dragging and release the mouse button when you have a command button similar to the one shown here:

A command button with selection handles appears on the form. The button is named Command1, the first command button in the program. (You might make a mental note of this button name—you'll see it again later when you write your program code.)

You can move command buttons by dragging them with the mouse and you can resize them by using the selection handles whenever Visual Basic is in *design mode* (whenever the Visual Basic programming environment is active). When a program is running, however, the user will not be able to move interface elements unless you have changed a special property in the program to allow this. You'll practice moving and resizing the command button now.

## Move and Resize a Command Button

1. Drag the command button to the right by using the mouse.

   The command button snaps to the grid when you release the mouse button. The form grid is designed to help you edit and align different user interface elements. You can change the size of the grid by clicking the Options command on the Tools menu and then clicking the General tab.

2. Position the mouse pointer on the lower-right corner of the command button.

   When the mouse pointer rests on a corner or a side of a selected object, it changes into a sizing pointer. You can use the sizing pointer to change the shape of an object.

3. Enlarge the object by holding down the left mouse button and dragging the pointer down and to the right.

   When you release the mouse button, the command button changes size and snaps to the grid.

4. Use the sizing pointer to return the command button to its original size, and then move the button back to its original location on the form.

Now you'll add a second command button to the form, below the first button.

## Add a Second Command Button

*CommandButton control*

1. Click the CommandButton control in the toolbox.

2. Draw a command button below the first button on the form. (For consistency, create a command button of the same size.)

3. Move or resize the button as necessary after you place it. If you make a mistake, feel free to delete the command button and start over.

---

 **TIP** You can delete an object by selecting the object on the form and then pressing Del.

---

## Add the Number Labels

Now add the labels used to display the numbers in the program. A *label* is a special user interface element designed to display text, numbers, or symbols when a program runs. When the user clicks the Lucky Seven program's Spin button, three random numbers appear in the label boxes. If one of the numbers is a seven, the user hits the jackpot.

*Label control*

1. Click the Label control in the toolbox, and then place the mouse pointer over the form.

   The Label control is selected, and the mouse pointer changes to cross hairs when it rests on the form.

2. Create a small rectangular box like the one shown in the figure on the top of the next page.

   The label object you have created is called Label1, the first label in the program. Now you'll create two more labels, named Label2 and Label3, on the form.

3. Click the Label control, and then draw a label box to the right of the first label.

   Make this label the same size as the first. The caption "Label2" will appear in the label.

4. Click the Label control again and add a third label to the form, to the right of the second label.

   The caption "Label3" will appear in the label.

---

 **IP**   As you create labels in this exercise, take a look at the pop-up box that appears next to the labels as you draw them. This box, which contains horizontal and vertical measurements, is called a sizing box. The numbers give the horizontal and vertical dimensions, respectively, of the object you are creating. The numbers are in units of measure called *twips*; a twip is one-twentieth of a point. (A point is 1/72 inch, so a twip is 1/1440 inch.) You can use the sizing box to compare the relative sizes of objects you're creating. After you create the object, the same information is also displayed on the right side of the toolbar.

---

Now you'll use the Label control to add a descriptive label to your form. This will be the fourth and final label in the program.

5. Click the Label control in the toolbox.

6. Create a larger rectangle directly below the two command buttons.

When you've finished, your four labels should look like those in the following illustration. (You can resize the label objects if they don't look quite right.)

Now you'll add an *image box* to the form to display the stack of coins the user wins when he or she draws a seven and hits the jackpot. An image box is designed to display bitmaps, icons, and other artwork in a program. One of the best uses for an image box is to display a piece of Visual Basic clip art.

## Add an Image

*Image control*

1. Click the Image control in the toolbox.

2. Using the Image control, create a large rectangular box directly beneath the three number labels.

   When you've finished, your image box object should look like the figure on the top of the next page.

   This object will be called Image1 in your program; you'll use this name later in the program code.

Now you're ready to customize your interface by setting a few properties.

# Setting the Properties

As you discovered in Lesson 1, you can change properties by selecting objects on the form and changing their settings in the Properties window. You'll start setting the properties in this program by changing the caption settings for the two command buttons.

## Set the Command Button Properties

1. Click the first command button (Command1) on the form.

   The command button is surrounded by selection handles.

2. Double-click the Properties window title bar.

   The Properties window is enlarged to full size, as shown in the illustration on the following page.

   The Properties window lists the settings for the first command button. These include settings for the background color, caption, font height, and width of the command button.

3. Double-click the Caption property in the left column of the Properties window.

   The current Caption setting ("Command1") is highlighted in the Properties window.

4. Type **Spin** and press Enter.

The Caption property changes to "Spin" in the Properties window and on the form. Now change the caption of the second button to "End." (You'll select the second button in a new way this time.)

5. Open the Object drop-down list box at the top of the Properties window.

A list of the interface objects in your program appears in the list box:

These properties for the objects on your form, and for the form itself, can be set with the object drop-down list box.

6. Click Command2 (the second command button) in the list box.

   The property settings for the second command button appear in the Properties window.

7. Double-click the current Caption property ("Command2"), type **End**, and then press Enter.

   The caption of the second command button changes to "End."

**IP**   Using the Object drop-down list box is a handy way to switch between objects in your program. You can also switch between objects on the form by clicking each object.

Now you'll set the properties for the labels in the program. The first three labels will hold the random numbers generated by the program and will have identical property settings. (You'll set most of them as a group.) The descriptive label settings will be slightly different.

## Set the Number Label Properties

1. Click the first number label, and then, holding down the Shift key, click the second and third number labels. (If the Properties window is in the way, move it to a new place.)

   A set of selection rectangles appears around each label that you click. When you've selected all three labels, release the Shift key.

**IP**   Because more than one object is selected, only those properties that can be changed as a group are displayed in the Properties window. You'll change the Alignment, BorderStyle, and Font properties now so that the numbers that appear in the labels will be centered, boxed, and identical in font and point size.

2. Click the Alignment property, and then click the drop-down list box arrow that appears to the right.

   A list of alignment options appears in the list box.

3. Click the 2 - Center option.

The Alignment property for each of the selected labels changes to 2 - Center.

Now you'll change the BorderStyle property.

4. Click the BorderStyle property, and then click the drop-down list box arrow that appears to the right.

   A list of the valid property settings (0 - None and 1 - Fixed Single) appears in the list box.

5. Click 1 - Fixed Single in the list box to add a thin border around each label.

   Now you'll change the font for the labels by changing settings for the Font property.

6. Double-click the Font property in the Properties window.

   The Font dialog box appears, as shown here:

7. Change the font to Times New Roman, the font style to Bold, and the point size to 24, and then click OK.

   The label captions appear in the font, style, and size you specified.

Now you'll delete the three captions so that the boxes will be empty when the program starts. (Your font selections will remain with the labels because they are stored as separate properties.) To complete this operation, you'll first need to select each of the labels individually.

8. Click the form to remove the selection handles from the three labels, and then click the first label.

9. Double-click the Caption property, and then press Del.

   The caption of the Label1 object is deleted. You'll use program code to put a random "slot machine" number in this property later in this lesson.

10. Delete the captions in the second and third labels on the form.

You've finished with the first three labels. Now you'll change the Caption, Font, and ForeColor properties of the last label.

## Set the Descriptive Label Properties

1. Click the fourth label object on the form.

2. Change the Caption property to "Lucky Seven."

3. Double-click the Font property, and use the Font dialog box to change the font to Arial, the font style to Bold, and the point size to 20. Click OK.

   The font in the label box is updated. Notice that the text in the box wrapped to two lines because it no longer fits on one. This is an important concept: the contents of an object must fit inside the object. If they don't, the contents will wrap or be truncated.

   Now you'll change the foreground color of the text.

4. Double-click the ForeColor property in the Properties window.

   A System tab and a Palette tab appear in a list box, providing you with two options to change the color of your object. The System tab displays the current colors used for user interface elements in your system. (The list reflects the current settings on the Appearance tab in your desktop's property sheet.) The Palette tab contains all the available colors in your system.

5. Click the Palette tab, and then click the box containing dark purple.

   The text in the label box changes to dark purple. The selected color is translated into a hexadecimal (base 16) number in the Properties window. Most programmers won't have to deal with this format often, but it is interesting to see how Visual Basic actually records such information inside the program.

Now you're ready to set the properties for the last object.

## The Image Box Properties

The image box object will contain the graphic of the stack of coins in your program. This graphic will appear when the user hits the jackpot (that is, when at least one seven appears in the number labels). You need to set the Stretch property to accurately size the graphic; the Picture property, which specifies the name of the graphics file to be loaded into the image box; and the Visible property, which specifies the picture state at the beginning of the program.

## Set the Image Box Properties

1. Click the image box object on the form.

2. Click the Stretch property in the Properties window, click the drop-down list box arrow, and then click True.

   Setting Stretch to True before you open a graphic will make Visual Basic resize the graphic to the exact dimensions of the image box. (Typically, you set this property before you set the Picture property.)

3. Double-click the Picture property in the Properties window.

   The Load Picture dialog box appears, as shown in the illustration on the top of the next page.

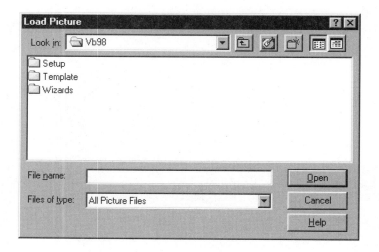

4. Navigate to the \LearnVb6 folder in the Load Picture dialog box.

   The subfolders in the \LearnVb6 folder appear.

5. Double-click the Less02 folder.

   The Windows metafile Coins.wmf appears in the Load Picture dialog box. Windows metafiles contain graphics objects that can be rendered in a variety of different sizes, so they look good in small and large boxes.

6. Select the file Coins.wmf in the dialog box, and then click Open.

   The Coins Windows metafile is loaded into the image box on the form.

   Now you'll change the Visible property to False so that the coins will be invisible when the program starts. (You'll make them appear later with program code.)

7. Click the Visible property. Click the Visible drop-down list box arrow.

   The valid settings for the Visible property appear in a list box.

8. Click False to make the image invisible when the program starts.

   The Visible property is set to False.

This affects the image box when the program runs, but not now while you are designing it. Your completed form looks like this:

9. Double-click the Properties window's title bar to return it to the docked position.

# Writing the Code

Now you're ready to write the code for the Lucky Seven program. Because most of the objects you've created already "know" how to work when the program runs, they're ready to receive input from the user and process it automatically. The inherent functionality of objects is one of the great strengths of Visual Basic—once objects are placed on a form and their properties are set, they're ready to perform many basic tasks without any additional programming. However, the "meat" of the Lucky Seven game—the code that actually calculates random numbers, displays them in boxes, and detects a jackpot—is still missing from the program. This computing logic can be built into the application only by using program statements—code that clearly spells out what the program should do each step of the way. Because the program is driven by the Spin and End buttons, you'll associate the code for the game with those buttons. The *Code window* is a special window in the programming environment that you use to enter and edit Visual Basic program statements.

In the following steps, you'll enter the program code for Lucky Seven in the Code window.

## Use the Code Window

1. Double-click the End command button on the form.

   The Code window appears, as shown on the top of the next page.

---

### Reading Properties in Tables

In this lesson, you've set the properties for the Lucky Seven program step by step. In future lessons, the instructions to set properties will be presented in table format unless a setting is especially tricky. Here are the properties you've set so far in the Lucky Seven program in table format, as they'd look later in the book.

| Object | Property | Setting |
|---|---|---|
| Command1 | Caption | "Spin" |
| Command2 | Caption | "End" |
| Label1, Label2, Label3 | BorderStyle | 1 – Fixed Single |
| | Alignment | 2 – Center |
| | Font | Times New Roman, Bold, 24-point |
| | Caption | (Empty) |
| Label4 | Caption | "Lucky Seven" |
| | Font | Arial, Bold, 20-point |
| | ForeColor | Dark purple (&H00800080&) |
| Image1 | Picture | "\LearnVb6\Less02\coins.wmf" |
| | Stretch | True |
| | Visible | False |

---

If the window is smaller than the one shown above, resize it with the mouse. (The exact size is not that important because the Code window includes scroll bars that you can use to examine long program statements.)

Inside the Code window are program statements that mark the beginning and the end of this particular Visual Basic subroutine, or *event procedure,* a block of code associated with a particular object in the interface:

```
Private Sub Command2_Click()
End Sub
```

The body of a procedure always fits between these lines and is executed whenever a user activates the interface element associated with the procedure. In this case, the event is a mouse click, but as you'll see later in the book, it could also be an event of a different type.

2. Type **End,** and press the Down arrow key.

   As you type the statement, the letters appear in black type in the Code window. When you press the Down arrow key (you could also press Enter or simply click a different line), the program statement turns blue, indicating that Visual Basic recognizes it as a valid statement, or *keyword,* in the program.

   You use the program statement End to stop your program and remove it from the screen. The Visual Basic programming system contains several hundred unique keywords such as this, complete with their associated operators and symbols. The spelling of and spacing between these items are critical to writing program code that will be accurately recognized by the Visual Basic compiler.

 **IP**  Another name for the exact spelling, order, and spacing of keywords in a program is *statement syntax*.

3.  Move the cursor to the beginning of the line with the End statement in it, and press the Spacebar four times.

    The indent moves the End statement four spaces to the right to set the statement apart from the Private Sub and End Sub statements. This indenting scheme is one of the programming conventions you'll use throughout this book to keep your programs clear and readable. The group of conventions regarding how program code is organized in a program is often referred to as *program style*.

Now that you've written the code associated with the End button, you'll write code for the Spin button. These programming statements will be a little more extensive and will give you a chance to learn more about program syntax and style. You'll study each of the program statements later in the book, so you don't need to know everything about them now. Just focus on the general structure of the program code and on typing the program statements exactly as they are printed. (Visual Basic is fussy about spelling and the order in which keywords and operators appear.)

## Write Code for the Spin Button

1.  Open the Object drop-down list box in the Code window.

    The Lucky Seven interface objects appear in the list box, as shown in the illustration on the top of the next page.

2.  Click Command1 in the list box.

    A procedure associated with the Command1 button appears above the first procedure.

Procedure View button

Full Module View button

By default, Visual Basic displays all the event procedures for a form in one window, so you can easily switch back and forth between them. (A horizontal line appears between the procedures so you can keep them apart.) Alternatively, you can view one procedure per window by clicking the tiny Procedure View button in the bottom-left corner of the Code window. To see all the procedures again in one window, click the Full Module View button located just to the right of the Procedure View button.

Although you changed the caption of this button to "Spin," its name in the program is still Command1. (The name and the caption of an interface element can be different to suit the needs of the programmer.) Each object can have several procedures associated with it, one for each event it recognizes. The click event is the one we're interested in now because users will click the Spin and End buttons when they operate the program.

3. Type the program lines shown on the following page between the Private Sub and End Sub statements, pressing Enter after each line and taking care to type the program statements exactly as they appear here. (The Code window will scroll to the left as you enter the longer lines.) If you make a mistake (usually identified by red type), delete the incorrect statements and try again.

---

**TIP** As you enter the program code, Visual Basic formats the text and displays different parts of the program in color to help you identify the various elements. When you begin to type a property, Visual Basic also displays the available properties for the object you're using in a list box, so you can double-click the property or keep typing to enter it yourself. If Visual Basic displays an error message, you may have misspelled a program statement. Check the line against the text in this book, make the necessary correction, and continue typing. (You can also delete a line and type it from scratch.) Readers of previous editions of this book have found this first typing exercise to be the toughest part of the lesson—"But Mr. Halvorson, I *know* I typed it just as written!"—so please give this program code your closest attention. I promise you, it works!

---

```
Image1.Visible = False          ' hide coins
Label1.Caption = Int(Rnd * 10) ' pick numbers
Label2.Caption = Int(Rnd * 10)
Label3.Caption = Int(Rnd * 10)
'if any caption is 7 display coin stack and beep
If (Label1.Caption = 7) Or (Label2.Caption = 7) _
  Or (Label3.Caption = 7) Then
    Image1.Visible = True
    Beep
End If
```

When you've finished, the Code window should look like the following:

## A Look at the Command1_Click Procedure

The Command1_Click procedure is executed when the user clicks the Spin button on the form. The procedure uses some pretty complicated statements, and because I haven't formally introduced them yet, the whole thing may look a little confusing. However, if you take a closer look you'll probably see a few things that look familiar. Taking a peek at the contents of the procedures will give you a feel for the type of program code you'll be creating later in this book. (If you'd rather not have a look, feel free to skip to the next section, "Saving the Program.")

The Command1_Click procedure performs three tasks: it hides the coin stack, creates three random numbers for the label windows, and displays the coin stack when the number seven appears. Let's look at each of these steps individually.

The first task in the procedure is accomplished by the line

```
Image1.Visible = False   ' hide coins
```

This line is made up of two parts: a program statement and a comment. The program statement (Image1.Visible = False) sets the Visible property of the first image box object (Image1) to False (one of two possible settings). You might remember that you set this property to False once before by using the Properties window. You're doing it again now in the program code because the first task is a spin and you need to clear away any coins that might have been displayed in a previous game. Because the property will be changed at run time and not at design time, the property needs to be set by using program code. This is a handy feature of Visual Basic, and we'll talk about it more in Lesson 3.

The second part of the first line (the part displayed in green type on your screen) is called a *comment*. Comments are explanatory notes included in program code following a single quotation mark ('). Programmers use comments to describe how important statements work in a program. These notes aren't processed by Visual Basic when the program runs; they exist only to document what the program does. You'll want to use comments often when you write Visual Basic programs to leave a "plain English" record of what you're doing.

The next three lines handle the random number computations. The Rnd function in each line creates a random number between 0 and 1 (a number with a decimal point), and the Int function multiplies the numbers by 10 and rounds them to the nearest decimal place. This computation creates random numbers between 0 and 9 in the program. The numbers are then assigned to the Caption properties of the first three labels on the form, and the assignment causes the numbers to be displayed in boldface, 24-point, Times New Roman type in the three label windows.

The last group of statements in the program checks whether any of the random numbers is seven. If one or more of them is, the stack of coins is made visible on the form and a beep announces a jackpot. Each time the user clicks the Spin button, the Command1_Click procedure is called and the program statements in the procedure are executed.

# Saving the Program

Now that you've completed the Lucky Seven program, you should save it to disk. Visual Basic saves your form's code and objects in one file and the "packing list" of project components in another file. (The project components are listed in the Project window.) You can use these component files individually in other programming projects by using the Add File command on the Project menu. To save a program in Visual Basic, click Save Project As on the File menu or click the Save Project button on the toolbar.

## Save the Lucky Seven Program

1. On the File menu, click the Save Project As command.

 **TIP** You can save your program at any time during the programming process.

The Save File As dialog box appears, prompting you for the name and storage location for your form.

2. Select the Less02 folder in the dialog box, if it's not already selected.

   You'll save your project files in the practice folder that the Learn Visual Basic Now installation program created on your hard disk. (You can specify a different folder if you like.)

3. Type **MyLucky** in the File Name text box, and press Enter.

---

⚑ **MPORTANT** I recommend that you save each project you create in this book by using the My prefix to keep a record of your progress and to preserve the original practice files. That way you can check the original files if you have any problems.

---

The Lucky Seven form is saved under the name MyLucky.frm. The Save Project As dialog box then appears:

4. Type **MyLucky** and press Enter.

   The Lucky Seven project is saved under the name MyLucky.vbp. To load this project again later, click the Open Project command on the File menu and click MyLucky in the Open Project dialog box. You can also load a recently used project by clicking the project name at the bottom of the Visual Basic File menu.

Congratulations! You're ready to run your first real program. To run a Visual Basic program from the programming environment, you can click Start on the Run menu, click the Start button on the toolbar, or press F5. Try running your Lucky Seven program now. If Visual Basic displays an error message, you may still have a typing mistake or two in your program code. Try to fix it by comparing the printed version in this book with the one you typed, or load Lucky from your hard disk and run it.

**TIP** The complete Lucky program is located in the \LearnVb6\Less02 folder.

---

### Can I Compile the Lucky Seven Program?

Are you interested in compiling your Lucky Seven project into a stand-alone Windows executable (.exe) file? That would be nice, wouldn't it?— and a fitting end to Visual Basic development life cycle, in computer science terms. However, the compilation capability has been disabled in the Visual Basic Working Model; the Visual Basic product group fears that if this feature were intact, you might not eventually upgrade to one of the full retail products: Visual Basic Learning Edition, Professional Edition, or Enterprise Edition.

All is not lost, however. You can still create, save, and run Visual Basic programs, and (most importantly) you can explore the depth of the Visual Basic programming language. If you want to share your programs, however, you'll need to save them as projects (.vbp files) and copy all of the project files to your colleagues' systems. In addition, they'll need to have their own copy of Visual Basic in order to load and run the project files. As a result, we won't be talking much about compiling your programs as executable files, but remember that if you do upgrade to a retail Visual Basic, you'll have this useful capability.

## Run the Program

*Start button*

1. Click the Start button on the toolbar.

   The Lucky Seven program runs in the programming environment. The user interface appears, just as you designed it.

2. Click the Spin button.

   The program picks three random numbers and displays them in the labels on the form, as follows:

   Because a "7" appears in the first label box, the stack of coins appears and the computer beeps. (The sound depends on your Windows Control Panel setting.) You win!

3. Click the Spin button 15 or 16 more times, watching the results of the spins in the number windows.

   About half the time you spin, you hit the jackpot—pretty easy odds. (The actual odds are about 2.7 times out of 10; you're just lucky at first.) Later on you might want to make the game tougher by displaying the coins only when two or three sevens appear. (You'll see how to do this when you learn more about modules and public variables in Lesson 10.)

4.  When you've finished experimenting with your new creation, click the End button.

    The program stops, and the programming environment reappears on your screen.

5.  Click Exit on the File menu to close Visual Basic. If Visual Basic prompts you to save your changes, click Yes.

# Adding to a Program

You can restart Visual Basic at any time and work on a programming project you have stored on disk. You'll restart Visual Basic now and add a special statement named Randomize to the Lucky Seven program.

## Reload Lucky Seven

1.  Click the Start button on the Windows taskbar, point to Programs, point to the Microsoft Visual Basic 6.0 folder, and then click the Microsoft Visual Basic 6.0 program icon.

2.  Click the Recent tab in the Open Project dialog box.

    A list of the most recent projects that you have worked on appears in a list box. Because you just finished working with Lucky Seven, MyLucky should be the first project on the list.

3.  Double-click MyLucky to load the Lucky Seven program from disk.

    The Lucky Seven program loads from disk, and the MyLucky form appears in a window. (If you don't see it, click the MyLucky form in the Project window and then click the View Object button.)

    Now you'll add the Randomize statement to the Form_Load procedure, a special procedure that's associated with the form and that's executed each time the program is started.

4.  Double-click the form (not one of the objects) to display the Form_Load procedure.

The Form_Load procedure appears in the Code window, as shown in the following illustration:

5. Press the Spacebar four times, type **Randomize**, and press the Down Arrow key.

   The Randomize statement is added to the program and will be executed each time the program starts. Randomize uses the system clock to create a truly random starting point, or "seed," for the Rnd statement used in the Command1_Click procedure. You might not have noticed, but without Randomize the Lucky Seven program produces the same string of random spins every time you restart the program. With Randomize in place, the program will spin randomly every time it runs. The numbers won't follow a recognizable pattern.

6. Run the new version of Lucky Seven, and then save the project to disk.

# 3

# Working with Controls

As you learned in Lessons 1 and 2, Microsoft Visual Basic controls are the graphical tools you use to build the user interface of a Visual Basic program. Controls are located in the toolbox in the programming environment, and you use them to create objects on a form with a simple series of mouse clicks and dragging motions. In this lesson, you'll learn how to display information in a text box, browse drives and folders on your system, process user input, launch Windows-based applications, and view database records. The exercises in this lesson will help you design your own Visual Basic applications and will teach you more about objects, properties, and program code. You'll also learn how to add ActiveX controls to the toolbox so that you can extend the functionality of Visual Basic.

# The Basic Use of Controls: The "Hello World" Program

A great tradition in introductory programming books is the "Hello World" program. Hello World is the name given to a short program that demonstrates how the simplest utility can be built and run in a given programming language. In the days of character-based programming, Hello World was usually a two-line or three-line program typed in a program editor and assembled with a stand-alone compiler. With the advent of graphical programming tools, however, the typical Hello World has grown into a complex program containing dozens of lines and requiring several programming tools for its construction. Fortunately, creating a Hello World program is still quite simple with Visual Basic. You can construct a complete user interface by creating two objects, setting two properties, and entering one line of code. Give it a try.

## Create a Hello World Program

1. Start Visual Basic and click the Open button to create a standard Visual Basic application.

TextBox control

CommandButton control

The Visual Basic programming environment appears, as shown in the previous illustration. The two controls you'll use in this exercise, TextBox and CommandButton, are labeled in the toolbox.

*TextBox control*

2. Click the TextBox control in the toolbox.

3. Move the mouse pointer to the center of the form. Note that the pointer turns into cross hairs as it passes over the form. Draw a text box similar to the following:

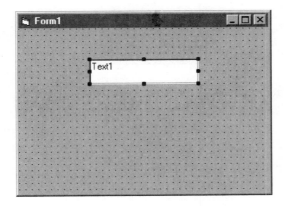

A *text box object* is used to display text on a form or to get user input while a Visual Basic program is running. How a text box works depends on how you set its properties and how you reference the text box in the program code. In this simple program, a text box object will be used to display the message "Hello, world!" when you click a command button on the form.

Now you'll add a command button to the form.

*CommandButton control*

4. Click the CommandButton control in the toolbox.

5. Move the mouse pointer below the text box on the form, and draw a command button.

Your form should look like the following:

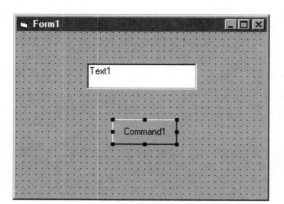

A *command button object* is used to get the most basic input from a user. When a user clicks a command button, he or she is requesting that the program perform a specific action immediately. In Visual Basic terms, the user is using the command button to create an *event* that needs to be processed in the program. Typical command buttons in a program are the OK button, which a user clicks to accept a list of options and indicate that he or she is ready to proceed; the Cancel button, which a user clicks to discard a list of options; and the Quit button, which a user clicks to exit the program. In each case, you should use command buttons in a recognizable way, so that they work as expected when the user clicks them. A command button's characteristics (like those of all objects) can be modified with property settings and references to the object in program code.

6. Set the properties for the text box and command button objects given on the following page, using the Properties window. The setting (Empty) means that you should delete the current setting and leave the property blank. Settings you need to type in are shown in quotation marks. You shouldn't type the quotation marks.

---

**IP** For more information about setting properties, see the section "Setting the Properties" in Lesson 2.

---

| Control | Property | Setting |
| --- | --- | --- |
| Text1 | Text | (Empty) |
| Command1 | Caption | "OK" |

7. Double-click the OK command button, and type the following program statement between the Private Sub and End Sub statements in the Code window:

```
Text1.Text = "Hello, world!"
```

 **TIP** After you type the Text1 object name and a period, Visual Basic displays a list box containing all the valid properties for text box objects to jog your memory if you've forgotten the complete list. You can select a property from the list by double-clicking it, or you can continue typing and enter it yourself. (I usually just keep on typing, unless I'm exploring new features.)

The statement you've entered changes the Text property of the text box to "Hello, world!" when the user clicks the command button at runtime. (The equal sign assigns everything between the quotation marks to the Text property of the Text1 object.) This example changes a property at runtime—one of the most common uses of program code in a Visual Basic program. Your statement is in an *event procedure*—an instruction that is executed when the Command1 command button is clicked. It changes the property setting (and therefore the text box contents) immediately after the user clicks the command button.

8. Use the Form Layout window to set the position of the form when the program runs. (If the Form Layout window is not visible, click the Form Layout Window command on the View menu.)

By default, the Form Layout window positions forms in the upper-left corner of the screen. However, you can customize this setting by dragging the tiny form icon within the Form Layout window. This feature is especially useful in programs that display more than one window.

Now you're ready to run the Hello World program and save it to disk.

## Run the Hello World Program

*Start button*

1. Click the Start button on the toolbar.

   The Hello World program runs in the Visual Basic programming environment.

2. Click the OK command button.

   The program displays the greeting "Hello, world!" in the text box, as shown here:

   When you clicked the OK command button, the program code changed the Text property of the empty Text1 text box to "Hello, world!" and displayed this text in the box. If you didn't get this result, repeat the steps in the previous section and build the program again. You might have set a property incorrectly or made a typing mistake in the program code. (Syntax errors appear in red type on your screen.)

*End button*

3. Click the End button on the toolbar to stop the program. You can also click the Close button on the program form to stop the program.

4. On the File menu, click the Save Project As command.

5. Select the \LearnVb6\Less03 folder, type **MyHello**, and click Save.

   Visual Basic saves your form to disk with the name MyHello.frm. Because Visual Basic saves forms separately from project files, you can reuse forms and procedures in future programming projects without rebuilding them from scratch.

After you enter the form name, you are prompted for a project filename for the file that Visual Basic uses to build your program. This Visual Basic project file has a .vbp filename extension.

6. Type **MyHello** again, and click Save.

Visual Basic saves your project to disk under the name MyHello.vbp. To open the program again later, you can select this file by clicking the Open Project command on the File menu. Visual Basic then loads all the files in the project list.

Congratulations—you've joined the ranks of programmers who have written a Hello World program. Now let's move on to some other objects.

# Using File System Objects

Visual Basic provides three very useful objects for gaining access to the file system. These are *drive list boxes,* which let you browse the valid drives on a system; *directory list boxes,* which let you navigate the folders on a particular drive; and *file list boxes,* which let you select a specific file in a folder. In the following exercise, you will use the three file system objects to build a program called Browser that locates and displays files containing artwork on your system.

---

 **IP**  You will also use an *image object* in this program. An image object can display six kinds of graphics formats: bitmaps (.bmp files), Windows metafiles (.wmf files, which are electronic artwork files that you can size), icons (.ico files), cursors (.cur files), JPEG format (.jpg files), and GIF format (.gif files).

---

## The Browser Program

The Browser program uses the three file system objects, an image object, and several lines of program code to create an artwork browser program. When you've finished creating Browser, you can use it routinely to examine the artwork on any floppy disk, hard disk, network drive, or CD-ROM. The file system objects support all drive types.

## Build the Browser Program

1. On the File menu, click New Project, and then click OK to create a new standard project.

   The Hello World program disappears, and a blank form appears on the screen. (You have a chance to save any unsaved changes in Hello World before it closes.)

2. On the Tools menu, click Options, and then click the Editor tab. If a check mark appears in the Require Variable Declaration box, click the box to remove the check mark. (This option will be discussed in Lesson 4.) Click OK.

3. Increase the size of your form so that it is big enough to hold file system controls and a good-sized window for viewing images.

   Scroll bars appear around your form so that you can view any hidden parts as you develop your program.

*DriveListBox
control*

4. Click the DriveListBox control in the toolbox.

5. Move the mouse pointer to the upper-left corner of the form, and then draw a drive list box, as shown in the following illustration:

Visual Basic includes the current drive and volume label in the object when you create it. This information is displayed to help the user identify the currently selected drive when he or she is using the program. It also lets you verify at design time whether you can see all the drive and volume information so that you can resize your drive list box accordingly.

*DirListBox control*

6. Click the DirListBox control in the toolbox, and then add a directory list box to the form, below the drive list box. Allow room for at least four or five folders to appear in the list box.

A directory list box object provides access to the folders in the file system. When you place the object on a Visual Basic form, the folders appear as they will when the program runs. It's tempting to start clicking folders now, but because the list box isn't active, nothing will happen. Folders appear now only so that you can size the object appropriately.

*FileListBox control*

7. Click the FileListBox control in the toolbox, and then add a file list box to the form, below the directory list box. Allow room for at least four or five filenames to be displayed.

A file list box object lets a user select a specific file in the file system. When the user selects a file, Visual Basic puts the filename in the Filename property of the file list box object. In a similar manner, the Drive property of the drive list box object and the Path property of the directory list box object receive the drive and folder selections the user makes in the drive and directory list boxes. You'll use these three properties together in the Browser program to open the artwork file the user selects.

This is a typical use of objects and properties in a program. The user changes a setting in an object while the program is running, the change is reflected in a property, and the property is processed in the program code.

---

 **IP**  The Drive, Path, and Filename properties are available only at runtime. (They contain values that are assigned when the file system list boxes are used.) You cannot set them by using the Properties window.

---

*Image control*

8. Click the Image control in the toolbox, and then add a large image box to the form, to the right of the drive, directory, and file list boxes.

   After you add the image object, your screen should look similar to the following:

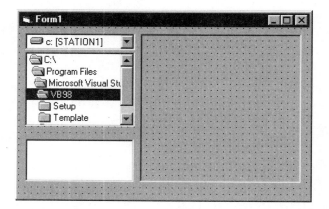

9. Now set the following properties by using the Properties window:

| Object | Property | Setting |
|--------|----------|---------|
| File1 | Pattern | *.bmp;*.wmf;*.ico |
| Image1 | Stretch | True |
| Image1 | BorderStyle | 1 – Fixed Single |

The Pattern setting in the file list box is especially important in this case. It lists the valid graphics formats that Visual Basic can display in a program by using an image box. If the property were left blank, the file list box would list all file types in a folder, and if the user selected a graphics format that Visual Basic doesn't support (such as .tif), the selection would result in a crash or a runtime error. If possible, it's best to eliminate such problems before they occur.

Now you'll add a few lines of program code to the procedures associated with the file system objects. These procedures are called *event procedures* because they are run when an event, such as a mouse click, occurs in the object.

 **IP** Double-click an object to display its default event procedure.

10. Double-click the drive list box object on the form, and then type the following program statement between the Private Sub and End Sub statements in the Drive1_Change event procedure:

```
Dir1.Path = Drive1.Drive
```

This statement updates the Path property in the directory list box when the user selects a drive in the drive list box. The statement hooks the two objects together so that the directory list box lists folders for the correct drive.

11. Close the Code window (click the Close button in the upper-right corner). Then double-click the directory list box on the form and add the following program statement to the Dir1_Change event procedure:

```
File1.Path = Dir1.Path
```

This statement links the file list box to the directory list box so that the files in the list box match the selected folder.

12. Close the Code window. Now double-click the file list box on the form and add the following code to the File1_Click event procedure:

```
SelectedFile = File1.Path & "\" & File1.Filename
Image1.Picture = LoadPicture(SelectedFile)
```

These two lines are the heart of the program. The first line uses the & operator to combine File1's Path property, the (\) character, and

File1's Filename property, and then stores the resulting pathname in the SelectedFile variable. A *variable* is a temporary storage space or holding tank for information in a program. In this case, the SelectedFile variable holds the complete name of the file that has been selected by the user (including drive and folder names). The second statement in the event procedure uses the SelectedFile variable when it loads the file into the image box (Image1) on the form with the LoadPicture function and the Picture property.

 **OTE** You'll learn more about operators, variables, and functions in Lesson 5.

After you enter the code for the File1_Click event procedure, the Code window should look similar to the following illustration. (This screen shot shows an enlarged Code window.)

Now you're ready to run the Browser program and save it to disk.

## Run the Browser Program

 **IP** The complete Browser.vbp program is located on disk in the \LearnVb6\Less03 folder.

*Start button*

1. Click the Start button on the toolbar.

   The Browser program starts to run in the programming environment.

2. Open the folder \LearnVb6\Less03 by using the directory list box.

   The Windows metafiles in the selected folder appear in the file list box.

3. Click the filename answmach.wmf.

   The selected file (a picture of an answering machine) appears in the image box, as shown here:

4. Scroll down the list and click the poundbag.wmf filename.

   A picture of an English money sack appears in the image box.

5. Use the drive, directory, and file list boxes to view other bitmaps, Windows metafiles, and icons on your system.

   You'll probably find several interesting bitmaps in the \Windows folder.

   When you've finished experimenting with Browser, stop the program and save it to disk.

6. Click the Close button on the form.

7. On the File menu, click Save Project As. Save the form as **MyBrowser** and the project as **MyBrowser**.

## What If My Program Crashes?

If you use the Browser program a lot, you might notice that it produces a runtime error, or *crashes*, in two specific situations. Because this program was created quickly for demonstration purposes, you didn't add the code necessary to protect the program against out-of-the-ordinary problems. As you begin to write more complex programs, however, you'll want to test your code carefully to make sure you can't break it under either normal or extreme operating conditions.

The first problem with Browser is that it crashes if the user selects a drive in the drive list box that doesn't contain a disk or is otherwise unready for work. (An example of an unready drive would be a drive containing a floppy disk that isn't formatted or an offline network drive.) To watch this happen, verify that drive A in your system doesn't have a disk in it, and then select A: in the Browser drive list box. The program immediately stops, and Visual Basic displays the message "Runtime error '68': Device unavailable." This statement means that Visual Basic couldn't find the floppy disk and quit running the program because it didn't know how to proceed. The Browser program relies on the user not making any mistakes with disks, which is probably not a wise assumption.

The second problem Browser has is with viewing artwork located in the root folder. Because files in the root folder have a pathname of only the backslash (\), the program statement

```
SelectedFile = File1.Path & "\" & File1.Filename
```

causes trouble because it creates a pathname containing two backslashes. (For example, the statement would describe a file named Truck.wmf in the root folder as C:\\Truck.wmf.) When Visual Basic tries to load a file whose name contains two backslashes side by side, it causes a run-time error and the program stops.

The way around these problems is to use program statements that avoid the error condition (you can do this with the pathname

*(continued)*

**What If My Program Crashes?** *(continued)*

> problem) or to create special routines called *error handlers* that will help your program recover if errors occur. Error handlers are beyond the scope of our current discussion, but for now you should note that although Visual Basic can handle most operating conditions, now and then users can create problems that make all but the sturdiest programs crash. We'll discuss tracking down and fixing bugs in Lessons 6 and 8.

# Objects for Gathering Input

Visual Basic provides several objects for gathering input in a program. *Text boxes* accept typed input, *menus* present commands that can be clicked, and *dialog boxes* offer a variety of elements that can be chosen individually or selected in a group. In this exercise, you'll learn how to use four important objects that will help you gather input in several different situations. You'll learn about option button objects, check box objects, list box objects, and combo box objects. You'll explore each of these objects as you use a Visual Basic program called Online Shopper, the user interface for an Internet application or other online utility that allows you to order computers and office equipment graphically. As you run the program, you'll get some hands-on experience with the input objects. In the next lesson, we'll discuss how these objects can be used along with menus in a full-fledged program.

## The Online Shopper Program

The Online Shopper program simulates an electronic ordering environment in which you see what you're ordering as you make your selection. If you work in a business that does a lot of order entry, you might want to expand this program into a full-featured graphical order entry program someday. (Graphical tools like this are popular on the Web.) As you experiment with Online Shopper, spend some time observing how the option button, check box, list box, and combo box elements work in the program. They were created in a few short steps by using Visual Basic.

## Run the Online Shopper Program

1. On the Visual Basic File menu, click Open Project.

   The Open Project dialog box appears.

2. Open the Online.vbp file in the \Vb6Sbs\Less03 folder.

*View Object button*

3. In the Project window, select the Online form and click the View Object button.

4. Close the Properties, Project, and Form Layout windows to see more of the Online Shopper form. If the Immediate window (a tool that is typically used only for debugging) is also open, close it now. You won't be using these tools in this exercise.

   The Online Shopper form appears, as shown in the illustration below.

The Online Shopper form contains option button, check box, list box, combo box, image box, command button, and label objects. These objects work together to create a simple order entry program that demonstrates how the Visual Basic input objects work. When the Online Shopper program is run, it loads Windows metafiles from the \LearnVb6\Less03 folder on drive C and displays them in the six image boxes on the form.

**IP** If you installed the practice files in a location other than the default C:\LearnVb6 folder, the statements in the program that load the artwork from the disk will contain an incorrect pathname. (Each statement begins with c:\LearnVb6\Less03, as you'll see soon.) If this is the case, you can make the program work by renaming the practice files folder to \LearnVb6 or by changing the pathnames in the Code window using the editing keys or the Replace command on the Edit menu.

*Start button*

5. Click the Start button on the toolbar.

   The program runs in the programming environment.

6. Click the Laptop option button in the Computer box.

   The image of a laptop computer appears in the Products Ordered area on the right side of the form. In the Computer box, a group of *option buttons* is used to gather input from the user. Option buttons force the user to choose one (and only one) item from a list of possibilities. The user can click the various option buttons repeatedly. After each click, the current choice is graphically depicted in the order area to the right.

7. Click the Answering Machine, Calculator, and Copy Machine check boxes in the Office Equipment box.

   *Check boxes* are used in a program when more than one option at a time can be selected from a list. Click the Calculator check box again, and notice that the picture of the calculator disappears from the order area. Because each user interface element is live and responds to click events as they occur, order choices are reflected immediately.

8. Click Satellite Dish in the Peripherals list box.

   A picture of a satellite dish is added to the order area. A *list box* is used to get a user's single response from a list of choices. List boxes can contain many items to choose from (scroll bars appear if the list is longer than the list box), and, unlike option buttons, a default selection is not required. In a Visual Basic program, items can be added to, removed from, or sorted in a list box while the program is running.

9. Now choose U.S. Dollars (sorry, no credit) from the payment list in the Payment Method combo box.

A *combo box,* or drop-down list box, is similar to a regular list box, but it takes up less space. Visual Basic automatically handles the opening, closing, and scrolling of the list box. All you do as a programmer is write code to add items to the list box before the program starts and to process the user's selection. You'll see examples of each task in the Online Shopper code.

After you make your order selections, your screen should look something like this:

10. Practice making a few more changes to the order list in the program (try different computers, peripherals, and payment methods), and then click the Quit button in the program to exit.

The program closes when you click Quit, and the programming environment appears.

## Looking at the Online Shopper Program Code

Although you haven't had much formal experience with program code yet, it's worth taking a quick look at a few event procedures in Online Shopper to see how the program processes input from the user interface elements. In these procedures, you'll see the If…Then and Select Case statements at work. You'll learn about these and other decision structures in Lesson 6. For now, concentrate on the Value property, which changes when a check box is selected, and the ListIndex property, which changes when a list box is selected.

---

 **OTE** Lessons 5, 6, and 7 discuss program code in detail.

---

## Examine the Check Box Code and List Box Code

1. Be sure the program has stopped running, and then double-click the Answering Machine check box in the Office Equipment box to display the Check1_Click event procedure in the Code window.

2. Resize the Code window, and you'll see the following program code:

```
Private Sub Check1_Click()
  If Check1.Value = 1 Then
    Image2.Picture = _
      LoadPicture("c:\learnvb6\less03\answmach.wmf")
    Image2.Visible = True
  Else
    Image2.Visible = False
  End If
End Sub
```

---

 **OTE** In program code, an underscore ( _ ) at the end of a line indicates that the program statement continues on the next line.

---

The Check1_Click event procedure contains the program code that is run when a user clicks the Answering Machine check box in the program. The important keyword here is Check1.Value, which should be read as "the Value property of the first check box object." Check1 is the name of the first check box created on a form; subsequent check boxes are named Check2, Check3, and so on. The Value property is the property that changes when a user clicks the check box on the form. When an "x" or a check mark appears in the check box, the Value property is set to 1; when the check box is blank, the Value property is set to 0 (zero).

The Value property can be set by using the Properties window when you are designing your check box (so that the check box can contain a default setting), or the property can be changed by the user when the program is running (when a check box is clicked). In the code above, the Value property is evaluated by an If…Then…Else decision structure. If the property evaluates to 1, the program loads the picture of an answering machine into the second image box on the form and makes the picture visible. Otherwise (if the Value property is 0), the answering machine picture is hidden from view. If this seems odd, don't worry. You'll learn about decision structures in detail in Lesson 6.

3. Close the Code window, and double-click the Peripherals list box on the form.

The List1_Click event procedure appears in the Code window. The following statements appear:

```
Private Sub List1_Click()
  Select Case List1.ListIndex
  Case 0
    Image3.Picture = _
      LoadPicture("c:\learnvb6\less03\harddisk.wmf")
  Case 1
    Image3.Picture = _
      LoadPicture("c:\learnvb6\less03\printer.wmf")
  Case 2
    Image3.Picture = _
      LoadPicture("c:\learnvb6\less03\satedish.wmf")
  End Select
  Image3.Visible = True
End Sub
```

Here you see code that executes when the user clicks an item in the Peripherals list box in the program. In this case, the important keyword is List1.ListIndex, which is read "the ListIndex property of the first list box object." After the user clicks an item in the list box, the ListIndex property returns a number that corresponds to the location of the item in the list box. (The first item is numbered 0, the second item is numbered 1, and so on.)

The actual text of the choice (the name of the list box item) is also returned in the List1.Text property. Visual Basic programmers often use this value in their programs. In the code on the previous page, List1.ListIndex is evaluated by the Select Case decision structure, and a different Windows metafile is loaded depending on the value of the ListIndex property. If the value is 0, a picture of a hard disk is loaded; if the value is 1, a picture of a printer is loaded; if the value is 2, a picture of a satellite dish (my dream peripheral) is loaded. You'll learn more about how the Select Case decision structure works in Lesson 6.

4. Close the Code window, and double-click the form (not any of the objects) to display the code associated with the form itself.

   The Form_Load event procedure appears in the Code window. This is the procedure that is executed each time the Online Shopper program starts, or *loads.* Programmers put program statements in this special procedure when they want them executed every time a program loads. Often, as in the Online Shopper program, the statements define an aspect of the user interface that couldn't be created by using toolbox controls or the Properties window.

---

 **IP** Statements in the Form_Load event procedure run when the program starts.

---

The Form_Load code follows:

```
Image1.Picture = _
    LoadPicture("c:\learnvb6\less03\pcomputr.wmf")
List1.AddItem "Extra hard disk"
List1.AddItem "Printer"
List1.AddItem "Satellite dish"
Combo1.AddItem "U.S. Dollars"
Combo1.AddItem "Check"
Combo1.AddItem "English Pounds"
```

The first line loads the personal computer Windows metafile into the first image box. This is the default setting reflected in the Computer option button box. The next three lines add items to the Peripherals list box (List1) in the program. The words in quotation marks will appear in the list box when it appears on the form. Below the list box program statements, the items in the Payment Method

## A Word About Terminology

So far in this book I've used several different terms to describe items in a Visual Basic program. Although I haven't defined each of them formally, it's worth listing several of them now to clear up any confusion. Can you tell the difference yet?

- **Control**  A control is a tool you use to create objects on a Visual Basic form. You select controls from the toolbox and use them to draw objects on a form by using the mouse. You use most controls to create user interface elements, such as command buttons, image boxes, and list boxes.

- **Object**  An object is the name of a user interface element you create on a Visual Basic form by using a toolbox control. You can move, resize, and customize objects by using property settings. Objects have what is known as *inherent functionality*— they know how to operate and can respond to certain situations on their own. (A list box "knows" how to scroll, for example.) You can program Visual Basic objects by using customized event procedures for different situations in a program. In Visual Basic, the form itself is also an object.

- **Property**  A property is a value or characteristic held by a Visual Basic object, such as Caption or ForeColor. Properties can be set at design time by using the Properties window or at run time by using statements in the program code. In code, the format for setting a property is

```
Object.Property = Value
```

where *Object* is the name of the object you're customizing, *Property* is the characteristic you want to change, and *Value* is the new property setting. For example,

```
Command1.Caption = "Hello"
```

*(continued)*

**A Word About Terminology** *(continued)*

could be used in the program code to set the Caption property of the Command1 object to "Hello."

- **Event procedure** An event procedure is a block of code that is executed when an object is manipulated in a program. For example, when the first command button in a program is clicked, the Command1_Click event procedure is executed. Event procedures typically evaluate and set properties and use other program statements to perform the work of the program.

- **Program statement** A program statement is a keyword in the code that does the work of the program. Visual Basic program statements create storage space for data, open files, perform calculations, and do several other important tasks.

- **Variable** A variable is a special container used to hold data temporarily in a program. The programmer creates variables to store the results of a calculation, create filenames, process input, and so on. Numbers, names, and property values can be stored in variables.

- **Method** A method is a special statement that performs an action or a service for a particular object in a program. In program code, the notation for using a method is

```
Object.Method Value
```

where *Object* is the name of the object you want to change, *Method* is the command you want to use to change the object, and *Value* is an optional argument to be used by the method. For example, the statement

```
List1.AddItem "Check"
```

uses the AddItem method to put the word *Check* in the List1 list box.

Method combo box (Combo1) are specified. The important keyword in both these groups is AddItem, which is a special function, or *method,* for the list box and combo box objects.

Methods are special statements that perform an action or a service for a particular object, such as adding items to a list box. Methods differ from properties, which contain a value, and event procedures, which execute when a user manipulates an object. Methods can also be shared among objects, so when you learn how to use one method, you'll often be able to apply it to several circumstances. We'll discuss several important methods as you work through this book.

You're finished using the Online Shopper program. Take a few minutes to examine any other parts of the program you're interested in, and then move on to the next exercise.

## Using an OLE Object to Launch Applications

One of the most exciting features of Visual Basic is its ability to work closely with other applications for Windows. Using an OLE object, you can launch applications or other components from your program while it is running and process several types of information. You can also run parts of other applications (such as the spelling checker in Microsoft Word) by using a special technology called *Automation* (formerly called OLE Automation).

We'll examine Automation in detail in Lesson 14. In the next exercise, you'll learn how an OLE object works and how it can be used (without program code) to create an application named Bid Estimator that launches Word, Microsoft Excel, and Microsoft Paint documents so that the user can enter estimate and bid information and site drawings for a construction project.

 **IP** An OLE object lets you start applications for Windows from inside a Visual Basic application.

To run the Bid Estimator program, you'll need copies of Word, Excel, and Paint on your hard disk. (Paint is included with Microsoft Windows.) When you first create an OLE object, an Insert Object dialog box appears, listing the available application objects you can use in your program. If you don't have Word, Excel, or Paint on your hard disk, the Insert Object dialog box won't list them, but feel free to choose another object instead. The purpose of this exercise is to practice using applications you'd like to start from a Visual Basic program. When you run it, the completed utility will look like the following illustration.

## Create the Bid Estimator Program

1. On the File menu, click New Project, and then click OK.

   The Online Shopper program closes, and a new form appears in the programming environment.

2. In the upper-left corner of the form, create a label that has the caption "Bid Estimator." Below the label, create a second label that has the caption "A construction estimate front end featuring Word, Excel, and Paint."

   Leave some extra space in the first label—you'll increase the point size of the caption when you set properties later.

3. Below the second label, spaced equally across the form (see the illustration on the previous page), create three additional labels that have the captions "Estimate scratchpad," "Bid calculator," and "Site drawings."

   These labels will be used to identify the OLE objects used to launch the Word, Excel, and Paint applications, respectively.

   Now you'll add the objects to the form.

*OLE control*

4. Click the OLE control in the toolbox.

5. Below the Estimate Scratchpad label, create a rectangle about the size of a matchbox by using the OLE control.

   When you release the mouse button, Visual Basic displays the Insert Object dialog box, shown below, which contains a list of all the application objects you can use in your program. (This will take a moment or two, because Visual Basic needs to gather the information from your system registry.) The exact list will vary from system to system.

6. Scroll down the list of objects, and click the Microsoft Word Document object if you have Word on your computer.

If you don't have Word, select another Windows-based word processor or a similar application in the dialog box.

7. Click the Display As Icon check box in the Insert Object dialog box so that the application will appear as an icon in your Visual Basic program.

   If you don't click this check box, the application object (typically a document) will be displayed in a window in your application. For now, however, just click Display As Icon.

8. Click OK to close the Insert Object dialog box and to open Word.

   Word opens and displays a blank word processing document in a window. This document will become a *template* in the Bid Estimator program.

   It should contain any information a contractor would find useful when using the program, such as information about the construction company, names, addresses, prices, materials, and so on.

9. For now just type **Estimate Notes—**. Then use the Date And Time command on the Insert menu to add today's date to the template.

   The text appears in the Word document as it will when you run the program.

10. On the Word File menu, click Exit.

    If you are asked whether you want to update the source document, click Yes. You will receive this prompt when you close certain application objects.

    When you're finished with the first object, your form should look like the illustration on the following page. Resize your object or label if any text is hidden from view.

---

**IP** The three-dimensional appearance of the OLE object is controlled by the Appearance property, which has 3-D and Flat settings. In step 13, you will set the Appearance property of each OLE object to Flat and the BackColor property of each OLE object to light gray to make the objects match the form.

---

11. Repeat steps 4 through 10 to add a Microsoft Excel Worksheet object (or its equivalent) to the form below the Bid Calculator label and a Bitmap Image object to the form below the Site Drawings label.

    Be sure to click the Display As Icon check box in the Insert Object dialog box both times, and add some template information (such as notes or instructions) to the Excel worksheet and the Paint canvas if you're comfortable using those programs. In the Excel worksheet, it is easy to imagine a well-organized contractor including several rows and columns of bidding information, including costs of lumber, paint, and labor. The beauty of using other Windows-based applications in your program is that you have access to all these applications' features automatically—you don't have to reinvent the wheel!

12. Place a command button at the bottom of the form. After you've added the button, double-click the object and type the statement **End** in the Command1_Click event procedure.

    The End program statement will terminate the program when the user is finished using it.

13. Set the following properties for the objects on the form by using the Properties window:

| Object | Property | Setting |
| --- | --- | --- |
| Command1 | Caption | "Quit" |
| Label1 | Font | Times New Roman, Bold, 18-point |
| OLE1 | BorderStyle | 0 – None |
| | Appearance | 0 – Flat |
| | BackColor | Light gray |
| OLE2 | BorderStyle | 0 – None |
| | Appearance | 0 – Flat |
| | BackColor | Light gray |
| OLE3 | BorderStyle | 0 – None |
| | Appearance | 0 – Flat |
| | BackColor | Light gray |

14. On the File menu, click Save Project As, and save the form to disk with the name **MyOleBid**. Save the project to disk with the name **MyOleBid**.

When you've finished, your MyOleBid form should look similar to the following illustration:

Now try running the program to see how the OLE objects operate at run-time.

## Run the My Bid Estimator Program

 **TIP** The complete OleBid program is located on disk in the \LearnVb6\Less03 folder.

1. Click the Start button on the toolbar.

   The program runs in the programming environment. The OLE1 object (the Document icon) is surrounded by a dotted line, indicating that it has the attention, or *focus*, of the program.

 **TIP** The focus is important for keyboard operations. When the user presses Enter, the object that has the focus is selected, or activated, in the program. The user can switch the focus to another object in the program by pressing the Tab key or by clicking the object. You can change the order in which objects receive the focus in the program by changing each object's TabIndex property.

2. Double-click the Document icon in the program.

   The word processor starts, and the Word template document appears in a window.

3. Type a few lines of text (pretend you're an important contractor), and then on the File menu, click Exit to return to the MyOleBid program.

4. Double-click the Worksheet icon in the program.

   The spreadsheet starts, and the Excel template appears in a window.

5. Enter a few rows and columns of information in the spreadsheet (feel free to use Excel functions and formatting features if you like). Then on the File menu, click Exit to return to the MyOleBid program.

6. Double-click the Bitmap Image icon.

   The Paint accessory program starts and appears in a window. Paint is a simple illustration program containing drawing tools and color palettes for creating rudimentary artwork.

7. Create a simple construction site sketch with the Paint accessory (or pretend you did), and then, on the File menu, click Exit & Return To.

8. Click the Quit button to end the program.

Congratulations! You've built your first program that uses Microsoft Office application objects. You can use this technique to include in a program any application object installed on your system. Now you'll try working with another type of file in the Windows environment— a preexisting database containing customer names and addresses.

## Using a Data Object to View a Microsoft Access Database

If you work in a corporate setting or share information with other computer users regularly, you might use databases to track important information about clients, employees, or ongoing projects. A *database* is an organized collection of information stored electronically in a file. Database applications, such as Microsoft Access, dBASE, and Paradox, are special programs that create and process information stored in databases. They provide the tools to design the database, manipulate the information in it, and search for specific items. To enhance your work with databases, Visual Basic provides three objects that let you display and modify the information in database files. The primary object, data, gives you access to the fields and records of a database file directly on your form. You'll practice using a data object now to display information in an Access database named Students.mdb.

## Fields and Records

Two important terms used to describe information in databases are *fields* and *records*. Fields are the categories of information stored in a database. Typical fields in a customer database might include customer names, addresses, phone numbers, and comments. All the information about a particular customer or business is called a record. When databases are created, information is entered in tables of fields and records. Often the records correspond to rows in the table, and the fields correspond to columns.

Fields

Records

| Instructor ID | Instructor | Phone Number | Extension |
|---|---|---|---|
| 1 | Delamare, Marie | 3105551234 | |
| 2 | Mackenzie, Wendy | 3105556543 | |
| 3 | Bein, Martin | 3105554321 | |
| 4 | Wilson, Peter | 3105550088 | |
| 5 | Burke, Shelley | 3105554567 | |
| * | (AutoNumber) | | |

 **IP** The Access file used in this exercise is on disk in the Less03 folder, so you can try this exercise even if you don't have Access installed. You can also substitute one of your own database files for the Access file if you like.

## Create a Data Object

1. On the File menu, click New Project, and then click OK.

   The MyOleBid program closes, and a new form appears in the programming environment. Save any changes to the MyOleBid program if you are prompted to.

2. Click the Data control in the toolbox.

*Data control*

3. Move the mouse pointer to the center of the form, near the bottom, and draw a rectangular box by using the control.

A data object named Data1 appears on the form:

The object contains arrows that let you scroll through the records of your database when the program runs. The object also contains a caption (currently Data1) that you can use to describe the database you'll access by using the object. Typically, the caption is set to the name of the database. The second set of arrows near the outside edges of the object are used to move to the beginning or the end of the database.

You can perform many sophisticated operations with a database in Visual Basic. In this exercise, you will display the Instructor field of the Students.mdb database. (You'll actually be able to scroll through the database and view each name in the file.) To display the Instructor field on the form, an additional object is needed to hold the data. Because the data you want to display is text, you'll add a text box object to the form. (You'll also place a label above the text box to identify the database field.) Finally, you'll establish a connection between the data object and the text box object, or *bind* them together, by using several property settings.

## Create Text Box and Label Objects

*TextBox control*

1. Click the TextBox control in the toolbox.

2. Create a text box on the form, above the data object.

The text box should be about the same size as the data object. The box should be wide enough to display instructor names (both first and last) up to 20 characters long.

*Label control*

3. Click the Label control in the toolbox.

4. Create a label above the text box on the form.

When you've finished creating the objects, your screen should look like this:

Now you'll set the properties for the objects.

## Set Object Properties

1. Click the data object, and then click the Properties Window button on the toolbar.

2. In the Properties window, verify that the Connect property is set to Access (the default).

   The Connect property records the database or spreadsheet format you'll be using. The formats Visual Basic can read include Access, Excel, Lotus 1-2-3, dBASE, FoxPro, and Paradox.

3. In the Properties window, set the DatabaseName property to c:\LearnVb6\Less03\students.mdb by selecting the file in the DatabaseName dialog box.

   Students.mdb is the sample Access database you'll open in this exercise. It contains a number of useful tables, fields, and records that an instructor or administrator might use to track academic data, including student names, teachers, classrooms, grades, and miscellaneous scheduling information. I've made this a fairly sophisticated database so that you can continue to experiment on your own if you like.

4. In the Properties window, click the RecordSource property, and then click the drop-down list box arrow. When a list of database tables appears, click Instructors in the list box.

   The RecordSource property lets you specify the table (the collection of data) you want to open in the database.

5. In the Properties window, set the Caption property of the data object to "Students.mdb."

   The caption in the control changes to Students.mdb to identify the database to the user.

   Now you'll change the DataSource property of the text box to link the text box to the data object.

6. Click the text box object, and then click the Properties Window button on the toolbar.

7. In the Properties window, click the DataSource property, click the drop-down list box arrow, and then click Data1.

8. In the Properties window, click the DataField property, click the drop-down list box arrow, and then click Instructor (the field you want to display) in the list.

9. Click the Label object, click the Properties button on the toolbar, and then change the Caption property to "Instructor."

   This will identify the database field in the text box when the program runs. Adding labels to your form to explain what objects are is always a good idea, especially when you're working with database fields.

10. Save your form as **MyData** and your project as **MyData**.

That's it! Now run your program.

## Run the MyData Program

 **TIP** The complete Data.vbp program is located on disk in the \LearnVb6 \Less03 folder.

1. Click the Start button on the toolbar.

   The program runs in the program environment, as shown in the following illustration:

   Visual Basic loads the Students.mdb database, opens the Instructor table, and places the first Instructor field in the text box. Examine other field entries now by clicking buttons in the data object.

2. Click the inner-right button in the data object.

   The second name in the database appears in the text window.

3. Click the outer-right button in the data object.

   Visual Basic displays the last name in the database.

4. Click the outer-left button in the data object.

   Visual Basic displays the first name in the database.

5. Click the Close button on the form to stop the program.

# Modifying a Database

A data object also lets you modify the information in databases. To change a name in the Students.mdb database, run the MyData program and scroll to the name you want to change. Then click in the Name text box and edit the name as you see fit. When you change to a different record, the edit you made is copied to the original database immediately. Give it a try now.

## Change a Name in the Database

1. Click Start on the toolbar to run the MyData program.

   The first name in the database appears in the text box.

2. Highlight the first name by using the mouse, press Del, and then type **Cocco, Sean.**

3. Click the inside right arrow in the data object to move to the next record.

   The first name in the database is changed to Cocco, Sean.

4. Click the inside left arrow in the data object to move back to the first record.

   The first name now appears as Cocco, Sean.

5. Click the Close button on the form to stop the program.

As you can see, a data object gives you quick access to preexisting databases. You can display any field in the database and process the information as you see fit. You'll learn more about data objects and how to manipulate database records in future lessons.

# Installing ActiveX Controls

You can extend the functionality of Visual Basic by installing the ActiveX controls that come with Visual Basic or by installing ActiveX controls that you create yourself or acquire from third-party tool vendors. To conserve system resources and desktop space, Visual Basic displays only the basic set of interface controls in the toolbox when you open a new project. However, you can customize the toolbox for each project individually by using the Components command on the Project menu. The ActiveX controls you install take advantage of 32-bit ActiveX technology, a Microsoft standard for programmable objects in application programs, operating systems, and Internet tools. You can recognize ActiveX controls by their .ocx filename extension. They are added to the operating system automatically each time you install a new application program. (Visual Basic "learns" about new ActiveX controls by looking for those associated with specific programs in the Windows system registry.)

## Install the Grid and the CommonDialog ActiveX Controls

Each version of Visual Basic (including the Working Model) features extra ActiveX controls you can use in your projects. For example, if you're writing a program to display data in a table, you can install the FlexGrid control, located in the file Msflxgrd.ocx, and use it to create a grid of cells on a form. (A grid object looks a lot like an Excel worksheet.) Another useful ActiveX control, the CommonDialog control, which is located in the file Comdlg32.ocx, creates standard dialog boxes, such as Open and Save As.

Follow these steps to install the ActiveX controls:

1. On the File menu, click New Project, and then click OK to create a standard .exe file.

   Save any changes to the MyData program if you are prompted to.

2. On the Project menu, click the Components command, and then click the Controls tab.

   The Components dialog box appears.

   The Controls tab presents an alphabetical list of the ActiveX controls in your system that can be added to your project's toolbox. To give you flexibility in how you create your programs, every project has its own unique toolbox containing the default Visual Basic controls and any ActiveX controls you select. Accordingly, any controls you add to this project now will appear only in this project's toolbox. In the following steps, you'll add the FlexGrid control (Msflxgrd.ocx) and the CommonDialog control (Comdlg32.ocx) to your toolbox.

> **TIP** The Components dialog box also contains an Insertable Objects tab, which you can use to add application objects to your project's toolbox. An *insertable object* is a program component supplied by another application for Windows, such as a Word document or an Excel worksheet. You'll find these tools just as useful as ActiveX controls.

3. Click the check box next to the control named Microsoft Common Dialog Control 6.0.

   The ActiveX control is selected, and the location of the .ocx file appears at the bottom of the dialog box.

4. As shown in the illustration, click the check box next to the control named Microsoft FlexGrid Control 6.0 to select it as well.

5. Click OK to add the selected ActiveX controls to this project's toolbox.

The toolbox displays two new controls, as shown in the following illustration:

CommonDialog control

FlexGrid control

The FlexGrid and CommonDialog controls work exactly like the rest of the Visual Basic controls in the toolbox. In fact, if you didn't know they were ActiveX controls, it would be difficult to tell them apart from the standard toolbox controls. You select the ActiveX controls by clicking them, and you use them to create objects on a form the same way you use the other controls. The ActiveX controls also have adjustable property settings and can be used in program code like the rest of the controls you've used in this lesson.

# Working with Menus and Dialog Boxes

In Lesson 3, you used several Microsoft Visual Basic objects to gather input from the user while he or she was using a program. In this lesson, you'll learn to present choices to the user by using professional-looking menus and dialog boxes. A *menu* is located on the menu bar and contains a list of related commands. When you click a menu title, a list of the menu commands appears in a list box. Most menu commands are executed immediately after they are clicked; for example, when the user clicks the Copy command on the Edit menu, information is copied to the Clipboard immediately. If a menu command is followed by an ellipsis (…), however, Visual Basic displays a dialog box requesting more information before the command is carried out. In this lesson, you'll learn to use the Menu Editor and the CommonDialog control to add menus and standard dialog boxes to your programs.

# Adding Menus by Using the Menu Editor

The Menu Editor is a graphical tool that manages menus in your programs. It lets you add new menus, modify and reorder existing menus, and delete old menus. It also lets you add special effects to your menus, such as access keys, check marks, and keyboard shortcuts. After you have added menus to your form, you can use event procedures to process the menu commands. In the following exercise, you'll use the Menu Editor to create a Clock menu containing commands that display the current date and time.

## Creating a Menu

1. Start Visual Basic and open a new project.

   If the programming environment is already running, on the File menu click New Project to open a new project.

*Menu Editor button*

2. Click the Menu Editor button on the toolbar.

   The Menu Editor appears, as shown in the following illustration:

The Menu Editor displays menu-building commands and options in a dialog box. You specify the caption for a menu (the name of the menu on the screen) in the Caption text box. You specify the name for a menu (the name it will have in the program code) in the Name text box. These are the two most important settings for a menu.

Additional settings, such as Index, HelpContextID, Shortcut, and Checked, are optional. You'll learn about the Shortcut setting at the end of this lesson.

When you click the Next button in the Menu Editor dialog box, the Menu Editor clears the dialog box so that you can enter specifications for the next menu item. The menu list box at the bottom of the dialog box displays menu items as you create them and shows the overall structure of the menu.

You'll use the Menu Editor now to create a Clock menu.

3. Type **Clock** in the Caption text box, and then press Tab.

   The word *Clock* is entered as the caption of your first menu, and the cursor moves to the Name text box. As you type the menu caption, the caption also appears in the menu list box at the bottom of the dialog box.

4. Type **mnuClock** in the Name text box.

   The word *mnuClock* is entered as the name of your menu in the program.

   By convention, the prefix *mnu* is used to identify a menu object in the program code. Prefixing user interface elements with a three-character label will help you differentiate event procedures as your programs get larger, and it will help you identify interface elements in the Code window.

---

 **IP**   Lesson 9 lists the naming conventions for all Visual Basic objects.

---

5. Click the Next button to add the Clock menu title to your program.

   The Clock menu is added to the menu bar, and the Menu Editor clears the dialog box for your next menu item. The menu title still appears in the menu list box at the bottom of the dialog box. As you build your menu, each item will be added to the menu list box so that you can see the structure of the menu.

6. Type **Date** in the Caption text box, press Tab, and then type **mnuDateItem** in the Name text box.

   The Date command appears in the menu list box. Because you want to make Date a command rather than a menu title, you use another naming convention—you add the word *Item* to the end of the name in the Name text box. This will help you differentiate menu commands from menu titles in the Code window.

7. With the Date item highlighted in the menu list box, click the Right arrow button in the Menu Editor.

   The Date command moves one indent (four spaces) to the right in the menu list box, indicating that the item is a menu command. The position of an item in the list box determines whether it is a menu title (flush left), a menu command (one indent), a submenu title (two indents), or a submenu command (three indents). You click the Right arrow button in the Menu Editor dialog box to move items to the right, and you click the Left arrow button to move items to the left.

   Now you'll add a menu command named Time to the Clock menu.

8. Click the Next button, type **Time**, press Tab, and then type **mnuTimeItem**.

   The Time command appears in the menu list box, as shown here:

The right arrow button creates a menu command or submenu

Menu list box

Notice that the Menu Editor assumed that the next item would be a menu command and indented Time one level. You've finished adding commands to the Clock menu, so you can close the Menu Editor.

9. Click OK to close the Menu Editor.

   The Menu Editor closes, and your form appears in the programming environment with a menu bar and a Clock menu. Now you'll open the Clock menu to see its contents.

10. Click the Clock menu.

    The Date and Time commands appear.

    Clicking a menu command in the programming environment displays the event procedure that is executed when the menu command is chosen. You'll create event procedures for Date and Time a little later. First, you'll add keyboard support to the menus.

11. Click the form (or press Esc twice) to close the Clock menu.

## Adding Access Keys to Menu Commands

Visual Basic makes it easy to provide *access key* support for menus and menu commands. The access key for a command is the keyboard key the user can press to execute the command. When the user opens a menu at runtime, the access key for a command is indicated by an underlined letter in the command name. To add an access key to a menu item, all you need to do is start the Menu Editor and prefix the access key letter in the menu item caption with an ampersand (&). From that time forward, your program will support the access key.

Try adding access keys to the Clock menu now.

### Adding access keys

*Menu Editor button*

1. Click the Menu Editor button on the toolbar.

   The Menu Editor appears, and the menu list box displays the menu items that are in your program. The caption and name for the Clock menu appear in the dialog box.

2. Click in front of the word *Clock* in the Caption text box.

   The cursor blinks before the letter "C" in *Clock.*

3. Type **&** to define the letter "C" as the access key for the Clock menu.

   An ampersand appears in the text box.

---

### Menu Conventions

By convention, each menu title and menu command in an application for Microsoft Windows has an initial capital letter. File and Edit are often the first two menu names on the menu bar, and Help is the last. Other common menu names are View, Format, and Window. No matter what menus and commands you use in your applications, take care to be clear and consistent with them. Menus and commands should be easy to use and should have as much in common with those in other Windows-based applications as possible. As you create menu items, use the following guidelines:

- Use short, specific captions consisting of one or two words at most.

- Assign each menu item in a program a unique access key. Use the first letter of the item if possible.

- If a command is used as an on/off toggle, place a check mark next to the item when it is active. You can add a check mark by clicking the Checked check box in the Menu Editor or by setting the menu item's Checked property to True.

- Place an ellipsis (...) after a menu command that requires the user to enter more information before the command can be executed.

- Use menu naming conventions such as the *mnu* prefix and the *Item* suffix when assigning menu names.

---

4. Click the Date command in the menu list.

   The caption and name for the Date command appear in the dialog box.

5. Type an ampersand before the letter "D" in the Caption text box.

   The letter "D" is now defined as the access key for the Date command.

6. Click the Time command in the menu list.

   The caption and name for the Time command appear in the dialog box.

7. Type an ampersand before the letter "T" in the Caption text box.

   The letter "T" is now defined as the access key for the Time command.

8. Click OK in the dialog box to close the Menu Editor.

   Now you'll run the program to see how the access keys look at runtime.

*Start button*

9. Click the Start button.

10. Click the Clock menu.

    The Clock menu and the menu commands are displayed with underlined access keys.

*End button*

11. Click the End button on the toolbar to quit the program.

Now you'll practice using the Menu Editor to switch the order of the Date and Time commands on the Clock menu. Changing the order of menu items is an important skill to have; at times you'll think better of a decision you made when you first defined your menus.

## Changing the Order of Menu Items

1. Click the Menu Editor button on the toolbar.

   The Menu Editor appears.

2. Click the Time command in the menu list.

   The caption and name for the Time command appear in the menu list.

3. Click the Up arrow button in the menu list.

   The Time menu item is moved above the Date menu item.

4. Click the OK button.

   The Menu Editor closes, and the order of the Date and Time commands is switched in the Clock menu. You can also use the Down arrow button in the Menu Editor to switch menu items; it moves commands down in the list.

You've finished creating the user interface for the Clock menu. Now you'll use the menu event procedures to process the user's menu selections in the program.

 **IP**   You can also insert new menu items and delete unwanted menu items by using the Menu Editor. To insert a new menu item, click the item in the menu list that should follow the new item and then click the Insert button. The Menu Editor will insert a blank item in the list. You can define this item by using the Caption and Name text boxes. To delete an unwanted menu item, click the unwanted item in the menu list and then click the Delete button.

# Processing Menu Choices

After menu items are placed on the menu bar, they become objects in the program. To make the menu objects do meaningful work, you need to write event procedures for them. Menu event procedures typically contain program statements that display or process information on the user interface form and modify one or more menu properties. If more information is needed from the user to process the selected command, an event procedure will often display a dialog box by using a common dialog object or one of the input objects.

---

 **IP**  A menu command is processed by an event procedure associated with the command.

---

In the following exercise, you'll add a label object to your form to display the output of the Time and Date commands on the Clock menu.

### Adding a label object to the form

*Label control*

1. Click the Label control in the toolbox.

2. Create a small label in the top middle area of the form.

   The label appears on the form. It is named Label1 in the program code. Your form should look like the following:

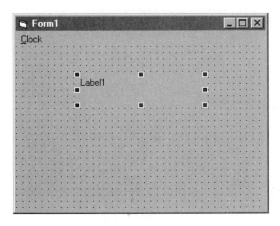

3. Set the following properties for the label:

| Object | Property | Setting |
| --- | --- | --- |
| Label1 | Alignment | 2 – Center |
| | Border Style | 1 – Fixed Single |
| | Caption | (none) |
| | Font | MS Sans Serif, Bold, 14-point |

 **IP** In the following exercises, you'll enter program code to process menu choices. Type in the program statements exactly as they are printed. You won't learn how program statements work yet—only how they are used to support a functional user interface. You'll learn how program statements work in Lessons 5 through 7.

Now you'll add program statements to the Time and Date event procedures to process the menu commands.

## Editing the Menu Event Procedures

1. Click the View Code button in the Project window to open the Code window.

2. Click the Object drop-down list box, and then click mnuTimeItem.

The object for the Time menu command

The mnuTimeItem_Click event procedure appears in the Code window. You assigned the name mnuTimeItem to the Time command in the Menu Editor. When the user clicks the Time command in the program, the mnuTimeItem_Click event procedure is executed.

3. Press the Spacebar four times, and then type

   ```
   Label1.Caption = Time
   ```

   This program statement displays the current time (from the system clock) in the caption of the Label1 object, replacing the previous Label1 caption. You can use the Time function at any time in your programs to display the time accurately down to the second.

---

**TIP** Visual Basic's Time function returns the current system time. You can set the system time by using the Date/Time option in Control Panel; you can change the system time format by using Control Panel's Regional Settings option.

---

4. Press the Down arrow key.

   Visual Basic interprets the line and adjusts capitalization and spacing, if necessary. (Visual Basic checks each line for syntax errors as you enter it. You can enter a line by pressing Enter, Up arrow, or Down arrow.)

5. Click the mnuDateItem object in the Object drop-down list box.

   The mnuDateItem_Click event procedure appears in the Code window. This event procedure is executed when the user clicks the Date command on the Clock menu.

6. Press the Spacebar four times, and then type

   ```
   Label1.Caption = Date
   ```

   This program statement displays the current date (from the system clock) in the caption of the Label1 object, replacing the previous Label1 caption. The Date function is also available for general use in your programs. Assign Date to an object caption whenever you want to display the current date on a form.

**IP** Visual Basic's Date function returns the current system date. You can set the system date by using the Date/Time option in Control Panel; change the system date format by using Control Panel's Regional Settings option.

7. Press the Down arrow key to enter the line.

Your screen should look like the following:

```
Project1 - Form1
mnuDateItem                    Click
    Private Sub mnuDateItem_Click()
        Label1.Caption = Date
    End Sub

    Private Sub mnuTimeItem_Click()
        Label1.Caption = Time
    End Sub
```

8. Close the Code window.

You've finished entering the menu demonstration program. Now you'll save the form and project to disk under the name MyMenu.

## Saving the MyMenu Program

*Save Project button*

1. Click the Save Project button on the toolbar.

The Save Project button is the toolbar alternative to the Save Project command on the File menu.

2. To enter the name of your project form, select the \LearnVb6 \Less04 folder, and then type **MyMenu** and press Enter.

The form is saved to disk with the name MyMenu.frm, and the Save Project As dialog box appears.

3. To enter the name of your project, type **MyMenu** and press Enter.

The project is saved to disk with the name MyMenu.vbp.

Now your program is ready to run.

**TIP** The complete Menu.vbp program is located on disk in the \LearnVb6 \Less04 folder.

## Running the MyMenu Program

*Start button*

1. Click the Start button on the toolbar.

   The MyMenu program runs in the programming environment.

2. Click the Clock menu on the menu bar.

   The contents of the Clock menu appear.

3. Click the Time command.

   The current system time appears in the label box, as shown here:

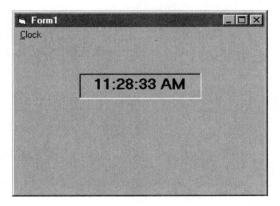

   Your time will probably differ from what appears here.

   Now you'll try displaying the current date by using the access keys on the menu.

4. Press and release the Alt key.

   The Clock menu on the menu bar is highlighted.

5. Press C to display the Clock menu.

   The contents of the Clock menu appear.

6. Press D to display the current date.

   The current date appears in the label box.

*End button*

7. Click the End button to stop the program.

Congratulations! You've created a working program that makes use of menus and access keys. In the next exercise, you'll learn how to use menus to display standard dialog boxes.

### System Clock Functions

You can use 10 functions to retrieve chronological values from the system clock. You can use these values to create custom calendars, clocks, and alarms in your programs. The following table lists the most useful system clock functions. For more information, check the Visual Basic online Help.

| Function | Description |
| --- | --- |
| Time | Returns the current time from the system clock. |
| Date | Returns the current date from the system clock. |
| Now | Returns an encoded value representing the current date and time. This function is most useful as an argument for other system clock functions. |
| Hour (*time*) | Returns the hour portion of the specified time (0 through 23). |
| Minute (*time*) | Returns the minute portion of the specified time (0 through 59). |
| Second (*time*) | Returns the second portion of the specified time (0 through 59). |
| Day (*date*) | Returns a whole number representing the day of the month (1 through 31). |
| Month (*date*) | Returns a whole number representing the month (1 through 12). |
| Year (*date*) | Returns the year portion of the specified date. |
| Weekday (*date*) | Returns a whole number representing the day of the week (1 is Sunday, 2 is Monday, and so on). |

# Using Common Dialog Objects

A *common dialog object* allows you to display any of five standard dialog boxes in your programs. Each common dialog box can be displayed from a single common dialog object by using the common dialog object method corresponding to that particular box. (As mentioned earlier, a method is a command that performs an action or a service for an object.) You control the contents of a common dialog box by setting its associated properties. When the user fills out a common dialog box in a program, the results are returned through one or more properties in the common dialog object, and can then be used in the program to perform meaningful work.

The five common dialog boxes provided by the common dialog object are listed here with the methods you use to specify them:

| Dialog box | Purpose | Method |
|---|---|---|
| Open | Get the drive, folder name, and filename for an existing file. | ShowOpen |
| Save As | Get the drive, folder name, and filename for a new file. | ShowSave |
| Print | Let the user set printing options. | ShowPrinter |
| Font | Let the user choose a new font type and style. | ShowFont |
| Color | Let the user select a color from a palette. | ShowColor |

In the following exercises, you'll add a new menu to the MyMenu program and practice using the Open and Color common dialog boxes. To retain a copy of the original MyMenu program, you'll save the MyMenu form and project with the name MyDialog before you start.

---

 **OTE**   Be sure to save both the form and the project under a new name when you're renaming a project. Always save the form first.

---

## Saving the MyMenu Files as MyDialog

1. If MyMenu.vbp is not already open, load it from disk by clicking Open Project on the File menu.

If you didn't create MyMenu, open Menu.vbp from the \LearnVb6 \Less04 folder. Its contents should match those of MyMenu.

2. On the File menu, click the Save MyMenu.frm As command.

The Save File As dialog box appears.

3. Specify the \LearnVb6\Less04 folder, type **MyDialog.frm**, and then press Enter.

A copy of the MyMenu form is saved to disk under the name MyDialog.frm.

---

 **MPORTANT** If you don't save the form under a new name first, the MyMenu and MyDialog programs will share the same form.

---

4. On the File menu, click the Save Project As command.

The Save Project As dialog box appears.

5. Specify the \Vb6Sbs\Less04 folder, type **MyDialog.vbp**, and then press Enter.

A copy of the MyMenu project file is saved to disk under the name MyDialog.vbp.

## Adding a Common Dialog Object

Now you'll use the CommonDialog control to add a common dialog object to the form. The common dialog object appears in only one size and is not visible to the user at runtime. (Because the object will not be visible, it can be placed anywhere on the form.) Placing the object on the form allows you to use any of the five common dialog boxes in your program.

### Adding the CommonDialog control to your toolbox

If the CommonDialog control is not in your toolbox, you can add it by clicking the Components command on the Project menu. Follow these steps:

1. On the Project menu, click the Components command.

2. Click the Controls tab, and place a check mark in the check box next to the Microsoft Common Dialog Control 6.0.

3. Click OK.

   The CommonDialog control appears in your toolbox, as shown in the following illustration:

CommonDialog control

### Adding a common dialog object

*CommonDialog control*

1. Click the CommonDialog control in the toolbox.

2. Draw a common dialog object in the lower-left corner of the form.

   When you finish drawing the object, it resizes itself. The common dialog object is ready for use in your program.

Now you'll create an image object by using the Image control. The image object displays artwork the user selects in your program by using the Open common dialog box.

### Adding an image object

*Image control*

1. Click the Image control in the toolbox.

2. Add an image object to the form, below the label.

3. Use the Properties window to set the image object's Stretch property to True.

   When you've finished, your screen should look like the one shown here.

CommonDialog object      Image object

Now you'll use the Menu Editor to add a File menu to the MyDialog program.

### Adding a File menu

1. Click the form to select the form object.

   The form must be selected before you can add or modify menu items.

*Menu Editor button*

2. Click the Menu Editor button on the toolbar.

   The Menu Editor appears, and the current menu structure of the MyDialog program appears in the dialog box. Now you'll add to the program a File menu that includes Open, Close, and Exit commands.

3. Click the Insert button four times.

   Four blank lines appear at the top of the menu item list. This creates space for the File menu commands you'll enter.

4. Click the Caption text box, type **&File**, press Tab, type **mnuFile**, and then click the Next button.

   The File menu is added to the program. The letter "F" is specified as the access key.

5. Type **&Open...**, press Tab, type **mnuOpenItem**, click the Right arrow button, and then click Next.

   The menu item Open—a command that will open Windows metafiles—is added to the menu list and indented one level. Because the command will display a dialog box, you added an ellipsis to the command caption.

6. Type **&Close**, press Tab, type **mnuCloseItem**, click the Right arrow button, and then click Next.

   The menu item Close (a command that will close the open file) is added to the menu list.

7. Type **E&xit**, press Tab, type **mnuExitItem**, and then click the Right arrow button.

   The menu item Exit—a command that will close the MyDialog application—is added to the menu list. It's traditional to use "x" as the access key for the Exit command. Your screen should look like the following:

## Disabling a Menu Command

In a typical application for Windows, not all menu commands are available at the same time. In a typical Edit menu, for example, the Paste command is available only when there is data on the Clipboard. You can disable a menu item by clearing the Enabled check box for that menu item in the Menu Editor. When a command is disabled, it appears in dimmed type on the menu bar.

In the following exercise, you'll disable the Close command. (Close is a command that can be used only after a file has been opened in the program.) Later in the lesson, you'll include a statement in the Open command event procedure that enables the Close command at the proper time.

### Disabling the Close command

1. Click the Close command in the menu list.

   The caption and name of the command appear in the dialog box.

2. Click the Enabled check box in the Menu Editor to remove the check mark.

The check mark is removed from the check box, and the setting is disabled.

Now you'll add a TextColor command to the Clock menu to demonstrate the Color common dialog box. The Color common dialog box returns a color setting to the program through the CommonDialog1.Color property. You'll use that property to change the color of the text in the label caption.

### Adding the TextColor Command to the Clock Menu

1. Click Date, the last menu item in the menu list.

   You'll place the TextColor command at the bottom of the Clock menu.

2. Click the Next button.

   A blank line appears at the bottom of the menu list.

3. Type **TextCo&lor...**, press Tab, and type **mnuTextColorItem**.

   The command TextColor is added to the Clock menu. The command contains a trailing ellipsis to indicate that it will display a dialog box when the user clicks it. The access key chosen for this command was "L" because "T" was already used in the menu, for Time. Your access keys won't behave correctly if you use duplicate keys at the same level within a particular menu or duplicate keys at the menu bar level.

4. Click OK to close the Menu Editor.

# Event Procedures That Manage Common Dialog Boxes

To display a common dialog box in a program, you need to call the common dialog object by using the appropriate object method in an event procedure. If necessary, you must also set one or more common dialog box properties before the call by using program code. After the user makes his or her selections in the common dialog box, you process the choices by using program code in the event procedure.

In the following exercise, you'll type in the program code for the mnuOpenItem_ Click event procedure, the routine that executes when the

Open command is clicked. You'll set the Filter property in the CommonDialog1 object to define the file type in the Open common dialog box. (You'll specify Windows metafiles.) Then you'll use the ShowOpen method to display the Open common dialog box. After the user has selected a file and closed the common dialog box, you'll display the file in the image object by setting the Picture property of the Image1 object to the filename the user selected. Finally, you'll enable the Close command so that the user can unload the picture if he or she wants.

## Editing the Open Command Event Procedure

*View Code button*

1. Click the View Code button in the Project window.

2. Click the Object drop-down list box, and then click the mnuOpenItem object.

   The mnuOpenItem_Click event procedure appears in the Code window.

3. Type the following program statements in the event procedure, between the Private Sub and End Sub statements. Indent each line four spaces to set the line off as the text of the event procedure. Be sure to type each line exactly as it is printed here, and press the Down arrow key after the last line.

```
CommonDialog1.Filter = "Metafiles (*.WMF)|*.WMF"
CommonDialog1.ShowOpen
Image1.Picture = LoadPicture(CommonDialog1.FileName)
mnuCloseItem.Enabled = True
```

Your screen should look like the following:

This statement displays the Open dialog box.

The first three lines in the event procedure refer to three different properties of the CommonDialog1 object. The first line uses the Filter property to define a list of valid files. (In this case, the list has only one item: *.WMF.) This is important for the Open dialog box because an image object, as you learned in Lesson 3, is designed for six types of files: bitmaps (.bmp files), Windows metafiles (.wmf files), icons (.ico files), cursors (.cur files), JPEG format (.jpg files), and GIF format (.gif files). (Attempting to display a .txt file in an image object would cause a runtime error, for example.)

---

**NOTE** The Filter property defines the file types that will be listed in the Open dialog box.

---

To add additional items to the Filter list, you can type a pipe symbol ( | ) between items. For example,

```
CommonDialog1.Filter = "Bitmaps (*.BMP)|*.BMP|Metafiles (*.WMF)|*.WMF"
```

allows both bitmaps and Windows metafiles to be chosen in the Open dialog box.

The second line in the event procedure displays the Open common dialog box in the program. Each common dialog box is displayed by using a different object method; the method for displaying the Open common dialog box is ShowOpen. (See the table earlier in this lesson for the methods that display other common dialog boxes.) This is the critical statement for the event procedure. Because the command's name is Open, the procedure needs to display an Open common dialog box and process the results.

The third line uses the filename selected in the dialog box by the user. When the user selects a drive, folder, and filename and then clicks OK, the complete pathname is passed to the program through the CommonDialog1.FileName property. The LoadPicture function, a routine that loads electronic artwork, is then used to copy the specified Windows metafile into the Image1 object.

The final line in the procedure enables the Close command on the File menu. Now that a file has been opened in the program, the Close command should be available so that users can close the file.

Now you'll type in the program code for the mnuTextColorItem_Click event procedure, the routine that runs when the TextColor command on the Clock menu is clicked.

## Editing the TextColor Command Event Procedure

1. Click the mnuTextColorItem object in the Object drop-down list box.

   The event procedure for the TextColor command appears in the Code window.

2. Type the following program statements (indented four spaces) in the event procedure, between the Private Sub and End Sub statements.

```
CommonDialog1.Flags = &H1&
CommonDialog1.ShowColor
Label1.ForeColor = CommonDialog1.Color
```

## Controlling Color Choices by Using Flags

The mnuTextColorItem_Click event procedure makes use of the common dialog object's properties and methods. The first line sets a property named Flags to &H1&, a hexadecimal value that directs the Color common dialog box to present a list of standard color choices to the user, with custom colors as an option and a default color choice highlighted. The following table shows the four possible values for the Flags property.

| Flag | Meaning |
|------|---------|
| &H1& | Display a standard Color common dialog box (with custom colors as an option), and specify the current color as the default. |
| &H2& | Display a standard and custom Color common dialog box. |
| &H4& | Display a standard Color common dialog box with the Define Custom Colors button disabled. |
| &H8& | Display a Help button in the Color common dialog box. |

You can use any combination of these values to prepare your Color common dialog box before you open it. To combine two or more values, use the Or operator. For example,

```
CommonDialog1.Flags = &H1& Or &H8&
```

displays the same Color common dialog box as before, but with an added Help button.

The second line in the event procedure uses the ShowColor method to open the Color common dialog box, and the third line assigns the selected color to the ForeColor property of the Label1 object. You might remember Label1 from the MyMenu program earlier in this lesson—it's the label box you used to display the current time and date on the form. You'll use the color returned from the Color common dialog box to set the color of the foreground text in the label.

---

 **TIP** The Color common dialog box can be used to set the color of any user interface element that supports color. Other possibilities include the form background color, the colors of shapes on the form, and the foreground and background colors of objects.

---

Now you'll type in the program code for the mnuCloseItem_Click event procedure, the routine that closes the file displayed in the image object when the Close command on the File menu is clicked.

## Editing the Close Command Event Procedure

1. Click the Object drop-down list box in the Code window, and then click the mnuCloseItem object in the list box.

   The event procedure for the File Close command appears in the Code window.

2. Type the following program statements (indented four spaces) in the event procedure, between the Private Sub and End Sub statements.

   ```
   Image1.Picture = LoadPicture("")
   mnuCloseItem.Enabled = False
   ```

The first line closes the open Windows metafile by loading a blank picture into the Image1 object. (This is the technique used to clear an image box or a picture box object.) The second line dims the Close command on the File menu as there is no longer an open file.

---

**TIP** Use the LoadPicture function with empty quotation marks to clear an image or image box.

---

Now you'll type in the program code for the mnuExitItem_Click event procedure, the routine that stops the program when the Exit command on the File menu is clicked. This is the last event procedure in the program.

## Editing the Exit Command Event Procedure

1. Click the mnuExitItem object in the Object drop-down list box.

   The event procedure for the File Exit command appears in the Code window.

2. Type the following program statement (indented four spaces) in the event procedure, between the Private Sub and End Sub statements.

   ```
   End
   ```

   This statement stops the program when the user is finished. (It might look familiar by now.)

3. Close the Code window.

*Save Project button*

4. Click the Save Project button on the toolbar to save the completed project to disk.

   Visual Basic saves your changes in the MyDialog form and project files.

Now you'll run the MyDialog program and experiment with the menus and dialog boxes you've created.

---

**TIP** The Dialog.vbp program is located in the \LearnVb6\Less04 folder.

---

## Running the MyDialog Program

*Start button*

1. Click the Start button on the toolbar.

   The program runs, and both the File and Clock menus appear on the menu bar.

2. On the form's File menu, click Open.

   The Open common dialog box appears. Notice the Metafiles (*.WMF) entry in the Files Of Type box. You defined this entry with the statement

   ```
   CommonDialog1.Filter = "Metafiles (*.WMF)|*.WMF"
   ```

   in the mnuOpenItem_Click event procedure. The first part of the text in quotation marks—Metafiles (*.WMF)—specifies which items are listed in the Files Of Type box. The second part—*.WMF—specifies the default filename extension of the files that are to be listed in the dialog box.

3. Open the \LearnVb6\Less03 folder on your hard disk.

   The sample Windows metafiles in the Less03 folder appear in the file list box, as shown in the following illustration:

4. Double-click the file pcomputr.wmf.

   A picture of a computer appears in the image box.

   Now you'll practice using the Clock menu.

5. On the Clock menu, click the Time command.

   The current time appears in the label box.

6. On the Clock menu, click the TextColor command.

   The Color common dialog box appears, as shown here:

   The Color common dialog box contains elements that let you change the color of the clock text in your program. The current color setting, black, is selected.

7. Click the light blue box, and then click the OK button.

   The Color common dialog box closes, and the color of the text in the clock label changes to light blue, as shown on the next page.

8. On the Clock menu, click the Date command.

   The current date is displayed in light blue type. Now that the text color has been set in the label, it will remain light blue until the color is changed again or the program closes.

9. Click the File menu.

   Notice that the Close command is now enabled. (You enabled it in the mnuOpenItem_Click event procedure by using the statement mnuCloseItem.Enabled = True.)

10. Press **C** to close the computer Windows metafile.

    The file closes, and the Windows metafile is removed.

---

### Adding Nonstandard Dialog Boxes to Programs

What if you need to add a dialog box to your program that isn't one of the five common dialog box types? No problem—but you'll need to do a little extra design work. As you'll learn in future lessons, a Visual Basic program can use more than one form to receive and display information. To create nonstandard dialog boxes, you'll need to add new forms to your program, add input and output objects, and process the dialog box clicks in your program code. (These techniques will be introduced in Lesson 8.) In the next lesson, you'll learn how to use two handy dialog boxes that are specifically designed for receiving text input (InputBox) and displaying text output (MsgBox). These dialog boxes will help bridge the gap between the common dialog boxes and those that you need to create on your own.

11.  Click the File menu.

     The Close command is now dimmed because there is no picture in
     the image box.

12.  Click the Exit command.

     The MyDialog program closes, and the Visual Basic programming
     environment appears.

That's it! You've learned several important commands and techniques for
creating menus and dialog boxes in your programs. After you learn more
about program code, you'll be able to put these skills to work in your own
programs.

# Assigning Shortcut Keys to Menus

The Menu Editor also lets you assign *shortcut keys* to your menus. Shortcut keys are key combinations that a user can press to activate a command without using the menu bar. For example, on a typical Edit menu
in an application for Windows (such as Visual Basic), you can copy
selected text to the Clipboard by pressing Ctrl+C. Try assigning shortcut
keys to the Clock menu in the MyDialog program now.

## Assigning Shortcut Keys to the Clock Menu

*Menu Editor
button*

1.  Click the form, and then click the Menu Editor button on the
    toolbar.

    The Menu Editor appears.

2.  Click the Time command in the menu list box.

    The caption and name of the Time command appear in the
    dialog box.

    You assign a shortcut key by selecting the desired key combination
    in the Shortcut drop-down list box. You'll assign Ctrl+T as the
    shortcut key for the Time command.

3.  Click the Shortcut drop-down list box, scroll down in the list box,
    and then click Ctrl+T.

**IP** You can't assign a shortcut key to a menu title.

Ctrl+T is assigned as the shortcut key for the Time menu item, and the key combination appears in the menu list box.

4. Click the Next button.

   The caption and name of the Date command appear in the dialog box. You'll assign Ctrl+D as the shortcut key for this command.

5. Click the Shortcut drop-down list box, and then click Ctrl+D.

   Your screen should look like the following:

— Shortcut keys

6. Click OK to close the Menu Editor.

   Now you'll run the program and try the shortcut keys.

*Start button*

7. Click the Start button on the toolbar.

8. Press Ctrl+T to choose the Time command.

   The current time appears in the program.

9. Press Ctrl+D to choose the Date command.

   The current date appears in the program.

10. Click the Clock menu.

    The shortcut keys are listed beside the Time and Date commands. Visual Basic adds these key combinations when you define the shortcuts by using the Menu Editor.

11. On the File menu, click the Exit command.

    The program stops, and the programming environment appears.

*Save Project button*

12. Click the Save Project button to save your shortcut keys to disk.

---

### If You Want to Boost Your Productivity

Spend a few minutes exploring the Magnify utility (magnify.vbp) in the \LearnVb6\Extras folder on your hard disk. I wrote this program as an extension of the Dialog program to give you a little more practice with the menu and dialog box concepts in this lesson. The application is a bitmap magnifier that lets you examine bitmaps up close on your system, in much closer detail than you can in a standard art program. I find it a useful tool for evaluating the dozens of bitmap (.bmp) files I routinely use in my programming projects for toolbars and other artwork. (Look in your \Windows folder for a few good examples.) If you like, you can try to expand the program yourself or simply use it as is for your daily work.

---

# Programming Fundamentals

# Visual Basic
# Variables and Operators

In Part 1, you learned how to create the user interface of a Microsoft Visual Basic program and how to build and run a program in the Visual Basic programming environment. In the next three lessons, you'll learn more about Visual Basic program code—the statements and keywords that form the core of a Visual Basic program. After you complete Part 2, you'll be ready for more advanced topics.

In this lesson, you'll learn how to use variables to store data temporarily in your program and how to use mathematical operators to perform tasks such as addition and multiplication. You'll also learn how to use mathematical functions to perform calculations involving numbers, and you'll use the InputBox and MsgBox functions to gather and present information by using dialog boxes.

# The Anatomy of a Visual Basic Program Statement

As you learned in Lesson 2, a line of code in a Visual Basic program is called a program statement. A *program statement* is any combination of Visual Basic keywords, properties, functions, operators, and symbols that collectively create a valid instruction recognized by the Visual Basic compiler. A complete program statement can be a simple keyword, such as

```
Beep
```

that sounds a note from your computer's speaker, or it can be a combination of elements, such as the following statement, which assigns the current system time to the Caption property of a label:

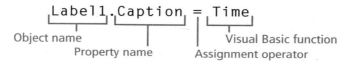

The rules of construction that must be used when you build a programming statement are called statement *syntax*. Visual Basic shares many of its syntax rules with earlier versions of the Basic programming language and with other language compilers. The trick to writing good program statements is learning the syntax of the most useful language elements and then using those elements correctly to process the data in your program. Fortunately, Visual Basic does a lot of the toughest work for you, so the time you spend writing program code will be relatively short, and the results can be used again in future programs.

In the following lessons, you'll learn the most important Visual Basic keywords and program statements. You'll find that they will complement nicely the programming skills you've already learned and will help you to write powerful programs in the future. Variables and data types, the first topics, are critical features of nearly every program.

# Using Variables to Store Information

A *variable* is a temporary storage location for data in your program. You can use one or many variables in your code, and they can contain words, numbers, dates, or properties. Variables are useful because they let you assign a short and easy-to-remember name to each piece of data you plan to work with. Variables can hold information entered by the user at runtime, the result of a specific calculation, or a piece of data you want to display on your form. In short, variables are simple tools you can use to track almost any type of information.

Using variables in a Visual Basic program is a little like getting a table at a fancy restaurant. You can start using one at any time, but the management is happiest if you make reservations for it in advance. I'll cover the process of making reservations for, or *declaring,* a variable in the next two sections.

## Making Reservations for Variables: The Dim Statement

To explicitly declare a variable before using it (typically, at the beginning of an event procedure), you type the variable name after the Dim statement. (Dim stands for *dimension.*) This declaration reserves room in memory for the variable when the program runs, and it lets Visual Basic know what type of data it should expect to see later. For example, the following statement creates space for a variable named LastName in a program:

```
Dim LastName
```

After the variable name, you can specify the variable type if you like. (You'll learn about several fundamental data types later in this lesson.) Visual Basic lets you identify the type in advance so that you can control how much memory your program uses. For example, if the variable will hold a small number without any decimal places (an integer), you can declare the variable as an integer and save some memory space. By default, however, Visual Basic reserves space for a variable type called a *variant,* which is a variable that can hold data of any size or format. The general-purpose variant variable is extremely flexible, and it may be the only variable you use in your programs.

After you declare a variable, you are free to assign information to it in your code. For example, the following program statement assigns the last name "Jefferson" to the LastName variable:

```
LastName = "Jefferson"
```

After this assignment, the LastName variable can be used in place of the name "Jefferson" in your code. For example, the assignment statement

```
Label1.Caption = LastName
```

would display *Jefferson* in the first label (Label1) on your form.

## Declaring Variables Without Dim

You can also declare a variable without the Dim statement; this process is called *implicit declaration*. To declare a variable in this way, you simply use the variable on its own, skipping the Dim statement altogether:

```
LastName = "Charles V"
```

Implicit declaration has the advantage of speed because you don't spend time typing the Dim statement. However, "the management" often discourages the use of implicit declaration because it doesn't force you to organize and list your variables in advance and because it prevents Visual Basic from displaying an error message if you mistype the variable name later. (See the following tip.) In this book, I'll declare variables by using both techniques.

 **IP** If you decide always to declare your variables by using the Dim statement, you might want to put the Option Explicit statement in the declarations section of your startup form for each new project. You can do this automatically by clicking the Options command on the Tools menu, clicking the Editor tab, and adding a check mark to the Require Variable Declaration check box.

When you use Option Explicit, Visual Basic generates an error message whenever it finds a variable that has not been explicitly declared in the code. (The likely cause is a spelling error in the variable name.) If you're worried about spelling errors, this statement can help you track them down.

## Using Variables in a Program

Variables can maintain the same value throughout a program or they can change values several times, depending on your needs. The following exercise demonstrates how a variable named LastName can contain both text and a number and how the variable can be assigned to object properties.

### Changing the value of a variable

1. Start Visual Basic.

2. On the File menu, click the Open Project command.

   The Open Project dialog box appears.

3. Open the sample project VarTest in the \LearnVb6\Less05 folder.

   The Variable Test project opens in the programming environment.
   Variable Test is a skeleton program—it contains a form with labels
   and buttons for displaying output, but little program code. You'll
   add code in this exercise.

*View Object
button*

4. If the Variable Test form is not visible, highlight the form name in
   the Project window, and then click the View Object button in the
   Project window.

   The Variable Test form appears on the screen, as follows:

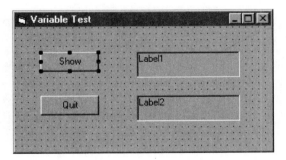

   The form contains two labels and two command buttons. You'll use
   variables to display information in each of the labels.

5. Double-click the Show command button.

   The Command1_Click event procedure appears in the Code
   window.

6. Type the following program statements to declare and use the LastName variable:

```
Dim LastName

LastName = "Smart"
Label1.Caption = LastName

LastName = 99
Label2.Caption = LastName
```

The program statements are arranged in three groups. The first statement declares the LastName variable by using the Dim statement. Because no type was specified, the variable is declared as a variant type—a variable that can hold text or numbers. The second and third lines assign the name "Smart" to the LastName variable and then display this name in the first label on the form. This example demonstrates one of the most common uses of variables in a program—transferring information to a property.

The fourth line assigns the number 99 to the LastName variable (in other words, it changes the contents of the variable). This operation removes the text string from the variable and replaces it with a number. The number wasn't placed in quotation marks. Text strings require quotation marks, but numbers don't. (If you had placed quotation marks around the number, the number would be treated as a text string and couldn't be used in mathematical formulas.)

Your screen should look like the following:

```
Project1 - Form1                                      _ □ ×
Command1              ▼   Click                   ▼
    Private Sub Command1_Click()                      ▲
        Dim LastName

        LastName = "Smart"
        Label1.Caption = LastName

        LastName = 99
        Label2.Caption = LastName
    End Sub
                                                      ▼
```

*Start button*

7. Click the Start button on the toolbar to run the program.

   The program runs in the programming environment.

8. Click the Show button.

---

## Variable Naming Conventions

Naming variables can be a little tricky because you need to use names that are short but intuitive and easy to remember. To avoid confusion, use the following conventions when naming variables:

- Begin each variable name with a letter. This is a Visual Basic requirement. Variable names must be fewer than 256 characters long and cannot contain periods.

- Make your variable names descriptive by combining one or more words when it makes sense to do so. For example, the variable name SalesTaxRate is much clearer than Tax or Rate.

- Use a combination of uppercase and lowercase characters and numbers if you wish. An accepted convention is to capitalize the first letter of each word in a variable; for example, DateOfBirth.

- Don't use Visual Basic keywords, objects, or properties as variable names.

- (Optional) Begin each variable name with a two-character or three-character abbreviation corresponding to the type of data that is stored in the variable. For example, use strName to show that the Name variable contains string data. Although you don't need to worry too much about this detail now, you might make a note of this convention for later—you'll see it in the Visual Basic online Help and many of the advanced books about Visual Basic programming. (See "Working with Specific Data Types" later in this lesson for more information about data types.)

The program declares the variable, assigns two values to it, and copies each value to the appropriate label on the form. The program produces the following output:

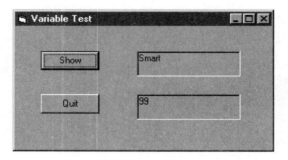

9. Click the Quit button to stop the program.

   The program stops, and the programming environment returns.

10. Save your form changes to disk under the name **MyVarTest.frm** by using the Save VarTest.frm As command. Save your project changes to disk under the name **MyVarTest.vbp** by using the Save Project As command.

# Using a Variable to Store Input

One practical use for a variable is to hold information input from the user. Although you can often use an object such as a file list box or a text box to retrieve this information, at times you may want to deal directly with the user and save the input in a variable rather than in a property. One way to do this is to use the InputBox function to display a dialog box on the screen and then store the text the user types in a variable. You'll try this approach in the following example.

## Getting Input by Using InputBox

1. On the File menu, click the Open Project command.

   The Open Project dialog box appears.

2. Open the project InputBox in the \LearnVb6\Less05 folder.

The InputBox project opens in the programming environment. InputBox is a skeleton program—it contains a form with buttons and a label for displaying output, but it contains little program code.

3. If the InputBox form is not visible, highlight the form in the Project window, and then click the View Object button in the Project window.

   The form contains one label and two command buttons. You'll use the InputBox function to get input from the user, and then you'll display the input in the label on the form.

4. Double-click the InputBox command button.

   The Command1_Click event procedure appears in the Code window.

5. Type the following program statements to declare two variables and call the InputBox function:

```
Dim Prompt, FullName
Prompt = "Please enter your name."
FullName = InputBox$(Prompt)
Label1.Caption = FullName
```

   This time you're declaring two variables by using the Dim statement: Prompt and FullName. The second line in the event procedure assigns a group of characters, or a *text string,* to the Prompt variable. This message will be used as a text argument for the InputBox function. (An *argument* is a value or an expression passed to a subprocedure or a function.) The next line calls the InputBox function and assigns the result of the call (the text string the user enters) to the FullName variable. InputBox is a special Visual Basic function that displays a dialog box on the screen and prompts the user for input.

   After InputBox has returned a text string to the program, the fourth statement in the procedure places the user's name in the Caption property of the Label1 object, which displays it on the form.

*Start button*

6. Click the Start button on the toolbar to run the program.

   The program runs in the programming environment.

**IP** In older versions of BASIC, the InputBox function was spelled with a $ character at the end to help programmers remember that the function returned information in the string ($) data type. You can call InputBox with or without the $ character in Visual Basic—I use it both ways in this book. (Sometimes I get sentimental for the old days.)

7. Click the Input Box button.

   Visual Basic executes the Command1_Click event procedure, and the InputBox dialog box appears on your screen:

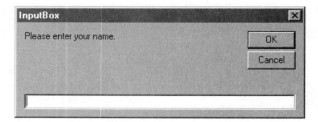

8. Type your full name, and click OK.

   The InputBox function returns your name to the program and places it in the FullName variable. The program then uses the variable to display your name on the form as shown in the following figure:

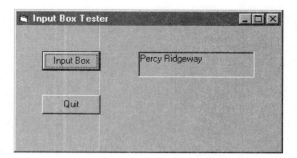

Use the InputBox function in your programs anytime you want to prompt the user for information. You can use this function in combination with the other input controls to regulate the flow of data into and out of a program. In the next exercise, you'll learn how to use a similar function to display text in a dialog box.

---

### What Is a Function?

InputBox is a special Visual Basic keyword known as a function. A *function* is a statement that performs meaningful work (such as prompting the user for information or calculating an equation) and then returns a result to the program. The value returned by a function can be assigned to a variable, as it was in the MyInputBox program, or it can be assigned to a property or another statement or function. Visual Basic functions often use one or more arguments to define their activities. For example, the InputBox function you just executed used the Prompt variable to display dialog box instructions for the user. When a function uses more than one argument, the arguments are separated by commas, and the whole group of arguments is enclosed in parentheses. The following statement shows a function call that has two arguments:

9. Click the Quit button on the form to stop the program.

   The program stops, and the programming environment returns.

10. Save your form and project changes to your hard disk under the name **MyInputBox**.

## Using a Variable for Output

You can display the contents of a variable by assigning the variable to a property (such as the Caption property of a label object) or by passing the variable as an argument to a dialog box function. One useful dialog box function for displaying output is the MsgBox function. Like InputBox, it takes one or more arguments as input, and the results of the function call can be assigned to a variable. The syntax for the MsgBox function is

```
ButtonClicked = MsgBox(Message, NumberOfButtons, Title)
```

where *Message* is the text to be displayed on the screen, *NumberOfBut-tons* is a button style number (1 through 5), and *Title* is the text displayed in the message box title bar. The variable *ButtonClicked* is assigned the result returned by the function, which indicates which button the user clicked in the dialog box.

If you're just displaying a message in MsgBox, the assignment operator (=), the *ButtonClicked* variable, and the *NumberOfButtons* argument are optional. You won't be using these in the following exercise.

Now you'll add a MsgBox function to the MyInputBox program to display the name the user enters in the InputBox dialog box.

## Displaying a Message by Using MsgBox

1. If you don't see the Code window now, double-click the InputBox button on the MyInputBox form.

   The event procedure for the Command1_Click procedure appears in the Code window. (This is the code you entered in the last exercise.)

2. Use the mouse to select the following statement in the event proce-dure (the last line):

   ```
   Label1.Caption = FullName
   ```

   This is the statement that displays the contents of the FullName variable in the label.

3. Press Del to delete the line.

   The statement is removed from the Code window.

4. Type the following line into the event procedure as a replacement:

   ```
   MsgBox (FullName), , "Input Results"
   ```

   This new statement will call the MsgBox function, display the con-tents of the FullName variable in the dialog box, and place the words *Input Results* in the title bar. (The optional *NumberOfBut-tons* argument and the *ButtonClicked* variable are irrelevant here and have been omitted.) Your event procedure should look like the following:

---

**TIP** When no *ButtonClicked* variable is included, the parentheses enclose only the first argument.

---

*Start button*

5. Click the Start button on the toolbar.

6. Click the Input Box button, type your name in the input box, and then click OK.

The input is stored in the program in the FullName variable and is then displayed in a message box like this:

7. Click OK to close the message box. Then click Quit to close the program.

The program closes, and the programming environment returns.

8. Save the form and project as **MyMsgBox** to keep a copy of your program.

# Working with Specific Data Types

In most cases, the variant data type will be the only data type you need. Variant variables can store all of Visual Basic's fundamental (predefined) data types and switch formats automatically. Variants are also easy to use and don't require you to give much thought to the eventual size of the variable when you declare it. If you want to create especially fast and concise code, however, you may want to use more specific data types when appropriate.

For example, if a variable will always contain small integer values (numbers without a decimal point), you can save space in memory when your program runs by declaring the variable as an integer rather than as a variant. You'll also gain a small performance advantage if your program performs calculations, because an integer variable speeds up arithmetic operations, too.

 **IP**  Variable storage size is measured in bytes—the amount of space required to store 8 bits (approximately 1 character).

The table on the following page lists the fundamental data types in Visual Basic. In the next exercise, you'll see how several of these data types work.

 **IP**  You can specify some fundamental data types by appending a type-declaration character to the variable's name. For example, you can declare a variable as type integer by adding a % character to the end of its name. So, in Visual Basic the following two declaration statements are equivalent:

```
Dim I As Integer
Dim I%
```

This is an older programming convention, but one that is still used by many programmers.

| Data type | Size | Range | Sample usage |
|-----------|------|-------|--------------|
| Integer | 2 bytes | −32,768 through 32,767 | `Dim Birds%`<br>`Birds% = 37` |
| Long integer | 4 bytes | −2,147,483,648 through 2,147,483,647 | `Dim Loan&`<br>`Loan& = 350,000` |
| Single-precision floating point | 4 bytes | −3.402823E38 through 3.402823E38 | `Dim Price!`<br>`Price! = 899.99` |
| Double-precision floating point | 8 bytes | −1.79769313486232D308 through 1.79769313486232D308 | `Dim Pi#`<br>`Pi# = 3.1415926535` |
| Currency | 8 bytes | −922337203685477.5808 through 922337203685477.5807 | `Dim Debt@`<br>`Debt@ = 7600300.50` |
| String | 1 byte per character | 0 through 65,535 characters | `Dim Dog$`<br>`Dog$ = "pointer"` |
| Boolean | 2 bytes | True or False | `Dim Flag as Boolean`<br>`Flag = True` |
| Date | 8 bytes | January 1, 100, through December 31, 9999 | `Dim Birthday as Date`<br>`Birthday = #3-1-63#` |
| Variant | 16 bytes (for numbers); 22 bytes + 1 byte per character (for strings) | All data type ranges | `Dim Total`<br>`Total = 289.13` |

## Using Fundamental Data Types in Code

1. On the File menu, click the Open Project command.

   The Open Project dialog box appears.

2. Open the Data project in the \LearnVb6\Less05 folder.

   The Data project opens in the programming environment. Data is a complete Visual Basic program that demonstrates how several fundamental data types work. You'll run the program to see what the data types look like, and then you'll look at how the variables are declared and used in the program code.

*Start button*

3. Click the Start button on the toolbar.

   The following application window appears.

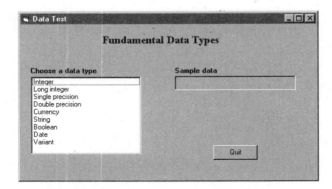

The Data program lets you experiment with nine data types, including integer, single-precision floating point, and date. The program displays an example of each type when you click its name in the list box.

4. Click the Integer type in the list box.

   The number 37 appears in the Sample Data box.

5. Click the Date type in the list box.

   The date Tuesday, November 19, 1963, appears in the Sample Data box.

6. Click each data type in the list box to see how Visual Basic displays it in the Sample Data box.

7. Click the Quit button to stop the program.

   Now you'll examine how the fundamental data types are declared and used in the List1_Click event procedure.

8. If the form is not visible, highlight the form in the Project window, and then click the View Object button.

9. Double-click the list box object on the form, and enlarge the Code window to see more of the program code.

The List1_Click event procedure appears as shown in the following figure:

```
Project1 - Form1                                        _ □ ×
List1                      ▼     Click                        ▼
    Private Sub List1_Click()                                ▲
        'Variable declaration section
        Dim Birds%, Loan&, Price!, Pie#, Debt@, Dog$, Total
        Dim Flag As Boolean
        Dim Birthday As Date

        'Select Case processes the user's choice
        Select Case List1.ListIndex
        Case 0
            Birds% = 37
            Label4.Caption = Birds%
        Case 1
            Loan& = 350000
            Label4.Caption = Loan&
        Case 2
            Price! = -1234.123                               ▼
```

The first few lines of the procedure declare variables with specific data types in the procedure. These variables will be *local* to the procedure: they'll have no meaning in other event procedures in the program. Several of the variables are declared using special data type characters, such as %, #, and @. These symbols identify each variable as a specific fundamental data type in the program and mark the variables for the Visual Basic compiler and for people reading your program code.

The next section of the event procedure is called a Select Case decision structure. In the next lesson, we'll discuss how this group of program statements selects one choice from many. For now, notice how each section of the Select Case block assigns a sample value to one of the fundamental data type variables and then assigns the variable to the caption of the Label4 object on the form. You can use both of these techniques to manipulate fundamental data types in your own programs.

The Date data type is especially useful if you work with date and time values regularly. The date, surrounded by # characters, is assigned to the variable Birthday and is formatted with the Format function.

**IP** Variables can also be *public*, or available in all form procedures and modules of a program. (*Modules* are special files that contain declarations and procedures not associated with a particular form.) For a variable to have this range, or scope, it needs to be declared in a standard module. For information about creating public variables in standard modules, see Lesson 10, "Using Modules and Procedures."

## User-Defined Data Types

Visual Basic also lets you create your own data types. This feature is most useful when you're dealing with a group of data items that naturally fit together but fall into different data categories. You create a *user-defined type* by using the Type statement, and you declare variables associated with the new type by using the Dim statement. (The Type statement must be located in the Declarations section of a standard module.) For example, the following declaration creates a user-defined data type named Employee that can store the name, date of birth, and hire date associated with a worker:

```
Type Employee
    Name As String
    DateOfBirth As Date
    HireDate As Date
End Type
```

After you create a new data type, you can use it in the program code. The following statements use the new Employee type. The first statement creates a variable named ProductManager, of the Employee type, and the second statement assigns the name "Erick Cody" to the Name component of the variable:

```
Dim ProductManager As Employee
ProductManager.Name = "Erick Cody"
```

This looks a little like setting a property, doesn't it? Visual Basic uses the same notation for the relationship between objects and properties as it uses for the relationship between user-defined data types and component variables.

10. Scroll through the Code window and examine each of the variable assignments closely.

    Try changing the data in a few variable assignment statements and running the program again to see what the data looks like.

11. When you've finished, close the Code window.

    If you made any changes you want to save to disk, click the Save Project button on the toolbar.

## Constants: Variables That Don't Change

If a variable in your program contains a value that never changes (such as $\pi$, a fixed mathematical entity), you might consider storing the value as a constant instead of as a variable. A *constant* is a meaningful name that takes the place of a number or text string that doesn't change. Constants are useful because they increase the readability of program code, using them can save memory, and they make global changes easier to accomplish later. Constants operate a lot like variables, but you can't modify their values at runtime. They are declared with the Const keyword, as shown in the following example:

```
Const Pi = 3.14159265
```

The statement above creates a constant called Pi that can be used in place of the value of $\pi$ in the program code. To make a constant available to all the objects and event procedures in your form, place the above statement in the Declaration section of your form (the top line in the Code window). To make the constant available to all the forms and modules in a program (not just Form1), create the constant in a standard module, with the Public keyword in front of it. For example:

```
Public Const Pi = 3.14159265
```

The following exercise demonstrates how you can use a constant in an event procedure.

---

 **IP**   For more information about standard modules, see Lesson 10, "Using Modules and Procedures."

---

### Using a constant in an event procedure

1. On the File menu, click the Open Project command.

   The Open Project dialog box appears.

2. Open the Constant project in the \LearnVb6\Less05 folder.

   The Constant program form appears on the screen. Constant is a skeleton program. The user interface is finished, but you need to type in the program code.

3. Double-click the Show Constant button on the form.

   The Command1_Click event procedure appears in the Code window.

4. Type the following statements in the event procedure:

```
Const Pi = 3.14159265
Label1.Caption = Pi
```

*Start button*

5. Click the Start button to run the program.

6. Click the Show Constant button in the program.

   The Pi constant appears in the label box, as shown here:

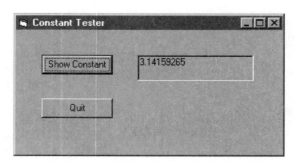

7. Click the Quit button to stop the program.

   If you would like to keep a copy of the modified Constant program, save the form and project on your hard disk with the name **MyConstant**.

Constants are useful in program code, especially in involved mathematical formulas, such as Area = $2\pi r^2$. The next section describes how you can use operators and variables to write similar formulas.

# Working with Visual Basic Operators

A *formula* is a statement that combines numbers, variables, operators, and keywords to create a new value. Visual Basic contains several language elements designed for use in formulas. In this section, you'll practice working with mathematical operators, the symbols used to tie together the parts of a formula. With a few exceptions, the mathematical symbols you'll use are the ones you use in everyday life, and their operations are fairly intuitive. You'll see each demonstrated in the following exercises.

 **IP** Visual Basic operators link the parts of a formula.

Visual Basic provides the following operators:

| Operator | Mathematical operation |
| --- | --- |
| + | Addition |
| – | Subtraction |
| * | Multiplication |
| / | Division |
| \ | Integer (whole number) division |
| Mod | Remainder division |
| ^ | Exponentiation (raising to a power) |
| & | String concatenation (combination) |

## Basic Math: The +, –, *, and / Operators

The operators for addition, subtraction, multiplication, and division are pretty straightforward and can be used in any formula where numbers or numeric variables are used. The following exercise demonstrates how you can use them in a program.

### Working with basic operators

1. On the File menu, click the Open Project command.

2. Open the BasicOp project in the \LearnVb6\Less05 folder.

   The form for the program appears on screen. The BasicOp program demonstrates how the addition, subtraction, multiplication, and division operators work with numbers you type in from the keyboard. It also demonstrates how you can use text box, option button, and command button objects to process user input in a program.

3. Click the Start button on the toolbar.

   The BasicOp program runs in the programming environment. The program displays two text boxes in which you enter numeric values, a group of operator option buttons, a box that displays results, and two command buttons.

4. Type **100** in the Variable 1 text box, and then press Tab.

   The cursor moves to the second text box.

5. Type **17** in the Variable 2 text box.

   You can now apply any of the mathematical operators to the values in the text boxes.

6. Click the Addition option button, and then click the Calculate command button.

   The operator is applied to the two values, and the number 117 appears in the Result box, as shown in the following illustration:

7. Practice using the subtraction, multiplication, and division operators with the two numbers in the variable boxes. (Click Calculate to
calculate each formula.)

    The results appear in the Result box. Feel free to experiment with
different numbers in the variable text boxes. (Try a few numbers
with decimal points if you like.)

8. When you've finished calculating, click the Quit button.

    The program stops, and the programming environment returns.

Now take a look at the program code to see how the results were calculated. Basic Operators uses a few of the standard input controls you
experimented with in Lesson 3 and an event procedure that uses variables and operators to calculate simple mathematical formulas. The procedure also uses the Val function to convert the string input received
from the text boxes to numbers.

## Examining the BasicOp Program Code

1. Double-click the Calculate button on the form.

    The Command1_Click event procedure appears in the Code
window:

The first statement in the procedure declares two general-purpose
variables of the variant type. The variants will hold the values

typed in the two text boxes, and they are flexible enough to handle any numeric data type you want to use. The next two statements load the data from the text boxes into the variables and convert the text strings to numbers by using the Val function:

```
First = Val(Text1.Text) 'fetch and convert numbers
Second = Val(Text2.Text)
```

## Visual Basic Mathematical Functions

Now and then you'll want to do a little extra number crunching in your programs. You may need to convert a value to a different type, calculate a complex mathematical expression, or introduce randomness to your programs. The following Visual Basic functions can help you work with numbers in your formulas. As with any function, the mathematical functions must be used in a program statement, and they will return a value to the program. In the following table, the argument $n$ represents the number, variable, or expression you want the function to evaluate.

| Function | Purpose |
| --- | --- |
| Abs($n$) | Returns the absolute value of $n$. |
| Atn($n$) | Returns the arctangent, in radians, of $n$. |
| Cos($n$) | Returns the cosine of the angle $n$. The angle $n$ is expressed in radians. |
| Exp($n$) | Returns the constant $e$ raised to the power $n$. |
| Rnd($n$) | Generates a random number between 0 and 1. |
| Sgn($n$) | Returns −1 if $n$ is less than 0, 0 if $n$ is 0, and +1 if $n$ is greater than 0. |
| Sin($n$) | Returns the sine of the angle $n$. The angle $n$ is expressed in radians. |
| Sqr($n$) | Returns the square root of $n$. |
| Str($n$) | Converts a numeric value to a string. |
| Tan($n$) | Returns the tangent of the angle $n$. The angle $n$ is expressed in radians. |
| Val($n$) | Converts a string value to a number. |

The Val function is a special routine that converts a text argument to a numeric value. This conversion is necessary for the addition operation to work correctly in this program. The default data type returned by a text box object is text. This isn't a problem for three of the operators. The −, *, and / operators work only with numbers, so when the user selects one of these three operators in the program, Visual Basic automatically converts the values returned to the First and Second variables to numbers.

The + operator works with both text strings and numbers. Because the default data type returned by the text box object is text, Visual Basic would treat First's and Second's values as text when the + operator is used. Visual Basic would combine, or *concatenate,* the two values rather than add them mathematically. (For example, "100" + "17" would equal "10017.")

You'll learn more about string concatenation in the next exercise. For now, make a mental note that even though the variant data type can hold any fundamental data type, you need to watch closely how it is used in a program. It might default to something you don't expect.

---

**IMPORTANT**  It is critical to test each calculation in a program to verify that the whole program is working correctly. Testing one part of the program is not enough.

---

2. Scroll down the Code window, and examine the four formulas that use the basic mathematical operators.

The first formula in the procedure uses the addition operator (+) in an If...Then decision structure.

```
'if first button clicked, add numbers
If Option1.Value = True Then
    Label1.Caption = First + Second
End If
```

If the Value property of the first option button is set to True (if the button has been clicked), the two variables are added together with the + operator, and the result is assigned to the label. The three remaining formulas have a similar logic, each using an If…Then decision structure and the Caption property of the Label1 object. Decision structures such as If…Then are extremely useful in determining which option a user selects in your program when several options are available. You'll learn more about If…Then in the next lesson.

3. Close the Code window.

You're done using the BasicOp program.

## Using Advanced Operators: \, Mod, ^, and &

In addition to the four basic mathematical operators, Visual Basic includes four advanced operators, which perform integer division (\), remainder division (Mod), exponentiation (^), and string concatenation (&). These operators are useful in special-purpose mathematical formulas and text processing applications. The following utility (a slight modification of the BasicOp program) shows how you can use each of these operators in a program.

### Working with advanced operators

1. On the File menu, click the Open Project command.

2. Open the AdvOp project in the \LearnVb6\Less05 folder.

   The form for the AdvOp program appears on the screen. The AdvOp program is identical to the BasicOp program, with the exception of the operators shown on the option buttons and the operators used in the program.

3. Click the Start button on the toolbar.

   The program displays two text boxes in which you enter numeric values, a group of operator option buttons, a box that displays results, and two command buttons.

4. Type **9** in the Variable 1 text box, and then press Tab.

5. Type **2** in the Variable 2 text box.

You can now apply any of the advanced operators to the values in the text boxes.

6. Click the Integer Division option button, and then click the Calculate button.

The operator is applied to the two values, and the number 4 appears in the Result box, as shown here:

Integer division produces only the whole number result of the division operation. Although 9 divided by 2 equals 4.5, the integer division operation returns only the first part, an integer (the whole number 4). You might find this result useful if you're working with quantities that can't easily be divided into fractional components, such as the number of adults that can fit in a car.

7. Click the Remainder option button, and then click the Calculate button.

The number 1 appears in the Result box. Remainder division (modulus arithmetic) returns the remainder (the part left over that won't evenly divide) after two numbers are divided. Because 9 divided by 2 equals 4 with a remainder of 1 ($2 \times 4 + 1 = 9$), the result produced by the Mod operator is 1. In addition to adding an early-seventies quality to your code, the Mod operator can help you track "leftovers" in your calculations, such as the amount of change left over after a financial transaction.

8. Click the Exponentiation option button, and then click the Calculate button.

The number 81 appears in the Result box. The exponentiation operator (^) raises a number to a power of itself. Because $9^2$ equals 81, the result produced by the ^ operator is 81. In a Visual Basic formula, $9^2$ is written 9 ^ 2.

9. Click the Concatenation option button, and then click the Calculate button.

The string "92" appears in the Result box. The string concatenation operator (&) combines two strings in a formula. The result ("92," in this case) is not a number; it is a combination of the "9" character and the "2" character. String concatenation can be performed only on text variables, strings delimited by quotation marks, and variant variables. Because the variables used in this program are variants, they were automatically converted to text for the operation. To see how this operator works with letters, type a few words in each variable box and then click the Calculate button again.

10. Click the Quit button to stop the program.

The program stops, and the programming environment returns.

Now take a look at the Command1_Click event procedure to see how the operators were used.

11. Double-click the Calculate button on the form.

The event procedure appears in the Code window, as shown in the following illustration:

This Command1_Click procedure looks similar to the Command1_Click procedure in the BasicOp program. The code declares two variant variables, assigns data to the variables from the text boxes, and computes the selected formula with If...Then decision structures.

There is one important difference, however: this event procedure doesn't use the Val function to convert the data to a numeric type when it reads it from the text box objects. The conversion isn't necessary for the advanced operators because, unlike the + operator, each of the advanced operators works with only one type of data: \, Mod, and ^ work only with numbers; & works only with text. Because there's no type ambiguity, the variant variables can adequately convert the strings returned by the text boxes to numbers for the operations that require numbers.

12. Close the Code window.

You're finished working with the AdvOp program.

## Operator Precedence

In the last two exercises, you experimented with seven mathematical operators and one string operator. Visual Basic lets you mix as many mathematical operators as you like in a formula, as long as each numeric variable and expression is separated from another by one operator. For example, this is an acceptable Visual Basic formula:

```
Total = 10 + 15 * 2 / 4 ^ 2
```

The formula processes several values and assigns the result to a variable named Total. But how is such an expression evaluated by Visual Basic? In other words, which mathematical operators does Visual Basic use first when solving the formula? You might not have noticed, but the order of evaluation matters a great deal in this example.

Visual Basic solves this dilemma by establishing a specific *order of precedence* for mathematical operations. This list of rules tells Visual Basic which operators to use first when evaluating an expression that contains more than one operator. The following table lists the operators from first to last in the order in which they will be evaluated. (Operators on the same level in this table are evaluated from left to right as they appear in an expression.)

| Operator(s) | Order of precedence |
| --- | --- |
| ( ) | Values within parentheses are always evaluated first. |
| ^ | Exponentiation (raising a number to a power) is second. |
| – | Negation (creating a negative number) is third. |
| * / | Multiplication and division are fourth. |
| \ | Integer division is fifth. |
| Mod | Remainder division is sixth. |
| + – | Addition and subtraction are last. |

Given the order of precedence in the table above, the expression

```
Total = 10 + 15 * 2 / 4 ^ 2
```

would be evaluated by Visual Basic in the following steps. (Boldface type is used to show each step in the order of evaluation and its result.)

```
Total = 10 + 15 * 2 / 4 ^ 2
Total = 10 + 15 * 2 / 16
Total = 10 + 30 / 16
Total = 10 + 1.875
Total = 11.875
```

## Using Parentheses in a Formula

You can use one or more pairs of parentheses in a formula to clarify the order of precedence. For example, Visual Basic would calculate the formula

```
Number = (8 - 5 * 3) ^ 2
```

by determining the value within the parentheses (–7) before doing the exponentiation—even though exponentiation is higher in order of precedence than subtraction and multiplication. You can further refine the calculation by placing nested parentheses in the formula. For example,

```
Number = ((8 - 5) * 3) ^ 2
```

directs Visual Basic to calculate the difference in the inner set of parentheses first, perform the operation in the outer parentheses next, and then determine the exponentiation. The result produced by the two formulas is different: the first formula evaluates to 49 and the second to 81. Parentheses can change the result of a mathematical operation, as well as make it easier to read.

# Using Decision Structures

In the last few lessons, you used several Microsoft Visual Basic tools to process user input. You used menus, objects, and dialog boxes to display choices for the user, and you processed input by using properties and variables. In this lesson, you'll learn how to branch conditionally to a specific program code section based on input you receive from the user. You'll also learn how to evaluate one or more properties or variables by using conditional expressions and then execute one or more program statements based on the results. Finally, you'll learn how to detect and fix programming mistakes in your code by using break mode.

# Event-Driven Programming

The programs you have written so far in this book have displayed menus, objects, and dialog boxes on the screen, and these programs have encouraged users to manipulate the screen elements in whatever order they saw fit. The programs put the user in charge, waited patiently for a response, and then processed the input predictably. In programming circles, this methodology is known as *event-driven programming.* You build a program by creating a group of "intelligent" objects that know how to respond when the user interacts with them, and then you process the input by using event procedures associated with the objects. The following diagram shows how an event-driven program works in Visual Basic:

Program input can also come from the computer system itself. For example, your program might be notified when a piece of electronic mail arrives or when a certain period of time has elapsed on the system clock. These events are triggered by the computer, not by the user. Regardless of how an event is triggered, Visual Basic reacts by calling the event procedure associated with the object that recognized the event. So far, you've dealt primarily with the Click and Change events. However, Visual Basic objects also can respond to several other types of events.

The event-driven nature of Visual Basic means that most of the computing done in your programs will be accomplished by event procedures.

These event-specific blocks of code process input, calculate new values, display output, and handle other tasks. In the previous lesson, you learned how to use variables, operators, and mathematical formulas to perform calculations in your event procedures. In this lesson, you'll learn

### Events Supported by Visual Basic Objects

Each object in Visual Basic has a predefined set of events it can respond to. These events are listed for each object in the Proc (Procedure) drop-down list box in the Code window. You can write an event procedure for any of these events, and if that event occurs in the program, Visual Basic will execute the event procedure that is associated with it. For example, a list box object supports the Click, DblClick, DragDrop, DragOver, GotFocus, ItemCheck, KeyDown, KeyPress, KeyUp, LostFocus, MouseDown, MouseMove, MouseUp, OLECompleteDrag, OLEDragDrop, OLEDragOver, OLEGiveFeedback, OLESetData, OLEStartDrag, Scroll, and Validate events. You probably won't need to program for more than one or two of these events in your applications, but it's nice to know that you have so many choices when you create elements in your interface. The following illustration shows a partial listing of the events for a list box object in the Code window:

how to use *decision structures* to compare variables, properties, and values, and you'll learn how to execute one or more statements based on the results. In the next lesson, you'll use *loops* to execute a group of statements over and over until a condition is met. Together, these powerful flow-control structures will help you build your procedures so that they can respond to almost any situation.

# Using Conditional Expressions

One of the most useful tools for processing information in an event procedure is a conditional expression. A *conditional expression* is a part of a complete program statement that asks a True-or-False question about a property, a variable, or another piece of data in the program code. For example, the conditional expression

```
Price < 100
```

evaluates to True if the Price variable contains a value that is less than 100, and it evaluates to False if Price contains a value that is greater than or equal to 100. You can use the comparison operators shown below in a conditional expression.

| Comparison operator | Meaning |
| --- | --- |
| = | Equal to |
| < > | Not equal to |
| > | Greater than |
| < | Less than |
| >= | Greater than or equal to |
| <= | Less than or equal to |

 **IP**  Expressions that can be evaluated as True or False are also known as *Boolean expressions*, and the True or False result can be assigned to a Boolean variable or property. You can assign Boolean values to certain object properties, variant variables, or Boolean variables that have been created by using the Dim statement and the As Boolean keywords.

The following table shows some conditional expressions and their results. In the next exercise, you'll work with the operators shown in the table.

| Conditional expression | Result |
|---|---|
| 10 < > 20 | True (10 is not equal to 20) |
| Score < 20 | True if Score is less than 20; otherwise, False |
| Score = Label1.Caption | True if the Caption property of the Label1 object contains the same value as the Score variable; otherwise, False |
| Text1.Text = "Bill" | True if the word *Bill* is in the first text box; otherwise, False |

# If...Then Decision Structures

Conditional expressions used in a special block of statements called a *decision structure* control whether other statements in your program are executed and in what order they are executed. An If...Then decision structure lets you evaluate a condition in the program and take a course of action based on the result. In its simplest form, an If...Then decision structure is written on a single line:

```
If condition Then statement
```

where *condition* is a conditional expression and *statement* is a valid Visual Basic program statement. For example,

```
If Score >= 20 Then Label1.Caption = "You win!"
```

is an If...Then decision structure that uses the conditional expression

```
Score >= 20
```

to determine whether the program should set the Caption property of the Label1 object to "You win!" If the Score variable contains a value that is greater than or equal to 20, Visual Basic sets the Caption property; otherwise, it skips the assignment statement and executes the next line in the event procedure. This sort of comparison always results in a True or False value. A conditional expression never results in maybe.

## Testing Several Conditions in an If...Then Decision Structure

Visual Basic also supports an If...Then decision structure that allows you to include several conditional expressions. This block of statements can be several lines long and contains the important keywords ElseIf, Else, and End If.

```
If condition1 Then
    statements executed if condition1 is True
ElseIf condition2 Then
    statements executed if condition2 is True
[Additional ElseIf clauses and statements can be placed here]
Else
    statements executed if none of the conditions is True
End If
```

In this structure, *condition1* is evaluated first. If this conditional expression is True, the block of statements below it is executed, one statement at a time. (You can include one or more program statements.) If the first condition is not True, the second conditional expression (*condition2*) is evaluated. If the second condition is True, the second block of statements is executed. (You can add additional ElseIf conditions and statements if you have more conditions to evaluate.) If none of the conditional expressions is True, the statements below the Else keyword are executed. Finally, the whole structure is closed by the End If keywords.

The following code shows how a multiline If...Then structure could be used to determine the amount of tax due in a hypothetical progressive tax return. (The income and percentage numbers are from the United States Internal Revenue Service 1998 Tax Rate Schedule for single filing status.)

```
If AdjustedIncome <= 25350 Then          '15% tax bracket
    TaxDue = AdjustedIncome * 0.15
ElseIf AdjustedIncome <= 61400 Then      '28% tax bracket
    TaxDue = 3802.50 + ((AdjustedIncome - 25350) * 0.28)
ElseIf AdjustedIncome <= 128100 Then     '31% tax bracket
    TaxDue = 13896.50 + ((AdjustedIncome - 61400) * 0.31)
ElseIf AdjustedIncome <= 278450 Then     '36% tax bracket
    TaxDue = 34573.50 + ((AdjustedIncome - 128100) * 0.36)
Else                                     '39.6% tax bracket
    TaxDue = 88699.50 + ((AdjustedIncome - 278450) * 0.396)
End If
```

---

**TIP** Multiline If...Then structures are perfect for calculating values that fall in different ranges, such as numbers in a tax return.

---

**IMPORTANT** The order of the conditional expressions in your If...Then and ElseIf clauses is critical. What if you reversed the order of the conditional expressions in the tax computation example and listed the rates in the structure from highest to lowest? Taxpayers in the 15 percent, 28 percent, and 31 percent tax brackets would all be placed in the 36 percent tax bracket, because they all would have an income that is less than or equal to 271,050. (Visual Basic stops at the first conditional expression that is True, even if others are also True.) Because all the conditional expressions in this example test the same variable, they need to be listed in ascending order to get the taxpayers to fall out at the right spots. Moral: When you use more than one conditional expression, consider their order carefully.

---

This useful decision structure tests the variable AdjustedIncome at the first income level and subsequent income levels until one of the conditional expressions evaluates to True and then determines the taxpayer's income tax accordingly. With some simple modifications, it could be used to compute the tax owed by any taxpayer in a progressive tax system such as the one in the United States. Provided that the tax rates are complete and up-to-date and that the value in the AdjustedIncome variable is correct, the program as written will give the correct tax for single U.S. taxpayers for 1997. If the tax rates change, it is a simple matter to update the conditional expressions. With an additional decision structure to determine taxpayers' filing status, the program readily extends itself to include all U.S. taxpayers.

In the next exercise, you'll use an If...Then decision structure to validate users as they log in to a program. You might use a similar program logic of user validation if you write a network application.

## Validating Users by Using If...Then

1. Start Visual Basic and create a new standard project.

   If Visual Basic is already running, open a new project.

*CommandButton control*

2. Use the CommandButton control to create a command button in the upper-left corner of the form.

3. Set the Caption property of the command button to "Log In".

4. Double-click the Log In button.

   The Command1_Click event procedure appears in the Code window.

5. Type the following program statements in the procedure:

```
UserName = InputBox("Enter your first name.")
If UserName = "Laura" Then
    MsgBox("Welcome, Laura!  Ready to start your PC?")
    Form1.Picture = _
      LoadPicture("c:\learnvb6\less06\pcomputr.wmf")
ElseIf UserName = "Marc" Then
    MsgBox("Welcome, Marc!  Ready to display your Rolodex?")
    Form1.Picture = _
      LoadPicture("c:\learnvb6\less06\rolodex.wmf")
Else
    MsgBox("Sorry, I don't recognize you.")
    End    'quit the program
End If
```

**IP** By convention, statements below If...Then, ElseIf, and Else clauses are indented.

The line continuation characters ( _ ) used after the Form1.Picture properties break two long program statements into four lines so that they can be printed in this book. If you choose, you can type each of these long statements on one line; the Code window will scroll to the right.

**IP** Program lines can be 1023 characters long in the Visual Basic Code window, but it is usually easiest to work with lines of 80 or fewer characters. You can divide long program statements among multiple lines by using a line continuation character ( _ ) at the end of each line in the statement except the last line. (You cannot use a line continuation character to break a string that is in quotation marks, however.)

When you've finished, your screen should look like the following:

```
Private Sub Command1_Click()
    UserName = InputBox("Enter your first name.")
    If UserName = "Laura" Then
        MsgBox ("Welcome, Laura!  Ready to start your PC?")
        Form1.Picture =
            LoadPicture("c:\learnvb6\less06\pcomputr.wmf")
    ElseIf UserName = "Marc" Then
        MsgBox ("Welcome, Marc!  Ready to display your Rolodex?")
        Form1.Picture =
            LoadPicture("c:\learnvb6\less06\rolodex.wmf")
    Else
        MsgBox ("Sorry, I don't recognize you.")
        End    'quit the program
    End If
End Sub
```

Line continuation characters

---

**TIP** The complete Login program is available on disk in the \LearnVb6 \Less06 folder.

---

*Start button*

6. Click the Start button on the toolbar.

The program runs in the programming environment. A blank form appears on the screen, with a Log In button in the upper-left corner.

7. Click the Log In button.

The InputBox function in the Command1_Click event procedure displays a dialog box that asks you to enter your first name.

8. Type **Laura** and press Enter.

The If…Then decision structure compares the name you typed with the text "Laura" in the first conditional expression. If you typed *Laura*, the expression evaluates to True and the If…Then statement displays a welcome message by using the MsgBox function.

9. Click OK in the message box.

The message box closes, and a Windows metafile of a PC is loaded on the form, as shown in the illustration on the following page.

In this program, the Windows metafile is loaded directly on the form by using the Picture property. (Forms have Picture properties, just as image objects and picture box objects do.) When a graphic is loaded on a form, it appears in the background. Any control visible on the form appears on top of the graphic.

10. Click the Log In button, type **Marc**, and click OK.

This time the decision structure selects the ElseIf clause and admits Marc to the program. A welcome message is displayed on the screen again by the MsgBox function.

11. Click OK to display the Rolodex artwork.

The Rolodex Windows metafile is loaded on the form.

12. Click the Log In button, type **Frasier**, and click OK.

The Else clause in the decision structure is executed, and as shown in the following illustration, a message appears in a MsgBox object.

13. Click OK to close the message box.

    The message box closes, and the program closes. An unauthorized user has been prohibited from using the program.

14. Save the form as **MyLogin.frm** and the project as **MyLogin.vbp**.

## Using Logical Operators in Conditional Expressions

Visual Basic lets you test more than one conditional expression in If...Then and ElseIf clauses if you want to include more than one selection criterion in your decision structure. The extra conditions are linked together by using one or more of the following logical operators:

| Logical operator | Meaning |
|---|---|
| And | If both conditional expressions are True, then the result is True. |
| Or | If either conditional expression is True, then the result is True. |
| Not | If the conditional expression is False, then the result is True. If the conditional expression is True, then the result is False. |
| Xor | If one and only one of the conditional expressions is True, then the result is True. If both are True or both are False, then the result is False. |

The following table lists some examples of the logical operators at work. In the expressions, it is assumed that the variable Vehicle contains the value "Bike" and the variable Price contains the value 200.

| Logical expression | Result |
|---|---|
| Vehicle = "Bike" And Price < 300 | True (both conditions are True) |
| Vehicle = "Car" Or Price < 500 | True (one condition is True) |
| Not Price < 100 | True (condition is False) |
| Vehicle = "Bike" Xor Price < 300 | False (both conditions are True) |

**IP** When your program evaluates a complex expression that mixes different operator types, it evaluates mathematical operators first, comparison
operators second, and logical operators third.

In the following exercise, you will modify the MyLogin program to
prompt the user for a password during the validation process. An input
box gets the password from the user, and you modify the If...Then and
ElseIf clauses in the decision structure so that they use the And operator
to verify the password.

## Adding Password Protection by Using the And Operator

1. Double-click the Log In button to open the Command1_Click event
   procedure in the Code window.

2. Insert the following statement between the InputBox statement and
   the If...Then statement in the procedure (between the first and second lines):

```
Pass = InputBox("Enter your password.")
```

3. Modify the If...Then statement to the following:

```
If UserName = "Laura" And Pass = "May17" Then
```

The statement now includes the And logical operator, which verifies the user name and password before Laura is admitted to the
program.

4. Modify the ElseIf statement to the following:

```
ElseIf UserName = "Marc" And Pass = "trek" Then
```

The And logical operator adds a check for the "trek" password in
Marc's account.

5. Save the form as **MyPass.frm** and the project as **MyPass.vbp**.

 **IP** The complete Password application is available in the \LearnVb6\Less06
folder.

6. Click the Start button on the toolbar.

*Start button*

The program runs in the programming environment.

7. Click the Log In button, type **Laura**, and then click OK.

   The program prompts you for a password.

8. Type **May17** and click OK.

   The And conditional expression evaluates to True, and Laura is welcomed to the program.

9. Click OK to close the message box.

*End button*

10. Click the End button on the toolbar to quit the program.

    The program stops, and the programming environment returns.

---

**IP** If you are writing a full-featured version of the MyPass program, consider using a text box object to receive the password input in the program. Text box objects support both the PasswordChar property, which lets you display a placeholder character such as an asterisk (*) as the user types, and the MaxLength property, which lets you limit the number of characters entered.

---

# Selecting Case Decision Structures

Visual Basic also lets you control the execution of statements in your programs by using Select Case decision structures. You used Select Case structures earlier in this book when you wrote event procedures to process list box, combo box, and menu item choices. A Select Case structure is similar to an If...Then...ElseIf structure, but it is more efficient when the branching depends on one key variable, or *test case*. You can also use Select Case structures to make your program code more readable.

The syntax for a Select Case structure looks like this:

```
Select Case variable
Case value1
    program statements executed if value1 matches variable
Case value2
    program statements executed if value2 matches variable
Case value3
    program statements executed if value3 matches variable
.
.
.
End Select
```

A Select Case structure begins with the Select Case keywords and ends with the End Select keywords. You replace *variable* with the variable, property, or other expression that is to be the key value, or test case, for the structure. You replace *value1*, *value2*, and *value3* with numbers, strings, or other values related to the test case being considered. If one of the values matches the variable, the statements below its Case clause are executed and Visual Basic continues executing program code after the End Select statement. You can include any number of Case clauses in a Select Case structure, and you can include more than one value in a Case clause. If you list multiple values after a case, separate them with commas.

The example below shows how a Select Case structure could be used to print an appropriate message about a person's age in a program. If the Age variable matches one of the Case values, an appropriate message appears as a label.

```
Select Case Age
Case 16
    Label1.Caption = "You can drive now!"
Case 18
    Label1.Caption = "You can vote now!"
Case 21
    Label1.Caption = "You can drink wine with your meals."
Case 65
    Label1.Caption = "Time to retire and have fun!"
End Select
```

A Select Case structure also supports a Case Else clause that you can use to display a message if none of the earlier cases matches. Here's how it works with the Age example:

```
Select Case Age
Case 16
    Label1.Caption = "You can drive now!"
Case 18
    Label1.Caption = "You can vote now!"
Case 21
    Label1.Caption = "You can drink wine with your meals."
Case 65
    Label1.Caption = "Time to retire and have fun!"
Case Else
    Label1.Caption = "You're a great age! Enjoy it!"
End Select
```

---

**IP** The organization of a Select Case structure can make it clearer than an equivalent If…Then structure.

---

## Using Comparison Operators with a Select Case Structure

Visual Basic lets you use comparison operators to include a range of test values in a Select Case structure. The Visual Basic comparison operators that can be used are =, < >, >, <, >=, and <=. To use the comparison operators, you need to include the Is keyword or the To keyword in the expression to identify the comparison you're making. The Is keyword instructs the compiler to compare the test variable to the expression listed after the Is keyword. The To keyword identifies a range of values. The following structure uses Is, To, and several comparison operators to test the Age variable and to display one of five messages:

```
Select Case Age
Case Is < 13
    Label1.Caption = "Enjoy your youth!"
Case 13 To 19
    Label1.Caption = "Enjoy your teens!"
Case 21
    Label1.Caption = "You can drink wine with your meals."
Case Is > 100
    Label1.Caption = "Looking good!"
Case Else
    Label1.Caption = "That's a nice age to be."
End Select
```

If the value of the Age variable is less than 13, the message "Enjoy your youth!" is displayed. For the ages 13 through 19, the message "Enjoy your teens!" is displayed, and so on.

A Select Case decision structure is usually much clearer than an If…Then structure and is more efficient when making three or more branching decisions based on one variable or property. However, when you're making two or fewer comparisons, or when you're working with several different values, you'll probably want to use an If…Then decision structure.

In the following exercise, you'll see how you can use a Select Case structure to process input from a list box. You'll use the List1.Text and List1.ListIndex properties to collect the input, and then you'll use a Select Case structure to display a greeting in one of four languages.

## Using a Select Case Structure to Process a List Box

1. On the File menu, click the New Project command and create a new standard application.

   A blank form appears in the programming environment.

*Label control*

2. Click the Label control in the toolbox, and then create a large box in the top middle of the form to display a title for the program.

*ListBox control*

3. Click the ListBox control in the toolbox, and then create a list box below the title label.

*CommandButton control*

4. Create a small label above the list box object, and then create two small labels below the list box to display program output.

5. Click the CommandButton control in the toolbox, and then create a small command button in the bottom of the form.

*Properties Window button*

6. Click the Properties Window button on the toolbar, and then set the object properties as shown below the form.

| Object | Property | Setting |
|--------|----------|---------|
| Label1 | Caption | "International Welcome Program" |
|        | Font | Times New Roman, Bold, 14-point |
| Label2 | Caption | "Choose a country" |
| Label3 | Caption | (Empty) |
| Label4 | Caption | (Empty) |
|        | BorderStyle | 1 – Fixed Single |
|        | ForeColor | Dark red (&H00000080&) |
| Command1 | Caption | "Quit" |

When you've finished setting properties, your form should look similar to the illustration at the top of the next page.

Now you'll enter the program code to initialize the list box.

7. Double-click the form.

   The Form_Load event procedure appears in the Code window.

8. Type the following program code to initialize the list box:

```
List1.AddItem "England"
List1.AddItem "Germany"
List1.AddItem "Spain"
List1.AddItem "Italy"
```

These lines use the AddItem method of the list box object to add entries to the list box on your form.

9. Open the Object drop-down list box, and then click the List1 object in the list box.

The List1_Click event procedure appears in the Code window.

10. Type the following lines to process the list box selection made by the user:

```
Label3.Caption = List1.Text
Select Case List1.ListIndex
Case 0
    Label4.Caption = "Hello, programmer"
Case 1
    Label4.Caption = "Hallo, programmierer"
Case 2
    Label4.Caption = "Hola, programador"
Case 3
    Label4.Caption = "Ciao, programmatori"
End Select
```

The first line copies the name of the selected list box item to the caption of the third label on the form. The most important property used in the statement is List1.Text, which contains the exact text of the item selected in the list box. The remaining statements are part of the Select Case decision structure. The structure uses the property List1.ListIndex as a test case variable and compares it to several values. The ListIndex property always contains the number of the item selected in the list box; the item at the top is 0 (zero), the second item is 1, the next item is 2, and so on. Using ListIndex, the Select Case structure can quickly identify the user's choice and display the correct greeting on the form.

11. Open the Object drop-down list box, and then click the Command1 object in the list box.

    The Command1_Click event procedure appears in the Code window.

12. Type **End** in the event procedure, and then close the Code window.

13. Save the form to disk under the name **MyCase.frm**, and then save the project to disk under the name **MyCase.vbp**.

*Start button*

14. Click the Start button on the toolbar to run the MyCase program.

15. Click each of the country names in the Choose A Country list box.

    The program displays a greeting for each of the countries listed. The following illustration shows the greeting for Italy.

16. Click the Quit button to stop the program.

   The program stops, and the programming environment returns.

You've finished working with Select Case structures in this lesson.

# Finding and Correcting Errors

The errors you have encountered in your programs so far have probably been simple typing mistakes or syntax errors. But what if you discover a nastier problem in your program—one you can't find and correct by a simple review of the objects, properties, and statements in your program? The Visual Basic programming environment contains several tools you can use to track down and fix errors, or *bugs,* in your programs. These tools won't stop you from making mistakes, but they'll often ease the pain when you encounter one.

 **OTE** The process of finding and correcting errors in programs is called *debugging.*

Consider the following If...Then decision structure, which evaluates two conditional expressions and then displays one of two messages based on the result:

```
If Age > 13 AND Age < 20 Then
    Text2.Text = "You're a teenager."
Else
    Text2.Text = "You're not a teenager."
End If
```

Can you spot the problem with this decision structure? A teenager is a person who is between 13 and 19 years old, inclusive, yet the structure fails to identify the person who is exactly 13. (For this age, the structure erroneously displays the message "You're not a teenager.") This type of mistake is not a *syntax error* (as the statements follow the rules of Visual Basic); it is a mental mistake, or *logic error.* The correct decision structure contains a greater than or equal to operator (>=) in the first comparison after the If...Then statement:

```
If Age >= 13 AND Age < 20 Then
```

Believe it or not, this type of mistake is the most common problem in a Visual Basic program. Code that works most of the time—but not all of the time—is the hardest to check out and fix.

## Using Break Mode

One way to identify a logic error is to execute your program code one line at a time and examine the content of one or more variables or properties as it changes. To do this, you can enter *break mode* while your program is running and then view your code in the Code window. Break mode gives you a close-up look at your program while the Visual Basic compiler is executing it. It's kind of like pulling up a chair behind the pilot and copilot and watching them fly the airplane. But in this case, you can touch the controls.

---

### Three Types of Errors

Three types of errors can occur in a Visual Basic program: syntax errors, runtime errors, and logic errors.

- **Syntax error (or compiler error)** This is a programming mistake (such as a misspelled property or keyword) that violates the rules of Visual Basic. Visual Basic points out several types of syntax errors in your programs while you type program statements and won't let you run a program until each syntax error is fixed.

- **Runtime error** This is a mistake that causes a program to stop unexpectedly during execution. Runtime errors occur when an outside event or an undiscovered syntax error forces a program to stop while it is running. A misspelled filename in a LoadPicture function or an open floppy drive are conditions that can produce runtime errors.

- **Logic error** This is a human error—a programming mistake that makes the program code produce the wrong results. Most debugging efforts are focused on tracking down logic errors introduced by the programmer.

---

While you are debugging your application, you might want to open the Debug toolbar, a special toolbar with buttons devoted entirely to tracking down errors. You might also want to open the Watches window, which can display the contents of critical variables you're interested in viewing. To enter program statements and see their immediate effect, use the Immediate window.

The following illustration shows the debugging toolbar, which you can open by pointing to the Toolbars command on the View menu and then clicking Debug.

In the following exercise, you'll use break mode to find and correct the logic error you discovered earlier in the If...Then structure. (The error is part of an actual program.) To isolate the problem, you'll use the Step Into button on the Debug toolbar to execute program instructions one at a time, and you'll use the Quick Watch button on the Debug toolbar to watch the content of the Age variable change. Pay close attention to this debugging strategy. You can use it to correct many types of glitches in your own programs.

### Debugging the IfBug program

*Open Project
button*

1. Click the Open Project button on the toolbar.

2. Open the project IfBug in the \LearnVb6\Less06 folder.

3. If the form isn't visible, highlight the IfBug form in the Project window, and then click the View Object button.

   The form for the IfBug program appears. This program prompts the user for his or her age. When the user clicks the Test button, the program lets the user know whether he or she is a teenager. The program still has the problem with 13-year-olds that we identified earlier in the lesson. You'll open the Debug toolbar now and use break mode to find the problem.

4. On the View menu, point to the Toolbars command and then click Debug if it is not already selected.

   The Debug toolbar opens. (It might appear docked to the right of the Standard toolbar.)

5. Drag the Debug toolbar below the IfBug form so that you have it handy while you work.

*Start button*

6. Click the Start button on the Debug toolbar.

7. The program runs. Remove the 0 from the Age text box, type **14**, and then click the Test button.

   The program displays the message "You're a teenager." So far, the program displays the correct result.

8. Type **13** in the Age text box, and then click the Test button.

   The program displays the message "You're not a teenager.", as shown in the following illustration:

This result
is a bug.

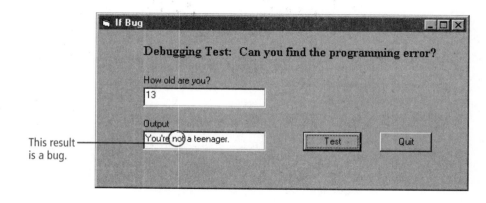

This answer is incorrect, and you need to look at the program code in order to fix the problem. Rather than quitting the program and searching the program code on your own, let Visual Basic help you out.

*Break button*

9. Click the Break button on the Debug toolbar. (The Break button is just to the right of the Start button.)

The program pauses, and Visual Basic displays the Code window, which shows your code as Visual Basic runs it. Your screen should look like the following:

*Step Into button*

10. Click the Step Into button on the Debug toolbar to execute the next program statement.

Visual Basic returns control to the form in the program and waits for input.

11. Click the IfBug form on the Windows taskbar, verify that 13 is still in the text box, and then click the Test button.

Because Visual Basic is in break mode, something unusual happens. Visual Basic opens the Code window and displays the

Command1_Click event procedure—the program code about to be executed by the compiler. The first statement in the procedure is highlighted with yellow. This gives you the opportunity to see how the logic in your program is evaluated.

12. Click the Step Into button to execute the first statement in the procedure.

The Sub statement is executed, and the statement containing the Age variable is highlighted. Age is the critical test variable in this program, so you'll place it in the Watches window now to see how it changes as the program executes.

---

 **IP**  When your program is in break mode, you can check the value of a variable in the Code window by holding the mouse button over it.

---

*Quick Watch button*

13. Select the Age variable by using the mouse, and then click the Quick Watch button on the Debug toolbar.

A dialog box appears on the screen showing the context, name, and value of the Age variable in the program. You'll also see this dialog box if you click the Quick Watch command on the Debug menu.

14. Click Add in the Quick Watch dialog box. The Watches window appears docked at the bottom of the screen. (You might need to resize the window to see all of it.)

---

 **IP**  The Watches window displays variables added by using the Quick Watch command. To remove a variable from the Watches window, click the line containing the variable in the Watches window and press Del.

---

The Age variable currently has no value because it hasn't been used yet in the event procedure. (Because the Age variable wasn't declared globally in the program, it is used as a local variable in the procedure and is reinitialized every time the procedure is called.)

15. Click the Step Into button to execute the next instruction.

Visual Basic copies the number 13 from the text box to the Age variable, and the Age variable in the Watches window is updated.

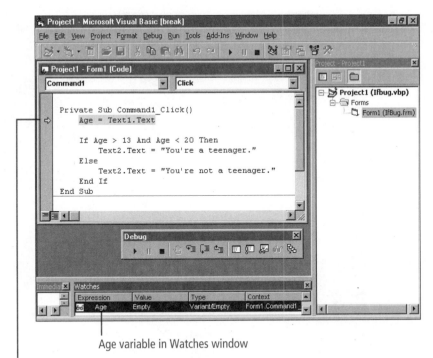

Age variable in Watches window

Next statement to be executed by Visual Basic

Visual Basic now highlights the first statement in the If...Then structure, the most important (and flawed) statement in the program. Because a 13-year-old is a teenager, Visual Basic should execute the Then clause after it evaluates this instruction.

**IP**   When a decision structure branches incorrectly, look for the bug in the conditional expression and fix it if possible.

16.   Click the Step Into button again.

Visual Basic highlights the Else clause in the If...Then structure instead. The test fails on this value, and you need to find and fix the problem now if possible. (Visual Basic helped you find the problem, but you still have to recognize and fix it.) This time, you already know the answer. The first comparison needs the >= operator.

17. Click after the > operator in the If...Then statement, and then type =. Your screen should look like the following:

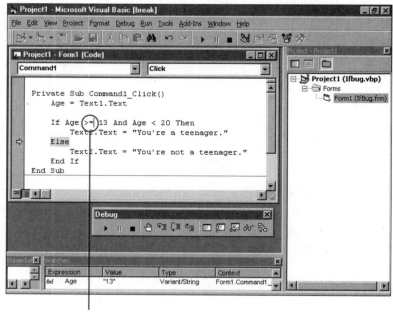

Fix for the bug!

Visual Basic lets you fix errors while in break mode, but if the changes you make are in statements that have already been executed, your corrections won't take effect until the next time the statements are run. To test your correction in this decision structure, you'll need to click the Test button again.

18. Click the Step Into button three times.

    Visual Basic finishes executing the decision structure.

19. Click the Start button (now labeled Continue) on the Debug toolbar to resume full-speed execution of the program.

    The IfBug form reappears.

20. Click the Test button to test your bug fix, verify the message "You're a teenager." in the Output box, and then click the Quit button to stop the program.

21. Click the Close button on the Debug toolbar and the Watches window (if it's still visible) to close them.

Congratulations! You've successfully used break mode to find and correct a logic error in a program. As you continue to work with Visual Basic, feel free to use break mode and the Debug toolbar to analyze your code.

# Using a Stop Statement to Enter Break Mode

If you know the exact place in the program code where you want to enter break mode and start debugging, you can place a Stop statement in your code at that place to pause the program and open the Code window. For example, as an alternative to clicking the Break button, you could have entered break mode in the previous exercise by inserting a Stop statement at the beginning of the Command1_Click event procedure, as shown below.

```
Private Sub Command1_Click()
    Stop      'enter break mode
    Age = Text1.Text
    If Age > 13 And Age < 20 Then
        Text2.Text = "You're a teenager."
    Else
        Text2.Text = "You're not a teenager."
    End If
End Sub
```

When you run a program that includes a Stop statement, Visual Basic enters break mode as soon as it hits the Stop statement. While in break mode, you can use the Code window and Debug toolbar just as you would if you had entered break mode manually. When you've finished debugging, remove the Stop statement.

# Using Loops and Timers

In Lesson 6, you learned how to use the If…Then and Select Case decision structures to choose which statements to execute in a program. In this lesson, you'll learn how to execute a block of statements over and over again by using a *loop*. You'll use a For…Next loop to execute statements a set number of times, and you'll use a Do loop to execute statements until a conditional expression in the loop evaluates to True. You'll also learn how to use the Print method to display text and numbers on a form and how to use a timer object to execute code at specific intervals in your program.

# Writing For...Next Loops

A For...Next loop lets you execute a specific group of program statements a set number of times in an event procedure. This approach can be useful if you're performing several related calculations, working with elements on the screen, or processing several pieces of user input. A For...Next loop is really just a shorthand way of writing out a long list of program statements. Because each group of statements in such a list would do essentially the same thing, Visual Basic lets you define just one group of statements and request that it be executed as many times as you want.

The syntax for a For...Next loop looks like this:

```
For variable = start To end
    statements to be repeated
Next variable
```

In this syntax statement, For, To, and Next are required keywords and the equal to operator (=) also is required. You replace *variable* with the name of a numeric variable that keeps track of the current loop count, and *start* and *end* with numeric values representing the starting and stopping points for the loop. The line or lines between the For and Next statements are the instructions that are repeated each time the loop is executed.

For example, the following For...Next loop sounds four beeps in rapid succession from the computer's speaker:

```
For i = 1 To 4
    Beep
Next i
```

This loop is the functional equivalent of writing the Beep statement four times in a procedure. It looks the same to the compiler as

```
Beep
Beep
Beep
Beep
```

The variable used in the loop is i, a single letter that, by convention, stands for the first integer counter in a For...Next loop. Each time the loop is executed, the counter variable is incremented by one. (The first time through the loop, the variable contains a value of 1, the value of *start*; the last time through, it contains a value of 4, the value of *end*.) As you'll see in the following examples, you can use this counter variable to great advantage in your loops.

## Displaying a Counter Variable by Using the Print Method

A counter variable is just like any other variable in an event procedure. It can be assigned to properties, used in calculations, or displayed in a program. One of the handiest techniques for displaying a counter variable is to use the Print method, a special statement that displays output on a form or prints output on an attached printer. The Print method has the following syntax:

```
Print expression
```

where *expression* is a variable, property, text value, or numeric value in the procedure. In the following exercise, you'll use the Print method to display the output of a For...Next loop on a form.

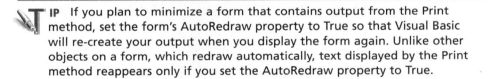

**IP** If you plan to minimize a form that contains output from the Print method, set the form's AutoRedraw property to True so that Visual Basic will re-create your output when you display the form again. Unlike other objects on a form, which redraw automatically, text displayed by the Print method reappears only if you set the AutoRedraw property to True.

### Displaying information by using a For...Next loop

1. In Microsoft Visual Basic, open a new project.

2. Increase the length of the form with the sizing pointer to create some extra room to display your output.

*CommandButton control*

3. Use the CommandButton control to create a command button on the right side of the form.

4. Open the Properties window, and then set the Caption property of the command button to "Loop."

5. Open the object drop-down list box at the top of the Properties window, and then click the Form1 object name.

   The properties for the form appear in the Properties window.

6. Change the Font property to Times New Roman.

   The Font property controls how text is displayed on the form. You can use any font on your system with the form, but TrueType fonts work the best because they can be displayed in many sizes and they look the same on screen as they do in print.

7. Change the AutoRedraw property to True.

   If your form is concealed, the AutoRedraw property will reprint any text displayed by the Print method.

8. Double-click the Loop button on the form.

   The Command1_Click event procedure appears in the Code window.

9. Type the following program statements in the procedure:

   ```
   For i = 1 To 10
       Print "Line"; i
   Next i
   ```

   This For...Next loop uses the Print method to display the word *Line*, followed by the loop counter, 10 times on the form. The semicolon (;) in the Print statement directs Visual Basic to display the counter variable next to the string "Line", with no additional spaces in between. (You will, however, see a space between "Line" and the counter variable when your program runs. When printing numeric values, the Print method reserves a space for a minus sign, even if the minus sign isn't needed.)

---

**T IP**   The Print method supports the semicolon (;) and the comma (,) symbols to separate elements in an expression list. The semicolon places the elements side by side, and the comma places the elements one tab field apart. You can use any combination of semicolon and comma symbols to separate expression list elements.

---

Now you're ready to run the program.

---

**T IP**   The complete ForLoop program is available in the \LearnVb6\Less07 folder.

---

*Start button*

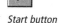

10. Click the Start button on the toolbar.

11. Click the Loop button.

   The For…Next loop prints 10 lines on the form, as shown in the following figure:

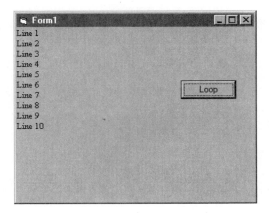

12. Click the Loop button again.

   The For…Next loop prints another 10 lines on the form (or as many as will fit). Each time a line is printed, the invisible insertion point moves down one line, until it is below the edge of the form.

13. Click the End button on the toolbar to stop the program.

*End button*

14. Click the Save Project button on the toolbar. Save the form as **MyForLoop.frm**, and then save the project as **MyForLoop.vbp**. Save the files in the \LearnVb6\Less07 folder.

*Save Project button*

### Changing a property in a For…Next loop

Visual Basic lets you change properties and update key variables in a loop. In the following exercise, you'll modify the MyForLoop program so that it changes the FontSize property in the For…Next loop. The FontSize property specifies the point size of the text on a form; you can use it as an alternative to changing the point size with the Font property.

### Changing the FontSize property

1. Open the Command1_Click event procedure if it is not already open.

   The For…Next loop appears in the Code window.

2. Insert the following instruction directly below the For statement:

```
FontSize = 10 + i
```

This statement sets the FontSize property of the form to 10 points greater than the value of the loop counter. The first time through the loop, the font size will be set to 11 points, the next time to 12 points, and so on until the last loop, when the font will be enlarged to 20 points. When you've finished, your For...Next loop should look like the following:

3. Click the Start button on the toolbar to run the program.

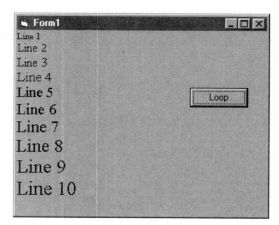

*Start button*

4. Click the Loop button.

The For...Next loop displays the following output on the form:

Each time the loop counter was incremented, it caused the point size on the form to grow.

*End button*

5. Click the End button to stop the program.

   The program stops, and the programming environment returns.

6. On the File menu, click the Save MyForLoop.frm As command. Save the modified form as **MyGrowFont.frm**.

7. On the File menu, click the Save Project As command. Save the project as **MyGrowFont.vbp**. (The complete GrowFont program is available in the \LearnVb6\Less07 folder.)

---

**MPORTANT** A For...Next loop can save considerable space in a program. In the previous example, a For...Next loop four lines long processed the equivalent of 20 program statements.

---

### Creating complex For...Next loops

The counter variable in a For...Next loop can be a powerful tool in your programs. With a little imagination, you can use it to create several useful sequences of numbers in your loops. To create a loop with a counter pattern other than 1, 2, 3, 4, and so on, you can specify a different value for *start* in the loop and then use the Step keyword to increment the counter at different intervals. For example, the loop

```
For i = 5 To 25 Step 5
    Print i
Next i
```

would print the following sequence of numbers on a form:

```
5
10
15
20
25
```

---

**IP** You can create a different sequence of numbers for your For...Next counter variable by using the Step keyword.

---

You can also specify decimal values in a loop. For example, the For...Next loop

```
For i = 1 To 2.5 Step 0.5
    Print i
Next i
```

would print the following numbers on a form:

```
1
1.5
2
2.5
```

In addition to displaying the counter variable, you can use the counter to set properties, calculate values, or process files. The following exercise shows how you can use the counter to open Visual Basic icons that are stored on your hard disk in files that have numbers in their names. The program also demonstrates how you can use a For...Next loop to work with several image objects as a group. To organize the image objects so that they can be processed efficiently, you'll place them in a container called a control array.

### Opening files by using a For...Next loop

1. On the File menu, click the New Project command, and click OK.

*Image control*

2. Click the Image control button in the toolbox, and then create a small, square image box near the upper-left corner of the form.

3. On the Edit menu, click the Copy command.

   A copy of the image box is moved to the Windows Clipboard. You'll use this copy to create three new image boxes on the form.

4. On the Edit menu, click the Paste command.

   Visual Basic displays a message asking whether you want to create a control array in your program. A *control array* is a collection of identical interface objects that you create by copying and pasting objects. Each object in the group shares the same object name, so the entire group can be selected and defined at once. However, the objects in a control array can also be referenced individually, giving you complete control over each item in your user interface.

5. Click Yes to create a control array.

   Visual Basic creates a control array of image boxes and pastes the second image box in the upper-left corner of the form. The new image box is selected.

6. Drag the second image box to the right of the first image box.

---

 **IP** After you select an object, you can drag it to any location on the form.

---

7. On the Edit menu, click the Paste command, and then drag the third image box to the right of the second image box.

8. Click the Paste command again, and then place the fourth image box to the right of the third image box.

   When you've finished pasting, your form should look like this:

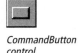

*CommandButton control*

9. Click the CommandButton control in the toolbox, and then create a command button at the bottom of the form.

   Now you'll set the properties of the objects on the form. First you'll set the properties of the image boxes in the control array. You work with all the objects in a control array by selecting them as a group.

10. Click the first image box, hold down the Shift key, and then click the second, third, and fourth image boxes. Release the Shift key.

    The image boxes in the control array appear selected on the form.

11. Open the Properties window and set the following properties. (After you set the image box properties, click the command button to set its property.)

| Object | Property | Setting |
|---|---|---|
| Image1 control array | BorderStyle Stretch | 1 – Fixed Single True |
| Command1 | Caption | "Display icons" |

12. Double-click the Display Icons button on the form to display the event procedure for the command button object.

    The Command1_Click event procedure appears in the Code window.

13. Widen the Code window, and type the following For...Next loop:

```
For i = 1 To 4
    Image1(i - 1).Picture = _
       LoadPicture("c:\learnvb6\less07\misc0" & i & ".ico")
Next i
```

**IP** The LoadPicture function in this event procedure is too long to fit on one line in this book, so I broke it into two lines by using the Visual Basic line continuation character (_). You can use this character anywhere in your program code except within a string expression.

The loop uses the LoadPicture function to load four icon files from the \LearnVb6\Less07 folder on your hard disk. The tricky part of the loop is the statement

```
Image1(i - 1).Picture = _
  LoadPicture("c:\learnvb6\less07\misc0" & i & ".ico")
```

which loads the files from your hard disk. The first part of the statement,

```
Image1(i - 1).Picture
```

accesses the Picture property of each image box in the control array. Control array items are referenced by their index values, so you would refer to the individual image boxes in this example as Image1(0), Image1(1), Image1(2), and Image1(3). The number in parentheses is the index value in the array. In this example, the correct index value is calculated by subtracting 1 from the counter variable.

The filename is created by using the counter variable and the concatenation operator you learned about in the previous lesson. The code

```
LoadPicture("c:\learnvb6\less07\misc0" & i & ".ico")
```

combines a pathname, a filename, and the .ico extension to create four valid filenames of icons on your hard disk. In this example, you're loading Misc01.ico, Misc02.ico, Misc03.ico, and Misc04.ico into the image boxes. This statement works because several files in the \LearnVb6\Less07 folder have the filename pattern Miscxx.ico. Recognizing the pattern lets you build a For...Next loop around the filenames.

*Save Project button*

14. Click the Save Project button on the toolbar.

    Save the form to disk as **MyCtlArray.frm**, and then save the project to disk as **MyCtlArray.vbp.**

*Start button*

15. Click the Start button on the toolbar to start the program, and then click the Display Icons button.

---

**IP**  The complete CtlArray program is available in the \LearnVb6\Less07 folder.

---

The For...Next loop loads the icons from your hard disk into the image boxes.

---

**IP**  If Visual Basic displays an error message, check your program code for typos and then verify that the icon files are in the path you specified in the program. If you installed the Learn Visual Basic Now practice files in a folder other than the default folder, or if you moved your icon files after installation, the pathname in the event procedure may not be correct.

---

The program displays the following output:

16. Click the Close button on the title bar to quit the program.

    The program stops, and the programming environment returns.

## Using the Step Keyword in the MyCtlArray Program

Imagine that the \LearnVb6\Less07 folder is full of files that have the filename pattern Miscxx.ico and try using the Step keyword to display a few more icons in the image boxes. To load filenames that follow a different pattern, you simply need to change the numbers that appear after the For statement and touch up the code that creates the control array index and the icon filename. You also need to change the image box indexes to match the new counter values you'll be using.

## Modifying the MyCtlArray Program

1. Click the first image box object on the form, and then open the Properties window.

    The properties for the Image1(0) image box appear in the Properties window.

2. Change the Index property to 22.

    The first item in a control array usually has an index value of 0, but you can change the index value to a different number if that makes the control array easier to use. In this exercise, the files you want to open are Misc22.ico, Misc24.ico, Misc26.ico, and Misc28.ico, so changing the object indexes to 22, 24, 26, and 28 will make the objects easier to reference.

3. Open the object drop-down list box in the Properties window, and then click the Image1(1) object name.

4. Change the Index property of the second image box to 24.

5. Open the object drop-down list box, and then click the Image1(2) object name.

6. Change the Index property of the third image box to 26.

7. Open the object drop-down list box, and then click the Image1(3) object name.

8. Change the Index property of the fourth image box to 28.

   Now you'll change the code in the For…Next loop.

9. Double-click the Display Icons button on the form.

   The Command1_Click event procedure appears in the Code window.

10. Change the For statement to the following:

```
For i = 22 To 28 Step 2
```

This code sets the counter variable to 22 in the first loop, 24 in the second loop, and 26 and 28 in subsequent loops.

Now you'll update the LoadPicture function in the loop.

11. Change the control array index from Image1(i − 1) to Image1(i).

Because the index now matches the loop and image object names exactly, no calculating is needed to determine the index.

12. Remove the second 0 (zero) from the pathname inside the LoadPicture function.

The Misc*xx*.ico filenames no longer contain zeros. When you've finished, your event procedure should look like the following:

13. Click the Start button on the toolbar, and then click the Display Icons button.

    The For...Next loop loads four new icons in the image boxes. Your screen should look like the figure at the top of the next page.

---

### Exit For Statements

An Exit For statement allows you to exit a For...Next loop before the loop has finished executing. This lets you respond to a specific event that occurs before the loop runs the preset number of times. For example, in the following For...Next loop,

```
For i = 1 To 10
    InpName = InputBox("Enter your name or type Done to quit.")
    If InpName = "Done" Then Exit For
    Print InpName
Next i
```

the loop prompts the user for 10 names and prints them on the form, unless the word *Done* is entered (in which case, the program jumps to the statement immediately following the Next statement). Exit For statements are usually used with If statements. You'll find them useful for handling special cases that come up in a loop, such as stopping when a predefined limit has been reached.

---

14. Click the Close button on the title bar.

    The program stops, and the programming environment returns.

 **OTE** The Visual Basic Working Model CD-ROM contains dozens of interesting icons like the ones shown above. To install these on your system, run Visual Basic Setup again and click Add/Remove. Then click the Graphics option and click Continue. After the installation is complete, you'll find several useful graphics folders in the \Program Files\Microsoft Visual Studio\ Common\Graphics folder.

15. Save the revised form and project to your hard disk under the name **MyStepLoop**. The complete StepLoop program is also located on disk in the \LearnVb6\ Less07 folder.

## Writing Do Loops

As an alternative to a For...Next loop, you can write a Do loop that executes a group of statements until a certain condition is True in the loop. Do loops are valuable because often you can't know in advance how many times a loop should repeat. For example, you may want to let the user enter names in a database until the user types the word *Done* in an input box. In that case, you can use a Do loop to cycle indefinitely until the text string "Done" is entered.

A Do loop has several formats, depending on where and how the loop condition is evaluated. The most common syntax is

```
Do While condition
    block of statements to be executed
Loop
```

For example, the following Do loop will process input until the word *Done* is entered:

```
Do While InpName <> "Done"
    InpName = InputBox("Enter your name or type Done to quit.")
    If InpName <> "Done" Then Print InpName
Loop
```

The conditional statement in this loop is InpName <> "Done", which the Visual Basic compiler translates to mean "loop as long as the InpName variable doesn't contain the word *Done*." This brings up an interesting fact about Do loops: if the condition at the top of the loop is not True when the Do statement is first evaluated, the Do loop is never executed. Here, if the InpName variable did contain the text string "Done" before the loop started (perhaps from an earlier assignment in the event procedure), Visual Basic would skip the loop altogether and continue with the line below the Loop keyword. Note that this type of loop requires an extra If...Then structure to prevent the exit value from being displayed when the user types it.

---

 **TIP** The placement of the conditional test affects how a Do loop runs.

---

If you always want the loop to run at least once in a program, put the conditional test at the bottom of the loop. For example, the loop

```
Do
    InpName = InputBox("Enter your name or type Done to quit.")
    If InpName <> "Done" Then Print InpName
Loop While InpName <> "Done"
```

is essentially the same as the previous Do loop, but here the loop condition is tested after a name is received from the InputBox function. This has the advantage of updating the InpName variable before the conditional test in the loop, so a preexisting "Done" value won't cause the loop to be skipped. Testing the loop condition at the bottom ensures that your loop will be executed at least once, but often it will force you to add a few extra statements to process the data.

## Avoiding an Endless Loop

Because of the relentless nature of Do loops, it's very important to design your test conditions so that each loop has a true exit point. If a loop test never evaluates to False, the loop will execute endlessly and your program will no longer respond to input. Consider the following example:

```
Do
    Number = InputBox("Enter a number to square. Type -1 to quit.")
    Number = Number * Number
    Print Number
Loop While Number >= 0
```

In this loop the user enters number after number, and the program squares each number and prints it on the form. Unfortunately, when the user has had enough, he or she can't quit because the advertised exit condition doesn't work. When the user enters –1, the program squares it and the Number variable is assigned the value 1. (The problem can be fixed by setting a different exit condition.) Watching for endless loops is essential when you're writing Do loops. Fortunately, they're pretty easy to spot if you test your programs thoroughly.

The following exercise shows how you can use a Do loop to convert Fahrenheit temperatures to Celsius temperatures. The simple program prompts the user for input by using the InputBox function, converts the temperature, and displays the output in a message box. The program also demonstrates how you can hide a form by setting its Visible property to False.

## Converting Temperatures by Using a Do Loop

1. On the File menu, click the New Project command and click OK.

   Visual Basic displays a new form in the programming environment.

2. Open the Properties window, and set the form's Visible property to False.

   When you set a form's Visible property to False, Visual Basic hides the form when you run the program. This essentially makes the entire user interface invisible at runtime—no objects can be displayed. You probably won't want to do this very often, but it's a useful technique when you want part or all of your program to work on a task in the background. Because this program only receives Fahrenheit temperatures and spits back Celsius temperatures, hiding its form is a good idea. You can handle the input by using the InputBox function and the output by using the MsgBox function.

3. Double-click the form.

The Form_Load event procedure appears in the Code window. In this program, all the code goes here. The Form_Load event procedure is executed when the program starts running.

4. Type the following program statements:

```
Prompt = "Enter a Fahrenheit temperature."
Do
    FTemp = InputBox(Prompt, "Fahrenheit to Celsius")
    If FTemp <> "" Then
        Celsius = Int((FTemp + 40) * 5 / 9 - 40)
        MsgBox (Celsius), , "Temperature in Celsius"
    End If
Loop While FTemp <> ""
End
```

These nine lines handle the calculations for the utility. The first line assigns a text string to the Prompt variable, which is then used to display a message of instruction in the input box. The Do loop repeatedly prompts the user for a Fahrenheit temperature, converts the number to Celsius, and then displays it on the screen by using the MsgBox function. The loop executes until the user clicks the Cancel button, which returns an empty, or *null*, value to the Ftemp variable. Finally, the loop checks for the null value by using a While conditional test at the bottom of the loop. The program statement

```
Celsius = Int((FTemp + 40) * 5 / 9 - 40)
```

handles the conversion from Fahrenheit to Celsius in the program. This statement employs a standard conversion formula, but it uses the Int function to return to the Celsius variable a value that contains no decimal places. (Everything to the right of the decimal point is discarded.) This cutting sacrifices accuracy, but it helps you avoid long, unsightly numbers, such as 21.1111111111111, the Celsius value for 70 degrees Fahrenheit.

Now try running the program.

*Start button*

5. Click the Start button on the toolbar.

   The program starts, and the InputBox function prompts you for a Fahrenheit temperature. (The form is invisible.) Your screen should look like the following:

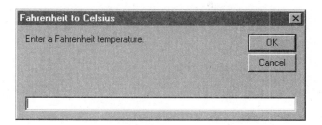

---

### Using the Until Keyword in Do Loops

The Do loops you have worked with so far have used the While keyword to execute a group of statements as long as the loop condition remains True. Visual Basic also lets you use the Until keyword in Do loops to cycle *until* a certain condition is True. The Until keyword can be used at the top or bottom of a Do loop to test a condition, just like the While keyword. For example, the following Do loop uses the Until keyword to loop repeatedly until the user enters the word *Done* in an input box:

```
Do
    InpName = InputBox("Enter your name or type Done to quit.")
    If InpName <> "Done" Then Print InpName
Loop Until InpName = "Done"
```

As you can see, a loop that uses the Until keyword is very similar to a loop that uses the While keyword, except that the test condition usually contains the opposite operator—the = (equal to) operator versus the <> (not equal to) operator, in this case. If using the Until keyword makes sense to you, feel free to use it with test conditions in your Do loops.

6. Type **32** and click OK.

The temperature 32 degrees Fahrenheit is converted to 0 degrees Celsius, as shown in the following message box:

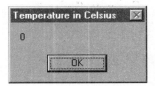

7. Click OK. Type **72** in the input box, and click OK.

The temperature 72 degrees Fahrenheit is converted to 22 degrees Celsius.

8. Click OK, and then quit the program by clicking Cancel in the input box.

The program quits, and the programming environment returns.

*Save Project button*

9. Click the Save Project button, and save the form and project to disk under the name **MyCelsius**. The complete Celsius program is also available in the \LearnVb6\Less07 folder.

# Using Timer Objects

Visual Basic lets you execute a group of statements for a specified *period of time* by using a timer object. A *timer object* is an invisible stopwatch that gives you access to the system clock from your programs. It can be used like an egg timer to count down from a preset time, to cause a delay in a program, or to repeat an action at prescribed intervals.

A timer object is accurate to 1 millisecond, or 1/1000 of a second. Although timers aren't visible at runtime, each timer is associated with an event procedure that runs every time the timer's preset *interval* has elapsed. You set a timer's interval by using the Interval property, and you activate a timer by setting the timer's Enabled property to True. Once a timer is enabled, it runs constantly—executing its event procedure at the prescribed interval—until the user stops the program or the timer is disabled.

## Creating a Digital Clock by Using a Timer Object

One of the most practical uses for a timer object is creating a digital clock. In the following exercise, you'll create a simple digital clock that keeps track of the current time down to the second. In the example, you'll set the Interval property for the timer to 1000, directing Visual Basic to update the clock time every 1000 milliseconds, or once a second. Because the Windows operating system is a multitasking environment and other programs will also require processing time, Visual Basic may not always get a chance to update the clock each second, but it will always catch up if it falls behind. To keep track of the time at other intervals (such as once every tenth of a second), simply adjust the number in the Interval property.

### Creating the DigClock program

1. On the File menu, click the New Project command and click OK.

2. Resize the form to a small window.

   You don't want the clock to take up much room.

*Timer control*

3. Click the Timer control in the toolbox.

4. Create a small timer object on the left side of the form.

   After you create the timer, Visual Basic resizes it to its standard size.

---

  **IP**   A timer object can be only one size.

---

*Label control*

5. Click the Label control in the toolbox.

6. In the center of the form, create a label that fills most of the form.

   You'll use the label to display the time in the clock. Your form should look like the following:

7. Open the Properties window and set the following properties in the program. To give the DigClock program a name that appears in its title bar, you'll set the Caption property of the Form1 object to "Digital Clock". Note that the Caption property of a form controls the name displayed in the program's title bar.

| Object | Property | Setting |
|--------|----------|---------|
| Label1 | Caption | (Empty) |
| | Font | Times New Roman, Bold, 24-point |
| | Alignment | 2 – Center |
| Timer1 | Interval | 1000 |
| | Enabled | True |
| Form1 | Caption | "Digital Clock" |

 **IP**  If you would like to put some artwork in the background of your clock, set the Picture property of the Form1 object to the pathname of an art file.

Now you'll write the program code for the timer.

8. Double-click the timer object on the form.

The Timer1_Timer event procedure appears in the Code window.

9. Type the following statement:

```
Label1.Caption = Time
```

This statement gets the current time from the system clock and assigns it to the caption property of the Label1 object. Only one statement is required in this program because you set the Interval property for the timer by using the Properties window. The timer object handles the rest.

*Start button*

10. Close the Code window, and then click the Start button on the toolbar to run the clock.

The clock appears, as shown at the top of the following page. (Your time may be different, of course.)

11. Watch the clock for a few moments.

    Visual Basic updates the time every second.

12. Click the Close button in the title bar to stop the clock.

    Clicking the Close button is an alternative to using the End button to stop the program. This is the method a user would use to close the clock if he or she were running it as a stand-alone program.

*Save Project button*

13. Click the Save Project button and save the form and project to disk under the name **MyDigClock**. The complete DigClock program is also available in the \LearnVb6\Less07 folder.

The MyDigClock program is so handy that you may want to use it on your computer. Feel free to customize it by using your own artwork, text, and colors.

---

 **IP** See the sidebar entitled "If You Want to Boost Your Productivity" at the end of this lesson for an alarm utility based on DigClock that will help you arrive on time for your appointments.

---

## Using a Timer Object to Set a Time Limit

Another interesting use of a timer object is to set it to wait for a given period of time and then either to enable or to prohibit an action. This is a little like setting an egg timer in your program—you set the Interval property with the delay you want, and then you start the clock ticking by setting the Enabled property to True.

The following exercise shows how you can use this approach to set a time limit for entering a password. (The password for this program is "secret.") The program uses a timer to close its own program if a valid password is not entered in 15 seconds. (Normally, a program like this would be part of a larger application.) You can also use this timer technique to display a welcome message or a copyright message on the screen, or to repeat an event at a set interval, such as saving a file to disk every 10 minutes.

## Setting a Password Time Limit

1. On the File menu, click the New Project command, and then click OK.

2. Resize the form to a small rectangular window about the size of an input box.

*TextBox control*

3. Click the TextBox control in the toolbox.

4. Create a rectangular text box in the middle of the form.

*Label control*

5. Click the Label control in the toolbox, and then create a long label above the text box.

*CommandButton control*

6. Click the CommandButton control in the toolbox, and then create a command button below the text box.

7. Click the Timer control in the toolbox.

*Timer control*

8. Create a timer object in the lower-left corner of the form.

9. Set the properties in the table below for the program.

| Object | Property | Setting |
|---|---|---|
| Text1 | Text | (Empty) |
| | PasswordChar | * |
| Label1 | Caption | "Enter your password within 15 seconds." |
| Command1 | Caption | "Try Password" |
| Timer1 | Interval | 15000 |
| | Enabled | True |
| Form1 | Caption | "Password" |

The PasswordChar setting will display asterisk (*) characters in the text box as the user enters a password. Setting the timer Interval property to 15000 will give the user 15 seconds to enter a password and click the Try Password button. Setting the Enabled property to True (the default) will start the timer running when the program

starts. (You could also disable this property and then enable it
in an event procedure if your timer was not needed until later in
the program.)

Your form should look like the following:

10. Double-click the timer object on the form, and then type the following statements.

```
MsgBox ("Sorry, your time is up.")
End
```

The first statement displays a message indicating that the time has
expired, and the second statement stops the program. Visual Basic
executes this event procedure if the timer interval reaches 15 seconds and a valid password has not been entered.

11. Click the Command1 object in the Code window drop-down list
box, and then type the following statements in the
Command1_Click event procedure:

```
If Text1.Text = "secret" Then
    Timer1.Enabled = False
    MsgBox ("Welcome to the system!")
    End
Else
    MsgBox ("Sorry, friend, I don't know you.")
End If
```

This program code tests whether the password entered in the text
box is "secret." If it is, the timer is disabled, a welcome message is
displayed, and the program ends. (A more useful program would
continue working rather than ending here.) If the password entered

is not a match, the user is notified with a message box and is given another chance to enter the password. But the user has only 15 seconds to do so!

---

 **IP**  The complete TimePass program is available in the \LearnVb6\Less07 folder.

---

*Start button*

12. Close the Code window, and then click the Start button to run the program.

    The program starts, and the 15-second clock starts ticking.

13. Type **open** in the text box, and then click the Try Password button.

    The following dialog box appears on the screen, noting your incorrect response:

14. Click OK, and then wait patiently until the sign-on period expires.

    The program displays the message shown in the following figure:

15. Click OK to end the program.

    The Visual Basic programming environment appears.

*Save Project button*

16. Click the Save Project button, and save the form and project to disk under the name **MyTimePass**.

### If You Want to Boost Your Productivity

Take a few minutes to explore the Alarm utility (alarm.vbp) in the \LearnVb6\Extras folder on your hard disk. I wrote this program as an extension of the DigClock program to give you a little more practice with the Timer control and the timekeeping concepts introduced in this lesson.

The application is a personal appointment reminder that sounds an alarm and displays a message when it is time for your next meeting or task. I find it a useful tool for keeping me on schedule when I'm working by my computer or in my office (it works better than those little yellow sticky notes, which seem to fall off). The Alarm program checks the current time stored in your computer's system clock, so before you use this program, open Control Panel and verify that the system time is correct. As you'll see, Alarm can be run in a window or minimized to the Windows taskbar, where it waits patiently until your appointment. You can customize the program yourself or simply use it as is for your daily work.

PART

# 3

# Creating the Perfect User Interface

# Working with Forms, Printers, and Error Handlers

In Part 2 you learned how to use a variety of Microsoft Visual Basic statements, functions, and control structures to do useful work in your programs. In Part 3 you'll focus again on the user interface and you'll learn how to create impressive effects and bulletproof applications. In this lesson, you'll learn how to add more forms to an interface to handle input, output, or special messages. You'll also learn how to send the output of a program to an attached printer and how to use error handlers to process unexpected results.

# Adding New Forms to a Program

Each program you have written so far has used only one form for input
and output. In many cases, one form will be sufficient for communication
with the user. But if you need to offer more information to (or obtain more
information from) the user, Visual Basic lets you add one or more extra
forms to your program. Each new form is considered an object and maintains its own objects, properties, and event procedures. The first form in a
program is named Form1. Subsequent forms are named Form2, Form3,
and so on. The following table lists several practical uses for extra forms
in your programs.

| Form or forms | Description |
| --- | --- |
| Introductory screen | A screen that displays a welcome message, artwork, or copyright information when the program starts |
| Program instructions | A screen that displays information and tips about how the program works |
| Dialog boxes | Custom dialog boxes that accept input and display output in the program |
| Document contents | A screen that displays the contents of one or more files and artwork used in the program |

## Blank or Predesigned Forms

You can create a new form by clicking the Add Form command on the
Project menu. A dialog box appears, prompting you for the type of form
you want to create (each version of Visual Basic has a different collection
of predesigned forms). You have the option of creating a new, blank form
or a partially completed form designed for a particular task.

## How Forms Are Used

In Visual Basic, you have significant flexibility when using forms. You
can make all of the forms in a program visible at the same time, or you
can load and unload forms as the program needs them. If you display
more than one form at once, you can allow the user to switch between the

forms or you can control the order in which the forms are used. A form that must be used when it is displayed on the screen is a *modal* form—a form that retains the focus until the user clicks OK, clicks Cancel, or otherwise dispatches it.

A form that the user can switch away from is a *nonmodal,* or *modeless,* form. Most applications for Microsoft Windows use nonmodal forms when displaying information because they give the user more flexibility, so nonmodal is the default when you create a new form. You can also independently set any property on a form, including the form's caption, form size, border style, foreground and background colors, display font, and background picture.

## Form Statements in Program Code

After you create a new form in the programming environment, you can load it into memory and access it by using specific statements in event procedures. The statement you use to load a new form has the syntax

```
Load formname
```

where *formname* is the name of the form you want to load. For example, the statement

```
Load Form2
```

would load the second form in a program into memory when the statement was executed by Visual Basic. After you have loaded a form, you can use it from any event procedure in the program and you can access any property or method you want to use with it. For example, to set the Caption property of the second form in your program to "Sorting Results," you could type the following program statement in any event procedure:

```
Form2.Caption = "Sorting Results"
```

When you are ready to display a loaded form, you call it by using the Show method and indicating whether it is modal or nonmodal. The syntax for the Show method is

```
formname.Show mode
```

where *formname* is the name of the form and *mode* is 0 for nonmodal (the default) or 1 for modal. For example, to display Form2 as a nonmodal form (the default), you could use the Show method without specifying a mode:

```
Form2.Show
```

To display Form2 as a modal form, you would type this statement:

```
Form2.Show 1
```

 **TIP** If you use the Show method before using the Load statement, Visual Basic will load and display the specified form automatically. Visual Basic provides a separate Load statement to let programmers preload forms in memory so that the Show method works quickly and users don't notice any performance lag. It's a good idea to preload your forms, especially if they contain several objects or pieces of artwork.

## Hiding and Unloading Forms

You can hide forms by using the Hide method, and you can unload forms by using the Unload statement. These keywords are the opposites of Show and Load, respectively. Hiding a form makes the form invisible but keeps it in memory for use later in the program. (Hiding a form is identical to making it invisible by using the Visible property.) Unloading a form removes the form from memory. This frees up the RAM used to store the objects and graphics on the form, but it doesn't free up the space used by the form's event procedures. These are always in memory. You could use the Hide and Unload keywords to hide and unload Form2 in the following manner:

```
Form2.Hide
Unload Form2
```

 **IMPORTANT** When you unload a form, its runtime values and properties are lost. If you reload the form later, it will contain the original values set in the program code.

## Minimizing Forms

You can minimize a form (place it on the taskbar) or maximize a form (expand it to fill the screen) by using the WindowState property. For example, the following statement would minimize Form1 in a program:

```
Form1.WindowState = 1
```

To maximize Form1, you would use the statement:

```
Form1.WindowState = 2
```

To return Form1 to its normal, default view, you would use:

```
Form1.WindowState = 0
```

The Alarm program in the \LearnVb6\Extras folder demonstrates how the WindowState property works.

---

### Adding Preexisting Forms to a Program

Visual Basic lets you reuse your forms in new programming projects. This is why you have been saving your forms as separate .frm files while using this book. To add a preexisting form to a programming project, click the Add Form command on the Visual Basic Project menu and then click the Existing tab. The Existing tab displays a dialog box that lists all the forms in the current folder (that is, the folder you used last in Visual Basic). To add an existing form, double-click the form filename in the dialog box. Visual Basic adds the specified form to the project, and you can view the form and modify its event procedures by clicking the View Object and View Code buttons in the Project window. You can specify the startup form in your program (the first form loaded) by clicking the Properties command on the Project menu, clicking the General tab, and choosing the appropriate form in the Startup Object drop-down list box. If you change a preexisting form in a new project, you should first save it with a different name. Otherwise, other projects using that form won't run correctly anymore.

---

# Working with Multiple Forms: The Italian Program

The following exercises demonstrate how you can use a second form to display graphics and text in a foreign-language vocabulary program named Italian. Right now, the program uses a MsgBox function to display a definition for each word, but you'll modify the program so that it uses a second form to display the information.

## Running the Italian Program

1. Start Visual Basic.

2. Click the Existing tab in the Open Project dialog box.

3. Open the Italian project in the \LearnVb6\Less08 folder.

4. If the Italian Step by Step form isn't open, click the Italian form in the Project window and then click the View Object button.

   The user interface for the program appears. You'll try running the utility now.

*Start button*

5. Click the Start button on the toolbar.

   A list of Italian verbs appears in the list box on the form. To get the definition for a word, you double-click the word in the list box.

6. Double-click *dormire.*

   A definition for the word *dormire* appears in a message box as shown on the next page.

The output is displayed by the MsgBox function in a plain but effective dialog box.

7. Click OK to close the dialog box.

   The dialog box closes, and the main form returns.

8. Click Quit to quit the program.

Now you'll remove the MsgBox function and replace it with an extra form used to display the information. You'll use the Form button on the toolbar to create the new form in the program.

## Creating a Second Form in the Program

1. On the Project menu, click the Add Form command.

   The Add Form dialog box appears, showing several predesigned forms in the New tab.

2. Click Open to open a new, blank form in the project.

   A blank form named Form2 appears in the programming environment.

3. Resize the second form so that it's about the size and shape of a small, rectangular dialog box.

   Make sure that you are resizing the Form2 window, not the Project1 window that contains the form!

*Image control*

4. Click the Image control in the toolbox, and then create a medium-size image box on the left side of the form.

   You'll use this image box to hold a bitmap of the Italian flag.

*Label control*

5. Click the Label control, and then create a label in the top middle area of the form.

*TextBox control*

*CommandButton control*

6. Click the TextBox control, and then create a large text box below the label in the middle of the form.

7. Click the CommandButton control, and then create a command button on the right side of the form.

8. Set the following properties for the objects on your new form:

| Object | Property | Setting |
|--------|----------|---------|
| Image1 | Stretch | True |
|        | Picture | "c:\learnvb6\less08\flgitaly.ico" |
| Label1 | Font | Times New Roman, Bold, 14-point |
| Text1 | TabStop | False |
| Command1 | Caption | "Close" |
| Form2 | Caption | "Definition" |

 **IP** Setting the TabStop property of the text box to False keeps the text box from getting the focus when the user presses the Tab key. If you don't set this property, the cursor will blink in the text box when the form appears.

When you've finished setting properties, your form should look similar to the following:

Now you'll save the new project and the new form. As you know, Visual Basic requires that each form be saved under its own filename. However, more than one project can share a form. Before you save Form2, be sure that it is the active, or selected, form in the programming environment (it should be now).

9. On the File menu, click the Save Form2 As command.

   The Save File As dialog box appears.

10. Save Form2 to disk under the name **MyDef.frm**. Store the form in the \LearnVb6\Less08 folder.

    The second form is saved to disk and is registered in the Project window. You can switch back and forth between forms by clicking a form or by highlighting a form name in the Project window and then clicking the View Object button.

11. Click Form1, and then click Save Italian.frm As on the File menu to save Form1. Type the name **MyWordList.frm** and press Enter.

    Now changes you make to Form1 won't be reflected in the Italian project. (You've created another copy of the form under a new name.)

12. On the File menu, click the Save Project As command, and then save the project under the name **MyItalian2.vbp**.

Now you'll modify the Text1_DblClick event procedure to display the new form.

## Accessing the Second Form in an Event Procedure

1. Click the first form (MyWordList), and then double-click the List1 object on the form.

   The List1_DblClick event procedure appears in the Code window. In this event procedure, I placed a Select Case decision structure that uses a MsgBox function to display the definition of the selected Italian word. The decision structure determines the list box pick and then assigns the appropriate definition to the Def variable. Take some time to examine the decision structure if you like, and then continue.

2. Scroll to the bottom of the event procedure in the Code window.

   The following MsgBox function appears:

   ```
   MsgBox (Def), , List1.Text
   ```

3. Delete the MsgBox function, and then type the following program statements in its place:

   ```
   Load Form2
   Form2.Label1 = List1.Text
   Form2.Text1 = Def
   Form2.Show
   ```

   The object name Form2 identifies the new form in the program. The first statement loads Form2 into memory. (You could also preload the form by placing this statement in the Form_Load event procedure.) After bringing the form into memory, you can change the form's properties and get it ready for viewing. The second line puts a copy of the selected Italian word into the first label on Form2. The third line assigns the Def variable (containing the word's definition) to the text box on the new form. You're using a text box to support longer definitions in the program. If the definition fills the text box, scroll bars will appear to provide access to the whole string. Finally, the Show method displays the completed form on the screen.

   Now you'll add a statement to the Close button on Form2 to close the form when the user is through with it.

4. Close the Code window, click Form2 (or display it by using the Project window), and then double-click the Close button.

   The Command1_Click event procedure appears in the Code window. This event procedure is associated with the first button on Form2—not the first button on Form1. Objects on different forms can have the same name, and Visual Basic has no trouble keeping them separate. However, if similar or identical names make it hard for you to tell the objects apart, you can change their names by using the Properties window.

5. Type the following program statement in the event procedure:

```
Form2.Hide
```

This statement uses the Hide method to make Form2 invisible when the user clicks the Close button. Because Form2 was displayed in a nonmodal state, the user is free to switch between Form1 and Form2 while the program runs. The user can close Form2 by clicking the Close button.

 **IP** To change an object's name, select the object on the form and then use the Properties window to change the object's Name property. The Name property holds the title that Visual Basic uses to identify the object, so if you change an object name, be sure to change it everywhere in your program code. An object name should be logical, so that you can easily remember what the object does. Object names, like variables, should also carry identifying prefixes. For example, a command button used to quit a program might be named cmdQuit.

*Save Project button*

6. Click the Save Project button to save your revised project to disk.

7. Click the Start button to run the program.

 **IP** The Italian2 program is available in the \LearnVb6\Less08 folder.

8. Double-click the verb *cucinare* in the list box.

The program displays the definition for the word on the second form, as shown in the following illustration:

Now you'll practice switching back and forth between the forms.

9. Click the first form, and then double-click the word *scrivere.*

The program displays the definition for *scrivere* (to write) on the second form. Because the forms are nonmodal, you can switch between them as you wish.

10. Click Close on the second form.

    The program hides the form.

11. Click Quit on the first form.

    The program stops, and Visual Basic unloads both forms. The programming environment returns.

# Sending Program Output to a Printer

Visual Basic lets you send output to an installed printer by using the Print method. You learned about the Print method in Lesson 7 when you used it in a loop to display text on a form. To send output to an attached printer, you use the Print method with the Printer object. For example, the following line sends the text string "Mariners" to the Windows default printer:

```
Printer.Print "Mariners"
```

Before printing, you can also use the Printer object to adjust certain font characteristics. For example, the following code prints "Mariners" in 14-point type:

```
Printer.FontSize = 14
Printer.Print "Mariners"
```

The Printer object has numerous properties and methods you can use to control different aspects of printing. Many of these are similar to keywords you've been using with forms and objects created by using toolbox controls. However, Printer properties differ in one crucial regard from the properties of forms and objects created by using controls in the toolbox: you can't set Printer properties by using the Properties window. Each Printer property must be set with program code at runtime.

The Form_Load event procedure is a good place to put standard Printer settings that you'll use every time your program runs. The tables on page 224 list some of the more useful Printer methods and properties.

## MDI Forms: Windows That Have Parent-Child Relationships

In most of the programs you'll write, you'll probably create a standard "home" form where the user does most of his or her work, and then you'll add special-purpose forms to handle the input and output of a program. However, Visual Basic also lets you set up a *hierarchy,* which is a special relationship among forms in a program that work best as a group. These special forms are called MDI (Multiple Document Interface) forms, and they are distinguished by their roles as *parent* and *child* forms. You create an MDI parent form by clicking the Add MDI Form command on the Project menu, and you create an MDI child form by clicking the Add Form command on the Project menu and then setting the form's MDIChild property to True. MDI forms perform like regular forms at runtime, with the following exceptions:

- All child forms are displayed within their parent form's window space.

- When a child form is minimized, it shrinks to a small title bar on the MDI form instead of appearing as a button on the taskbar.

- When the parent form is minimized, the parent and all its children appear as one button on the taskbar.

- All child menus are displayed on the parent form's menu bar. When a child form is maximized, its caption is displayed in the parent's title bar.

- You can display all the child forms of a parent form by setting the AutoShowChildren property of the parent form to True.

Parent and child forms are especially useful in so-called *document-centered applications,* in which many windows are used to display or edit a document.

| Method | Description |
|--------|-------------|
| Print | Prints the specified text on the printer |
| NewPage | Starts a new page in the print job |
| EndDoc | Signals the end of a print job |
| KillDoc | Terminates the current print job |

| Property | Description |
|----------|-------------|
| FontName | Sets the font name for the text |
| FontSize | Sets the font size for the text |
| FontBold | True sets the font style to bold |
| FontItalic | True sets the font style to italic |
| Page | Contains the number of the page that is being printed |

In the following exercise, you'll add basic printing support to the MyItalian2 program you created earlier in this lesson. You'll use the FontName, FontSize, and FontBold properties to change the style of the text; the Print method to send definitions to the printer; and the EndDoc method to signal the end of the printing job.

## Adding Printer Support to the MyItalian2 Program

1. Open the MyItalian2 project file if it isn't already open.

   If you didn't create MyItalian2.vbp, you can load Italian2.vbp from your hard disk, in the \LearnVb6\Less08 folder.

2. Display the second form in the project (MyDef.frm, or Def.frm if you're using Italian2.vbp).

   This form displays the definition for the Italian word that the user double-clicks in the list box. You'll add a Print button to this form to give the user the option of printing a copy of the definition.

3. Click the CommandButton control in the toolbox, and then create a command button to the left of the Close button.

*CommandButton control*

You may need to make room for the button by widening the form and moving the Close button to the right or by adjusting the size of the Label1 object. When you've finished, your revised form should look similar to the following illustration:

4. Change the caption of the button to "Print" by using the Properties window.

5. Double-click the new Print button to edit its event procedure.

   The Command2_Click event procedure appears in the Code window.

6. Type the following printing statements in the event procedure:

```
Printer.Print ""
Printer.FontName = "Arial"
Printer.FontSize = 18
Printer.FontBold = True
Printer.Print Label1.Caption
Printer.FontBold = False
Printer.Print Text1.Text
Printer.EndDoc
```

Here are some of the important elements in the print routine:

■ The first statement initializes the printer object to prepare it for output.

■ The FontName property sets the printer font to Arial, a TrueType font.

---

**TIP**   Using one of the TrueType fonts that was supplied with Windows will make your program compatible with most printers.

---

■ The FontSize property sets the font size to 18 point.

- Setting the FontBold property to True turns bold type on.

- The fifth and seventh lines use the Print method to print the Italian word and its definition.

- The last line ends the print job and sends it to the printer.

---

 **IP**   If you want to allow the user to print several word definitions on one page, you might want to postpone using the EndDoc method until the user clicks Quit to end the program.

---

7. On the File menu, click the Save MyDef.frm As command, and then save the second form as **MyPrintFrm.frm**. This will preserve the original MyDef.frm form on disk.

8. On the File menu, click the Save Project As command, and then save the new project as **MyPrintFrm.vbp**.

   Because you didn't save MyWordList.frm under a new name, the MyPrintFrm.vbp project and the MyItalian2.vbp project will share its form and code. Whenever you make a change to the MyWordList.frm file (on the form or in the event procedures), the change will be reflected in both projects.

## Running the MyPrintFrm Program

Now you'll run the program if you have a printer attached to your system. Your application will use the default printer specified in the Windows Printers folder, so the device can be a local printer, a network printer, or a fax modem program. Verify that the printer is online and ready to go.

*Start button*

1. Click the Start button on the toolbar.

   The program runs in the programming environment.

---

 **IP**   The complete PrintFrm project is located on disk in the \LearnVb6 \Less08 folder.

---

2. Double-click the Italian word *bere* in the list box.

   The definition appears in the form shown on the next page.

3. Click the Print button on the form to print the definition on paper.

   Visual Basic sends your document to the default printer.

---

> **MPORTANT** If your printer is not ready to print, Windows may return an error to Visual Basic—an error that your program is not ready to handle. This could result in a runtime error or program crash. You'll learn how to handle runtime errors associated with disk drives, printers, and other devices later in this lesson.

---

4. Click Close to close the definition window, and then click Quit to end the program.

   The program stops, and the programming environment returns.

## Printing an Entire Form by Using the PrintForm Method

As an alternative to printing individual lines by using the Print method, you can send the entire contents of one or more forms to the printer by using the PrintForm method. This technique lets you arrange the text, graphics, and user interface elements you want on a form and then send the entire form to the printer. You can use the PrintForm keyword by itself to print the current form, or you can include a form name to print a specific form. For example, to print the contents of the second form in a program, you could enter the statement

```
Form2.PrintForm
```

in any event procedure in the program.

The following example shows how to use the PrintForm method to print a form containing both text and graphics. In most situations, PrintForm is the easiest way to send artwork to a printer.

---

 **IP**  The PrintForm method prints your form at the current resolution of your display adapter, typically 96 dots per inch.

---

## Using PrintForm to Print Text and Graphics

1. On the File menu, click the New Project command, and then click OK to create a new, standard application.

*Label control*

2. Click the Label control, and then create a medium-size label near the center of the form.

*CommandButton control*

3. Click the CommandButton control, and then create a button in the lower-right corner of the form.

4. Set the following properties for the objects in the program:

| Object | Property | Setting |
|--------|----------|---------|
| Label1 | Caption | "Quarterly Report" |
|        | BackStyle | 0 – Transparent |
|        | Font | MS Sans Serif, Bold, 14-point |
| Command1 | Caption | "Print this!" |
| Form1 | Picture | "c:\learnvb6\less08\prntout2.wmf" |

5. Double-click the Print this! button to open its event procedure.

6. Type the following program statement:

```
Form1.PrintForm
```

*Save Project button*

7. Click the Save Project button on the toolbar to save the form and the project. Type **MyPrintWMF** for the form name and for the project name.

*Start button*

8. Click the Start button on the toolbar to run the program.

---

 **IP**  The complete PrintWMF project is located on disk in the \LearnVb6 \Less08 folder.

---

The program displays the following:

9.  Click the Print this! button to print the contents of the form.

Visual Basic sends the entire contents of the form (label, Windows metafile, and command button) to the printer. While the document prints, you might see the following Visual Basic dialog box:

Soon, the output of the program emerges from the printer.

10.  Click the Close button on the form to end the program.

---

**MPORTANT**  The PrintForm method prints only the objects that are currently visible on the form. To remove unwanted objects from a printout (such as the Print this! button in the last example), set the Visible property of those objects to False before calling the PrintForm method. Then add a statement to make the objects visible again after you have sent the form to the printer.

---

# Processing Errors by Using Error Handlers

Have you experienced a runtime error in a Visual Basic program yet? A *runtime error,* or *program crash,* is an unexpected problem that occurs in a Visual Basic program—a problem from which it can't recover. You may have experienced your first program crash in this lesson when you were trying to print, if something didn't work right. (Perhaps the printer was out of paper or was turned off and you received a printer error message from Visual Basic or Windows.) A runtime error happens anytime Visual Basic executes a statement that for some reason can't be completed "as dialed" while the program is running. It's not that Visual Basic isn't tough enough to handle the glitch; it's just that the compiler hasn't been told what to do when something goes wrong.

Fortunately, you don't have to live with occasional errors that cause your programs to crash. Visual Basic lets you write special routines, called *error handlers,* to respond to runtime errors. An error handler handles a runtime error by telling the program how to continue when one of its statements doesn't work. Error handlers are placed in the same event procedures where the potentially unstable statements are. As their name implies, error handlers handle, or *trap,* a problem by using a special error handling object named Err. The Err object has a Number property that identifies the error and lets your program respond to it. For example, if a floppy disk causes an error, your error handler might display a custom error message and then disable disk operations until the user fixes the problem.

## When to Use Error Handlers

You can use error handlers in any situation in which an unexpected action might result in a runtime error. Typically, error handlers are used to process external events that influence a program—for example, events caused by a failed network drive, an open floppy drive door, or a printer that is offline. The following table lists potential problems that can be addressed by error handlers.

| Problems | Description |
|---|---|
| Network problems | Network drives or resources that fail, or "go down," unexpectedly |
| Floppy disk problems | Unformatted or incorrectly formatted disks, open drive doors, or bad disk sectors |
| Printer problems | Printers that are offline, out of paper, or otherwise unavailable |
| Overflow errors | Too much printing or drawing information |
| Out-of-memory errors | Application or resource space is not available in Windows |
| Clipboard problems | Problems with data transfer or the Windows Clipboard |
| Logic errors | Syntax or logic errors undetected by the compiler and previous tests (such as an incorrectly spelled filename) |

## Setting the Trap: The On Error Statement

The program statement used to detect a runtime error is On Error. You place On Error in an event procedure right before you use the statement you're worried about. The On Error statement sets, or *enables,* an event trap by telling Visual Basic where to branch if it encounters an error. The syntax for the On Error statement is

```
On Error GoTo label
```

where *label* is the name of your error handler.

Error handlers are typed near the bottom of an event procedure, following the On Error statement. Each error handler has its own label, which is followed by a colon (:) for identification purposes—ErrorHandler: or PrinterError:, for example. An error handler usually has two parts. The first part typically uses the Err.Number property in a decision structure (such as If...Then or Select Case) and then displays a message or sets a property based on the error. The second part is a Resume statement that sends control back to the program so that the program can continue.

## Dealing with the Resume Statement

In the Resume statement, you can use the Resume keyword alone, use the Resume Next keywords, or use the Resume keyword with a label you'd like to branch to, depending on which part of the program you want to continue next.

The Resume keyword returns control to the statement that caused the error (in hopes that the error condition will be fixed or won't happen again). Using the Resume keyword is a good strategy if you're asking the user to fix the problem, for example, by closing the floppy drive door or by tending to the printer.

The Resume Next keywords return control to the statement *following* the one that caused the error. Using the Resume Next keywords is the strategy to employ if you want to skip the problem command and continue working. You can also follow the Resume keyword with a label you'd like to branch to. This gives you the flexibility of moving to any place in the event procedure you want to go. A typical location to branch to is the last line of the procedure.

## Creating a Floppy Drive Error Handler

The following example shows how you can create an error handler to recover from errors associated with floppy disk drives. You'll add the error handler to a program that attempts to load a Windows metafile from a disk in drive A. You can use the same technique to add error handling support to any Visual Basic program—just change the error numbers and messages.

### Creating a disk drive error handler

1. Open the DriveErr project file in the \LearnVb6\Less08 folder.

   The DriveErr form appears in the Project window.

2. If the form is not visible, click the DriveErr form in the Project window, and then click the View Object button.

3. Double-click the Check Drive button on the form.

The event procedure for the Command1_Click object appears in the Code window. This event procedure loads a Windows metafile named Prntout2.wmf from the root folder of drive A, but it currently generates an error if the file does not exist or if the floppy drive door is open.

4. Type the following statement at the top of the event procedure:

```
On Error GoTo DiskError
```

This statement enables the error handler in the procedure and tells Visual Basic where to branch if runtime error occurs. Now you'll add the DiskError error handler to the bottom of the event procedure.

5. Move one line below the LoadPicture statement, and then type the following program code:

```
Exit Sub   'exit procedure
DiskError:
    If Err.Number = 71 Then   'if DISK NOT READY
        MsgBox ("Please close the drive latch."), , _
          "Disk Not Ready"
        Resume
    Else
        MsgBox ("I can't find prntout2.wmf in A:\."), , _
          "File Not Found"
        Resume StopTrying
    End If
StopTrying:
```

The conditional expression in the error handler's If...Then statement tests the Err.Number property to see if it contains the number 71, the error code that is returned whenever a disk drive is not functioning. If a disk error has occurred, the program gives the user the opportunity to fix the problem (either by closing the drive latch or by inserting a new disk) and then continue with the loading operation. (The LoadPicture function is attempted again with the Resume keyword.)

If the error was not related to the disk drive, the program assumes that the disk is valid but that the file cannot be located in the root folder. Then the error handler branches to the StopTrying: label at the bottom of the procedure. In either case, the error handler prints a message for the user and stops the program from being prematurely terminated. You could add more ElseIf statements and error numbers to the error handler to give the user more specific and useful information about the disk problem.

If the program encounters no disk problems or if the user fixes an initial problem, the program proceeds until the Exit Sub statement ends the event procedure. Exit Sub is a general-purpose statement that you can use to exit any Visual Basic procedure before the End Sub statement is executed. In this case, Exit Sub prevents the error handler from running after the program successfully loads the Windows metafile.

---

 **TIP** You can use the Exit Sub statement to skip over an error handler in a procedure.

---

6. On the File menu, click the Save DriveErr.frm As command, and then save the form as **MyFinalErr**.

7. On the File menu, click the Save Project As command, and then save the project as **MyFinalErr**. The complete FinalErr program is also available in the \LearnVb6\Less08 folder.

8. Use Windows Explorer to copy the file Prntout2.wmf from the \LearnVb6\Less08 folder to a floppy disk in drive A. (You need a spare floppy disk to complete this step.)

   Be sure to copy the file to the root folder on the disk (A:\).

9. Remove the floppy disk from drive A, or open the drive latch.

10. Click the Start button to run the program.

11. Click the Check Drive button on the form.

   Visual Basic generates a runtime error, and the error handler displays the error message shown at the top of the next page.

12. Insert the floppy disk that has the Windows metafile on it or close the drive door.

13. Click OK to close the error handler and retry the loading operation.

    After a few moments, the Prntout2.wmf Windows metafile is displayed on the form, as shown in the following illustration:

**TIP** If an error message still appears, you may have a different error in your program. Try stepping through your program code by using break mode. Errors are easy to spot by using Quick Watch expressions, and the process shows you graphically how error handlers work.

14. Click the Close button on the form to end the program.

## More Techniques for Error Handlers

The Err object contains a few other properties that you might want to use to display additional information in your error handlers. The Err.Description property contains the error message returned to Visual Basic when a runtime error occurs. You can use this message as an additional source of information for the user, whether or not you plan to respond to the error programmatically. For example, the error handler code shown below uses the Description property to display an error message if an error occurs when you are loading artwork from a floppy disk.

```
On Error GoTo DiskError
Image1.Picture = LoadPicture("a:\prntout2.wmf")
Exit Sub                    'exit procedure
DiskError:
MsgBox (Err.Description), , "Loading Error"
Resume                      'try LoadPicture function again
```

You can use this technique to trap floppy disk problems such as unformatted disks, missing files, or an open drive door. The error handler uses the Resume statement to try the loading operation again when the user fixes the problem and clicks OK in the message box. When the file eventually loads, the Exit Sub statement ends the event procedure.

 **TIP** If you get stuck in an error loop and can't get out, press Ctrl+Break.

## Specifying a Retry Period

Another strategy you can use in an error handler is to try an operation a few times and then jump over the problem if it isn't resolved. For example, the following error handler uses a counter variable named Retries to track the number of times an error message has been displayed, and then it forces the program to skip the loading statement if it fails twice:

```
Retries = 0                 'initialize counter variable
On Error GoTo DiskError
Image1.Picture = LoadPicture("a:\prntout2.wmf")
Exit Sub                    'exit the procedure
DiskError:
MsgBox (Err.Description), , "Loading Error"
```

```
Retries = Retries + 1        'increment counter on error
If Retries >= 2 Then
    Resume Next
Else
    Resume
End If
```

This is a useful technique if the error you're handling is a problem that can occasionally be fixed by the user. The important thing to remember here is that Resume retries the statement that caused the error and that Resume Next skips the statement and moves on to the next line in the event procedure. When you use Resume Next, be sure that the next statement really is the one you want to execute, and when you continue, make sure that you don't accidentally run the error handler again. A good way to skip over the error handler is to use the Exit Sub statement; or you can use Resume Next with a label that directs Visual Basic to continue executing below the error handler.

# 9

# Adding Artwork
# and Special Effects

For most developers, adding artwork and special effects to an application is the most exciting—and addicting—part of programming. Fortunately, creating impressive and useful graphical effects with Microsoft Visual Basic is both satisfying and easy. In this lesson, you'll learn how to add interesting "bells and whistles" to your programs. You'll learn how to create compelling artwork on a form, build graphical command buttons, and change the shape of the mouse pointer. You'll also learn how to add drag-and-drop support to your programs and how to create simple animation by using image and timer objects. When you've finished, you'll have the skills you need to create the ultimate user interface.

# Adding Artwork by Using the Line and Shape Controls

You've already learned how to add bitmaps, icons, and Windows metafiles to a form by creating picture box and image objects. Adding ready-made artwork to your programs is easy in Visual Basic, and you've had practice doing it in almost every lesson. Now you'll learn how to create original artwork on your forms by using the Line and Shape controls. These handy tools are located in the toolbox, and you can use them to build a variety of images of different shapes, sizes, and colors. The objects you create by using these controls do have a few limitations—they can't receive the focus at runtime, and they can't appear on top of other objects—but they are powerful, fast, and easy to use.

 IP    The Line and Shape controls let you create geometric images.

## The Line Control

*Line control*

You can use the Line control to create a straight line on a form. You can then set a variety of properties to change the appearance of the line object you create, just as you can for other objects. The most important line object properties are BorderWidth, BorderStyle, BorderColor, and Visible.

The BorderWidth property adjusts the thickness of the line on your form. This option is especially useful when you're creating an underline or a line that separates one object from another. The BorderStyle property lets you make the line solid, dotted, or dashed, and the BorderColor property lets you set the color of the line to any of Visual Basic's standard colors. Finally, the Visible property lets you hide the line or display it as it becomes necessary in your program.

You'll get a chance to work with the Line control after you learn a little about the Shape control.

## The Shape Control

*Shape control*

You can use the Shape control to create rectangles, squares, ovals, and circles on your forms. You use the Shape control to draw the image you want, and then you use the Properties window to adjust the image characteristics. The Shape property controls the shape of the image; you can select a rectangle, rounded rectangle, square, rounded square, oval, or circle shape after you create the image. You can build complex images by drawing several shapes and lines.

Other important shape object properties include FillColor, which lets you specify the object's color; FillStyle, which lets you specify a pattern for the fill color; and BorderColor, which lets you specify a separate color for the shape's border. A shape object also has a Visible property, which lets you hide or display your artwork as necessary.

The following exercise gives you hands-on practice using the Line and Shape controls. You'll use the controls to create a welcome screen used by a fictitious business named Northwest Window Screens. The welcome screen will look like this:

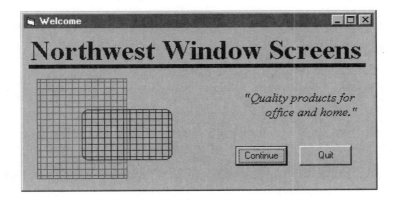

## Using the Line and Shape Controls

1. Start Visual Basic and open a new, standard project.

   If Visual Basic is already running, click the New Project command on the File menu, and open a new, standard project.

2. Widen the form so that you have room for large type, shape objects, and command buttons.

*Label control*

3. Click the Label control in the toolbox, and then create a long label across the top of the form.

4. Open the Properties window, and then set the Caption property of the label to "Northwest Window Screens."

5. Set the Font property of the label to Times New Roman, Bold, 26-point. Set the ForeColor property to Dark Blue.

   Your label should now take up most of the width of the screen. Adjust the label width and height, if necessary, so that the business name fits on one line.

*Line control*

6. Click the Line control in the toolbox, and then create a line under the business name. Make the line stretch across most of the form, just as the label does.

   The Line control places selection handles on either side of the line after you create it. You can use these handles to resize the line, if necessary.

*Properties
Window button*

7. Click the Properties Window button to display the Properties window, and then set the following properties for the line object:

| Object | Property | Setting |
|--------|----------|---------|
| Line1 | BorderWidth | 5 |
| | BorderColor | Dark blue |

The name of your new line object is Line1. The BorderWidth setting changes the width of the line to 5 twips. (A twip is 1/20 point, or 1/1440 inch.) The BorderColor setting changes the color of the line to dark blue.

Now you'll create two window screen images on the form.

*Shape control*

8. Click the Shape control in the toolbox, and then create a rectangle on the left side of the form.

   This rectangle is the outline of the first window screen. You'll set the FillStyle property of this object a little later to make the rectangle look like a screen.

9. Click the Shape control again, and then create a second rectangle on the left side of the form, partially overlapping the first rectangle.

The Shape control works a lot like a general-purpose drawing tool in an art program. The control creates the basic shape, and then you set properties to refine that shape.

10. Click the Properties Window button, and then set the following properties for the two shapes:

| Object | Property | Setting |
| --- | --- | --- |
| Shape1 | Shape | 0 – Rectangle |
| | FillColor | Dark yellow |
| | FillStyle | 6 – Cross |
| | BorderColor | Dark yellow |
| Shape2 | Shape | 4 – Rounded rectangle |
| | FillColor | Light blue |
| | FillStyle | 6 – Cross |
| | BorderColor | Light blue |

11. Create a label on the right side of the form. Make it a fairly narrow label so that the label caption wraps over two lines. Then set the properties as shown in the following table:

| Object | Property | Setting |
| --- | --- | --- |
| Label2 | Caption | ""Quality products for office and home."" |
| | Font | Times New Roman, Italic, 12-point |
| | Alignment | 1 – Right Justify |

*CommandButton control*

12. Click the CommandButton control in the toolbox, and then create a command button in the lower-right corner of the form. Create a second button to the left of the first command button.

13. Set the following properties for the command buttons:

| Object | Property | Setting |
| --- | --- | --- |
| Command1 | Caption | "Quit" |
| Command2 | Caption | "Continue" |

14. Double-click the Quit command button, type **End** in the Command1_Click event procedure, and then close the Code window.

    The welcome form you're creating is intended to be a gateway to the program, but if users want to quit without moving on in the program, the Quit button gives them a way out. Because the welcome screen is the only part of this program that exists now, you'll also use the Quit button to end the program.

15. Change the Caption property of the form to "Welcome," and then resize the objects and the form so that the screen looks well proportioned.

    When you've finished, your form should look similar to the following:

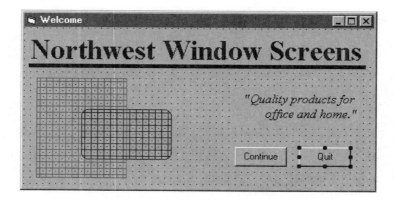

You can use a welcome form like this for any program you write. Its purpose is to welcome users to the program gracefully and then let them continue or exit as they see fit. When users click the Continue button, the program should hide the welcome form and then display the main form of the application.

## Running the StartFrm Program

1. Click the Start button on the toolbar.

 **TIP** The complete StartFrm program is available in the \LearnVb6\Less09 folder.

The Welcome form appears, as shown in the illustration at the top of the next page.

---

### Using Graphics Methods to Create Shapes

Visual Basic supports several method keywords for adding artwork to your programs. You can use these graphics methods to create special visual effects. Graphics methods are commands you use in event procedures to create images on a form or send images to a printer.

The disadvantage of graphics methods is that they take considerable planning and programming to use. You need to learn the syntax of the commands, understand the coordinate system used on your form, and refresh the images if they become covered by another window. However, you can use graphics methods to create some visual effects that you can't create by using the Line control or the Shape control, such as arcs and individually painted pixels.

The most useful graphics methods are Line, which creates a line, rectangle, or solid box; Circle, which creates a circle, ellipse, or "pie slice;" and PSet, which sets the color of an individual pixel on the screen.

For example, the following Circle statement draws a circle with a radius of 750 twips at (x, y) coordinates (1500, 1500) on a form:

```
Circle (1500, 1500), 750
```

---

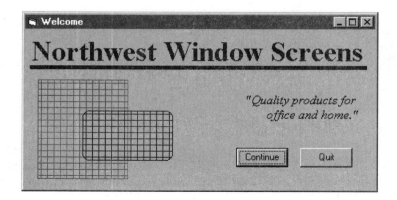

The line and shape objects appear immediately on the form and add to the general character of the welcome screen. Line and shape objects always appear faster than does artwork loaded from disk.

2. Click the Quit button to end the program.

*Save Project button*

3. Click the Save Project button on the toolbar, and then save your form in the Less09 folder as **MyStartFrm.frm**. Save the project file as **MyStartFrm.vbp**.

## Creating Graphical Command Buttons

You've used command buttons throughout this book to give the user an intuitive method for issuing commands. As you've learned, you create a command button by using the CommandButton control, and then you set the caption property of the button to a word that describes the command the button executes.

As an alternative to creating text-based buttons, Visual Basic lets you use the Image control to create graphical buttons in your programs. A *graphical button* contains artwork that is a visual representation of the command executed by the button. For example, a button containing a floppy disk icon could represent a command that saves information to your computer or to a disk drive. Graphical buttons can be placed individually in programs, or they can be grouped in collections called *toolbars.* The Visual Basic toolbar is an example of this type of button grouping. In this section, you'll learn how to create authentic graphical command buttons that "push in" and "pop out" when you click them, just like the buttons you've seen in other applications for Microsoft Windows.

## Detecting a MouseDown Event

To give your graphical buttons a realistic look and "feel," you'll want your program to respond as soon as the user places the mouse pointer over a graphical button and holds down the mouse button. So far, you've been using the Click event to take action in your programs, but in this case Click isn't good enough. Your program needs to respond when the user first *presses* the button, not after the button is released. You can track mouse activity in Visual Basic by using the MouseDown event.

 **IP** The MouseDown event detects the first half of a mouse button click.

*MouseDown* is a special event that executes an event procedure whenever the user places the mouse pointer over an object on the form and then holds down the mouse button. If you write a special event procedure for the MouseDown event (such as Image1_MouseDown in the next section), your program can take action whenever the user holds down the mouse button while the mouse pointer is over the object. When you're creating graphical command buttons, you'll want your program to change the button when the user clicks, to give the button that "pushed in" look, and then execute the specified command in the program.

 **IP** In addition to recognizing MouseDown events, your programs can recognize MouseUp events (generated whenever the user releases the mouse button) and MouseMove events (generated whenever the user moves the mouse).

## Swapping Out Buttons

So how do you make graphical command buttons look pushed in and popped out when they are clicked in a program? As you might suspect, the icon pictures aren't modified on the screen when the user clicks the icons. Instead, the icons are replaced by other icons, or *swapped out,* by a MouseDown event procedure. As the illustration on the following page shows, each graphical command button has three states: up, down, and disabled.

Up is the normal, or popped out, state—the appearance of the button when it's at rest, or in its default position. Down is the selected, or pushed in, state—the appearance of the button when it's been selected (clicked) or is active. Disabled is an optional state that's used when a button isn't currently available for use in the program. Some graphical command buttons never use this state.

In a Visual Basic program, button states are controlled by swapping icons in and out of the image object used to hold the button. The MouseDown event procedure associated with the image object handles the swapping. For the event procedure to work correctly, it must read the current state of the button (up, down, or disabled), change to the requested state, and then execute the requested command (such as changing text to boldface). The button icons can be loaded at runtime by using the LoadPicture function, or they can be swapped on the form by using assignment statements. Some programmers put all three button states on the form to make the updating quicker.

You can update button states by using the MouseDown event procedure.

---

 **IP**  You can create graphical buttons and toolbars on any Visual Basic form, but MDI forms have special built-in properties that make working with collections of buttons easier. In addition, the Toolbar ActiveX control (a component of the Windows Common Control), helps you create and manage toolbars on your MDI forms. For more information about using "professional" ActiveX controls, see Lesson 15.

---

In the following exercise, you'll create a program that uses three graphical command buttons (Bold, Italic, and Underline) to format text on a form. The program uses six icons from the Less09 folder to display the buttons on the form, and it uses three MouseDown event procedures to update the buttons and format the text. The illustration at the top of the next page shows the form you'll build.

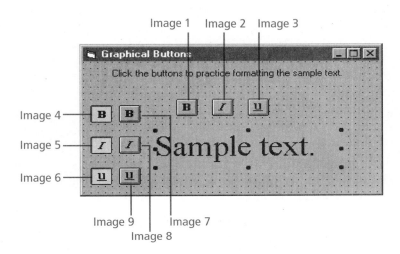

## Creating Toolbar Buttons

1. On the File menu, click the New Project command, and then click OK.

2. Resize the form so that it resembles a medium-size dialog box.

*Label control*

3. Click the Label control, and then create a long label along the top edge of the form.

*Image control*

4. Use the Image control to create three small image boxes centered below the label on the form.

   These image boxes will hold the Bold, Italic, and Underline buttons you'll use in the program.

5. Create six image boxes on the left side of the form. See the illustration above for the suggested placement of these objects and try to create them like I did.

   These image boxes will hold the six button states you'll be swapping in and out of the first three image boxes. (Alternatively, you could load these buttons from disk or store some of the states in global variables, but keeping them all on the form is fast and convenient for this example.)

6. Create a large label in the middle of the form to hold the sample text.

   This is the label you'll format by using the toolbar buttons. You'll adjust the text by using the FontBold, FontItalic, and FontUnderline properties in the MouseDown event procedures.

   Now you'll set the properties for the objects on the form. First, you'll make the six swapping icons invisible on the form, and then you'll change and format the text in the labels. Next, you'll record the opening button states in a special image box property named *Tag*. You can use the Tag property to include descriptive notes in an object you're working with. Often, Tag is used to store the name of the object, but in this case you'll use it to store the button state: "Up" or "Down."

7. Set the following properties for the objects.

| Object | Property | Setting |
| --- | --- | --- |
| Label1 | Caption | "Click the buttons to practice formatting the sample text." |
| Label2 | Caption<br>Font | "Sample text."<br>Times New Roman, 28-point |
| Form1 | Caption | "Graphical Buttons" |
| Image1 | Picture<br>Tag | "c:\learnvb6\less09\bld-up.bmp"<br>"Up" |
| Image2 | Picture<br>Tag | "c:\learnvb6\less09\itl-up.bmp"<br>"Up" |
| Image3 | Picture<br>Tag | "c:\learnvb6\less09\ulin-up.bmp"<br>"Up" |
| Image4 | Picture<br>Visible | "c:\learnvb6\less09\bld-dwn.bmp"<br>False |
| Image5 | Picture<br>Visible | "c:\learnvb6\less09\itl-dwn.bmp"<br>False |
| Image6 | Picture<br>Visible | "c:\learnvb6\less09\ulin-dwn.bmp"<br>False |

*(continued)*

*(continued)*

| Object | Property | Setting |
|--------|----------|---------|
| Image7 | Picture | "c:\learnvb6\less09\bld-up.bmp" |
|        | Visible  | False |
| Image8 | Picture | "c:\learnvb6\less09\itl-up.bmp" |
|        | Visible  | False |
| Image9 | Picture | "c:\learnvb6\less09\ulin-up.bmp" |
|        | Visible  | False |

When you've finished, your form should look similar to the following:

Now you'll enter the code for the three MouseDown event procedures.

8. Double-click the Image1 object (the Bold button above the sample text) on the form.

   The Image1_Click event procedure appears in the Code window. This time you'll write code for the MouseDown event rather than for the Click event. To open a different event procedure for an object, you click the event in the Procedure drop-down list box.

9. Open the Procedure drop-down list box in the Code window.

   The drop-down list box displays the events that can be recognized by the image object.

10. Click the MouseDown event in the list box.

---

 **TIP**   The MouseDown event procedure supplies four variables you can use in your programs.

---

The Image1_MouseDown event procedure appears in the Code window. This event procedure receives four pieces of information about the MouseDown event: the mouse button pressed; the combination of Alt, Ctrl, and Shift keys being held down (if any); the *x* (horizontal) screen coordinate of the mouse pointer; and the *y* (vertical) screen coordinate of the mouse pointer. These values are returned, or *passed,* to the event procedures in variables that you can use in your code. Although you won't use event procedure variables, or *parameters,* in this program, they can be useful tools, and many event procedures provide them. You'll learn a little about using parameters in the DragDrop program later in this lesson.

11. Type the following program statements in the Image1_MouseDown event procedure:

```
If Image1.Tag = "Up" Then
    Image1.Picture = Image4.Picture
    Label2.FontBold = True
    Image1.Tag = "Down"
Else
    Image1.Picture = Image7.Picture
    Label2.FontBold = False
    Image1.Tag = "Up"
End If
```

**TIP** The FontBold property controls boldfaced formatting.

This simple If decision structure processes the two types of Bold button clicks the user can perform in the program. If the Bold button is initially in the up state, the procedure replaces the Bld-up.bmp icon with the Bld-dwn.bmp icon, changes the text to boldface, and sets the image box tag to "Down." If the button is initially in the down state, the procedure replaces the Bld-dwn.bmp icon with the Bld-up.bmp icon, cancels the boldface setting, and sets the image box tag to "Up." Whichever state the button is in, the decision structure changes it to the opposite state.

12. Open the Object drop-down list box in the Code window, and then select the Image2 object. Open the Procedure drop-down list box, and then select the MouseDown event.

    The Image2_MouseDown event procedure appears.

13. Type the following program statements:

```
If Image2.Tag = "Up" Then
    Image2.Picture = Image5.Picture
    Label2.FontItalic = True
    Image2.Tag = "Down"
Else
    Image2.Picture = Image8.Picture
    Label2.FontItalic = False
    Image2.Tag = "Up"
End If
```

 **TIP** The Tag property is used to determine the current button state.

This decision structure controls the operation of the Italic button in the program. The code is almost identical to the Image1_Mouse-Down procedure. The only differences are the names of the image boxes and the use of the FontItalic property instead of the FontBold property.

14. Open the Object drop-down list box, and then select the Image3 object. Open the Procedure drop-down list box, and then select the

MouseDown event. When the Image3_MouseDown event procedure appears, type the following program statements:

```
If Image3.Tag = "Up" Then
    Image3.Picture = Image6.Picture
    Label2.FontUnderline = True
    Image3.Tag = "Down"
Else
    Image3.Picture = Image9.Picture
    Label2.FontUnderline = False
    Image3.Tag = "Up"
End If
```

 **IP**  The Picture property is used to switch the buttons.

This decision structure controls the operation of the Underline button. It's nearly identical to the two previous procedures. You've finished building the program, so now you'll save it to disk.

*Save Project button*

15. Click the Save Project button on the toolbar. Specify the \LearnVb6 \Less09 folder, and then save your form as **MyButtons.frm**. Save your project as **MyButtons.vbp** in the same folder.

Now you'll run the program.

### Running the program and testing the buttons

*Start button*

1. Click the Start button on the toolbar.

 **IP**  The complete Buttons program is available in the \LearnVb6\Less09 folder.

The MyButtons program runs, as shown in the illustration at the top of the next page.

The instructions, toolbar buttons, and sample text appear on the form. You can use the three buttons in any order and as many times as you like.

2. Click the Italic button.

As soon as you press the mouse button, the Italic button "pushes in" and the sample text is italicized.

3. Click the Underline button.

---

 **IP** If you wanted to wait until the mouse button was released to format the text, you could still handle the icon swap in the MouseDown procedure—but you could use a MouseUp event to change the font. As the programmer, you have complete control over how the buttons affect the text.

---

Your screen should look like this:

4. Click the Italic and Underline buttons again.

   The buttons "pop out," and the text returns to normal.

5. Experiment with the Bold button to see how it works. Try using different buttons in different combinations.

*End button*

6. When you've finished testing the buttons, click the End button on the toolbar.

   The program stops, and the programming environment returns.

# Adding Drag-and-Drop Support to Your Programs

In applications for Windows, users execute many commands by clicking menus and buttons with the mouse. Visual Basic lets you provide another way to perform some actions in your programs—you can allow users to *drag and drop*. To drag and drop, the user holds down the mouse button, drags an object from one location to another, and then releases the mouse button to relocate the object or to issue a command. One application of drag and drop is to move text from one location to another in a word processing program. Another is to drag unwanted items to a "recycle bin" to remove them from the screen.

**TIP**  Drag-and-drop support can make your user interface more intuitive and easier to use.

You can use several properties and two event procedures to control drag-and-drop operations. You can set an object's DragMode property to 1 to allow the user to drag the object. You can also use the DragIcon property to specify that the mouse pointer appears as a picture of the dragged object while the object is being dragged. When the user drops an object on the form or on another object, Visual Basic responds to the event by executing the DragDrop event procedure for the object on which the icon was dropped. When one object is dragged over another object on the form, Visual Basic executes the DragOver event procedure for the object over which the object is being dragged.

## Drag and Drop Step by Step

To add drag-and-drop support to a program, follow three steps:

1. **Enable drag and drop for the object.**   Visual Basic requires that you enable objects on your form for drag and drop individually. To add drag-and-drop support to an object, you set its DragMode property to 1 by using program code or the Properties window.

2. **Select a drag icon.**   Visual Basic uses a rectangle to represent an object being dragged, but you can substitute a different drag icon if you like. To specify a different icon, set the DragIcon property of

the object to the bitmap or icon you want by using program code or the Properties window.

3. **Write a DragDrop or DragOver event procedure for the target object.**   Write an event procedure for the object that is the target, or *destination*, object of the dragging motion. Visual Basic executes the event procedure for the object onto which the dragged object is dragged or dropped. The event procedure should perform some appropriate action, such as relocating or hiding the dragged object, executing a command, or changing the destination object in some way. You open the event procedure by clicking the destination object on the form, opening the Code window, and then clicking the DragDrop or DragOver event in the Procedure drop-down list box.

The following illustration shows the three programming steps visually:

## The DragDrop Program

The following program shows you how to add drag-and-drop functionality to your applications. The program lets the user drag three items to a burn barrel on the form and then drop in a match and torch the items. The burn barrel is similar in some ways to the Microsoft Windows Recycle Bin or a Macintosh-style trash can. You can use the burn barrel in your programs to let users dispose of a variety of objects, including unwanted documents, files, artwork, email, network connections, screen elements, and so on. The program uses image boxes for the screen elements, and it hides objects by setting their Visible properties to False.

### Using drag and drop to create a burn barrel

1. On the File menu, click the New Project command, and then click OK.

2. Resize the form so that it resembles a medium-size dialog box.

*Label control*

3. Click the Label control in the toolbox, and then create a long label across the top of the form.

   This label will contain the program instructions for the user.

4. Use the Image control to create the six image boxes shown in the following illustration. Be sure to create the image boxes in the order indicated. (Create Image1 first, Image2 second, and so on.) When you set the image box properties in the next step, this will ensure that the correct icon will be placed in each image box.

5. Set the properties shown in the table on the next page for the objects in the program. As you do this, note the "Fire" setting for the Image3 Tag property. You'll use this tag to identify the match when the user drops it in the burn barrel.

**TIP** You must set the Stretch property before the Picture property for the icons to size correctly.

| Object | Property | Setting |
| --- | --- | --- |
| Label1 | Caption | "Throw everything away, and then drop in the match." |
| | Font | Times New Roman, Bold, 10-point |
| Form1 | Caption | "Burn Barrel" |
| Image1 | Stretch | True |
| | Picture | "c:\learnvb6\less09\trash02a.ico" |
| Image2 | Picture | "c:\learnvb6\less09\cdrom02.ico" |
| | DragIcon | "c:\learnvb6\less09\cdrom02.ico" |
| | DragMode | 1 – Automatic |
| Image3 | Picture | "c:\learnvb6\less09\fire.ico" |
| | DragIcon | "c:\learnvb6\less09\fire.ico" |
| | DragMode | 1 – Automatic |
| | Tag | "Fire" |
| Image4 | Picture | "c:\learnvb6\less09\gaspump.ico" |
| | DragIcon | "c:\learnvb6\less09\gaspump.ico" |
| | DragMode | 1 – Automatic |
| Image5 | Picture | "c:\learnvb6\less09\point11.ico" |
| | DragIcon | "c:\learnvb6\less09\point11.ico" |
| | DragMode | 1 – Automatic |
| Image6 | Stretch | True |
| | Picture | "c:\learnvb6\less09\trash02b.ico" |
| | Visible | False |

When you've finished setting the properties, your form should look similar to the figure at the top of the next page.

6. Double-click the Image1 object (the empty burn barrel) on the form.

The Image1_Click event procedure appears in the Code window.

7. Open the Procedure drop-down list box in the Code window, and then click the DragDrop event in the list box.

   The Image1_DragDrop event procedure appears. The Sub statement of the procedure lists three parameters that are returned when an object is dropped: Source, X, and Y. The Source parameter identifies the source object that was dragged in the program. You'll use this parameter to hide the source object on the form to make it look as if the object has been thrown away. You won't use the X and Y parameters in this procedure.

8. Type the following program statements in the event procedure:

```
Source.Visible = False
If Source.Tag = "Fire" Then
    Image1.Picture = Image6.Picture
End If
```

 **IP**   The Source variable identifies the object dropped in the burn barrel.

These are the only program statements in the program. The first line uses the Source variable and the Visible property to hide the object that was dragged and dropped. This makes the item appear to have been thrown into the burn barrel. The remaining lines check whether the object thrown away was the match icon.

Remember that when you set the properties for this program, you set the Tag property of the Image3 object to "Fire" to identify it as the match that would light the burn barrel. The If...Then decision structure uses Tag now to check whether the match is being thrown into the barrel. If it is, the decision structure "lights the fire" by copying the burning barrel icon over the empty barrel icon.

*Save Project
button*

9.  Click the Save Project button on the toolbar. Specify the \LearnVb6 \Less09 folder, and then save your form as **MyDragDrop.frm**. Save your project as **MyDragDrop.vbp** in the same folder.

### Running the MyDragDrop program

*Start button*

1.  Click the Start button on the toolbar.

**TIP**    The complete DragDrop program is available in the \LearnVb6\Less09 folder.

The MyDragDrop program appears, as shown here:

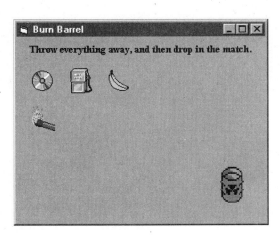

2.  Drag the CD-ROM icon into the burn barrel, and then release the mouse button.

    As you drag the icon, the mouse pointer changes to the original CD-ROM icon (the DragIcon property at work). When you release the mouse button over the burn barrel, the mouse pointer changes back to its original shape and the original CD-ROM icon disappears.

## Changing the Mouse Pointer

In the DragDrop program, you learned how to use the DragIcon property to change the mouse pointer during a drag-and-drop operation. You can also change the mouse pointer to one of 12 predefined pointers by using the MousePointer property, or you can load a custom pointer by using the MouseIcon property.

Predefined mouse pointers let the user know graphically how the mouse should be used. If you set the MousePointer property for an object on the form, the mouse pointer will change to the specified shape when the user moves the mouse pointer over that object. If you set the MousePointer property for the form itself, the mouse pointer will change to the shape you specify unless it's over another object that already has a predefined shape or custom pointer.

The table below lists a few of the pointer shapes you can select by using the MousePointer property. (You can check the Properties window for a complete list.) If you specify shape 99 (Custom), Visual Basic uses the MouseIcon property to set the pointer shape.

| Pointer | MousePointer setting | Description |
| --- | --- | --- |
| + | 2 | Crosshairs pointer for drawing |
| I | 3 | Insertion pointer for text-based applications |
| ✥ | 5 | Sizing pointer (pointers whose arrows point in other directions are available) |
| ⧗ | 11 | Hourglass pointer, which indicates that the user needs to wait |
| ⊘ | 12 | No-drop pointer, which indicates that the action the user is attempting to perform can't be performed |

3. Drag and drop the gas pump icon and the banana icon into the burn barrel.

   The mouse pointer changes to the appropriate drag icons as you drag the elements. (The gas pump will really get the fire going.)

4. Now drop in the match.

   As soon as you release the mouse button, the burn barrel starts burning, as shown in the following illustration:

5. Click the Close button to stop the program.

---

 **IP** This general drag-and-drop technique has several applications. Consider using it whenever you want to give users visual feedback when the program is processing or deleting an object. For example, you could change the barrel icon to another shape and use drag and drop to process artwork, print files, send faxes and electronic mail, work with databases, or organize resources on a network.

---

# Adding Animation to Your Programs

Switching icons and dragging objects adds visual interest to a program, but for programmers, the king of graphical effects has always been animation. *Animation* is the simulation of movement produced by rapidly displaying a series of related images on the screen. In a way, drag and drop is a "poor man's animation" because it lets you move images from one place to another on a form.

Real animation involves moving objects programmatically, and it often involves changing the size or shape of the images along the way.

In this section, you'll learn how to add simple animation to your programs. You'll learn how to use the Move method, update a picture box's Top and Left properties, and control the rate of animation by using a timer object.

## Using a Form's Coordinate System

A common trait of animation routines is that they move images in relation to a predefined coordinate system on the screen. In Visual Basic, each form has its own coordinate system. The coordinate system's starting point, or *origin*, is in the upper-left corner of a form. The default coordinate system is made up of rows and columns of device-independent twips. (Recall that a twip is 1/20 point, or 1/1440 inch.)

In the Visual Basic coordinate system, rows of twips are aligned to the *x*-axis (horizontal axis) and columns of twips are aligned to the *y*-axis (vertical axis). You define locations in the coordinate system by identifying the intersection of a row and column with the notation (*x*, *y*). Although you can change the coordinate system to a scale other than twips, the (*x*, *y*) coordinates of the upper-left corner of a form are always (0, 0). The following illustration shows how an object's location is described in the Visual Basic coordinate system.

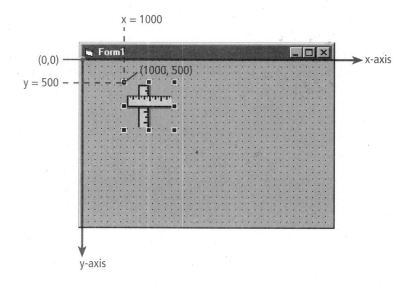

## Moving Objects in the Coordinate System

Visual Basic includes a special method named Move that lets you move objects in the coordinate system. The basic syntax for the Move method is

```
object.Move left, top
```

where *object* is the name of the object on the form that you want to move, and *left* and *top* are the screen coordinates of the new location for the object, measured in twips. The *left* measurement is the distance between the left edge of the form and the object, and the *top* measurement is the distance between the top edge of the form and the object. (The Move method also lets you adjust the height and width of an object. See "Expanding and Shrinking Objects While a Program is Running" later in this lesson for an example.)

The Visual Basic statement

```
Picture1.Move 1440, 1440
```

moves the Picture1 object to the location (1440, 1440) on the screen, or exactly 1 inch from the top edge of the form and 1 inch from the left edge of the form.

You can also use the Move method to specify a relative movement. A relative movement is the distance the object should move from its *current location*. When specifying relative movements, you use the Left and Top properties of the object (values that maintain its *x*-axis and *y*-axis location) and a + (plus) or − (minus) operator. For example, the statement

```
Picture1.Move Picture1.Left - 50, Picture1.Top - 75
```

moves the Picture1 object from its current position on the form to a location 50 twips closer to the left edge and 75 twips closer to the top edge.

---

**TIP**   A picture box object is usually used with the Move method because it creates less flicker on the screen than an image box object.

---

## Creating Animation by Using the Move Method and a Timer Object

The trick to creating animation in a program is placing one or more Move methods in a timer event procedure so that at set intervals the timer will cause one or more objects to drift across the screen. In Lesson 7, you learned to use a timer object to update a simple clock utility every second so that it displayed the correct time. When you create animation, you set the Interval property of the timer to a much faster rate—1/5 second (200 milliseconds), 1/10 second (100 milliseconds), or less. The exact rate you choose depends on how fast you want the animation to run.

Another trick is to use the Top and Left properties to "sense" the top edge and the left edge of the form. Using these values in an event procedure will let you stop the animation (disable the timer) when an object reaches the edge of the form. You can also use the Top property or the Left property, or both, in an If...Then or Select Case decision structure to make an object appear to bounce off one or more edges of the form.

## Adding a Smoke Cloud to the DragDrop Program

The following exercise demonstrates how you can animate a picture box in a program by using the Move method and a timer object. In this exercise, you'll add a smoke cloud to the DragDrop program. The smoke cloud is made visible when the user drops the match into the burn barrel. Using the Move method and a timer object, the program makes the smoke cloud appear to drift gently in the wind until it flies off the form.

### Creating smoke animation

1. On the File menu, click the Save MyDragDrop.frm As command, and then save the DragDrop form as **MySmoke.frm**.

2. On the File menu, click the Save Project As command, and then save the DragDrop project as **MySmoke.vbp**.

   Saving the form and project in new files will preserve the original DragDrop program on your disk.

*PictureBox control*

3. Click the PictureBox control in the toolbox, and then draw a small rectangle above the empty burn barrel on the form.

You'll place a cloud icon in this picture box when you set properties.

*Timer control*

4. Click the Timer control in the toolbox, and then draw a timer object in the lower-left corner of the form.

   The timer object (Timer1) resizes itself on the form.

5. Set the following properties for the picture box and timer:

| Object | Property | Setting |
| --- | --- | --- |
| Picture1 | Appearance | 3D |
| | BackColor | Light gray |
| | BorderStyle | 0 – None |
| | Picture | "c:\learnvb6\less09\cloud.ico" |
| | Visible | False |
| Timer1 | Enabled | False |
| | Interval | 65 |

After you set these properties, your form will look similar to the following:

6. Double-click the empty burn barrel (the Image1 object) to edit its event procedure.

   The Image1_DragDrop event procedure appears in the Code window.

7. Update the event procedure so that it looks like the one below. (The fourth and fifth lines are new.)

```
Source.Visible = False
If Source.Tag = "Fire" Then
    Image1.Picture = Image6.Picture
    Picture1.Visible = True
    Timer1.Enabled = True
End If
```

The new statements make the cloud icon visible when the barrel lights, and they start the timer running to get the cloud moving. Because you've already set the timer interval to 65 milliseconds, the timer is ready to go. You only need to add the Move method.

8. Open the Object drop-down list box in the Code window, and then click the Timer1 object.

The Timer1_Timer event procedure appears in the Code window.

9. Type the following program statements:

```
If Picture1.Top > 0 Then
    Picture1.Move Picture1.Left - 50, Picture1.Top - 75
Else
    Picture1.Visible = False
    Timer1.Enabled = False
End If
```

As long as the timer is enabled, this If...Then decision structure is executed every 65 milliseconds. The first line in the procedure checks whether the smoke cloud has reached the top of the form. If it hasn't (if its Top property is still positive), the procedure uses a relative Move method to move the cloud 50 twips closer to the left edge of the form and 75 twips closer to the top edge of the form.

As you'll see when you run the program, this movement gives the cloud animation a gentle drift quality. To make the cloud drift to the right, you would simply add a positive value to the Left property. To make the cloud move down, you would add a positive value to the Top property. When the cloud reaches the top of the form, the Else clause in the Timer1_Timer procedure makes the picture invisible and disables the timer. Disabling the timer ends the animation.

*Save Project button*

10. Close the Code window, and then click the Save Project button to save your changes.

Now you'll run the program.

---

IP The complete Smoke program is available on disk in the \LearnVb6 \Less09 folder.

---

*Start button*

11. Click the Start button on the toolbar to run the program.

The MySmoke program runs in the programming environment.

12. Drag and drop the CD-ROM, gas pump, and banana into the burn barrel, and then drop in the match.

The burn barrel lights, and the smoke cloud starts moving:

After a few moments, the cloud drifts off the edge of the screen and the animation stops.

*End button*

13. Click the End button to stop the program.

---

IP For another example of animation with the Move method, load and run the StepUp program in the \LearnVb6\Less01 folder. The StepUp program bounces a stick of dynamite down a few steps and displays a smoke cloud when the dynamite explodes. (The animation code is in the timer event procedures.) You might remember StepUp as the welcome program you ran in the first lesson. You've certainly come a long way since then!

---

Congratulations! You've added animation—and a number of other useful programming skills—to your graphics repertoire. Feel free to continue to experiment on your own with Visual Basic graphics. You'll learn a lot about programming in the process, and your users will appreciate the results.

## Expanding and Shrinking Objects While a Program Is Running

Interested in one last special effect? In addition to maintaining a Top property and a Left property, Visual Basic maintains a Height property and a Width property for most objects on a form. You can use these properties in clever ways to expand and shrink objects while a program is running. The following exercise shows you how to do it.

### Expanding a picture box at runtime

1. On the File menu, click the New Project command, and then click OK to open a new, standard project.

*Image control*

2. Click the Image control in the toolbox, and then draw a small image box near the upper-left corner of the form.

3. Set the following properties for the image box and the form. When you set the properties for the image box, note the current values in the Height and Width properties. (You can set these at design time, too.)

| Object | Property | Setting |
|--------|----------|---------|
| Image1 | Stretch | True |
|        | Picture  | "c:\learnvb6\less09\earth.ico" |
| Form1  | Caption  | "Approaching Earth" |

4. Double-click the Image1 object on the form.

   The Image1_Click event procedure appears in the Code window.

5. Type the following program code in the event procedure:

```
Image1.Height = Image1.Height + 200
Image1.Width = Image1.Width + 200
```

These two lines increase the height and width of the Earth icon by 200 twips each time the user clicks the picture box. If you let your imagination run a little, watching the effect makes you feel like you're approaching the Earth in a spaceship.

*Start button*

6. Close the Code window, and then click the Start button to run the program.

   The Earth icon appears alone on the form, as shown here:

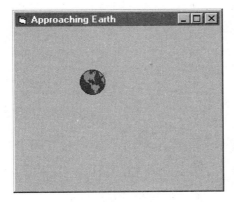

7. Click the Earth icon several times to expand it on the screen.

   After 10 or 11 clicks, your screen should look similar to the following:

**TIP**  The complete Zoom program is available on disk in the \LearnVb6 \Less09 folder.

8. When you get close enough to establish a standard orbit, click the Close button to quit the program.

   The program stops, and the programming environment returns.

9. Click the Save Project button, and then save the form as **MyZoom.frm**. Save the project as **MyZoom.vbp**.

# Naming Objects in a Program

Earlier in this lesson you created the MyButtons program, which demonstrated how graphical command buttons are created and processed in a Visual Basic program. The program contains nine image box objects (Image1 through Image9) and three event procedures that display and process the buttons. In addition to showing how graphical buttons are used in a program, the exercise demonstrates the inadequacy of using the default object names to manage objects of the same type in a program. If you (or another programmer) revisit the MyButtons program in a few weeks, it will probably take you some time to figure out which object is doing what in the program code.

**IMPORTANT**  Naming interface objects helps you identify them in the program code.

The solution to the problem of object name ambiguity is to assign each object a unique name by using the Name property. Each object name (like any variable name) should clearly identify the purpose of the object in the program and the control that created the object. The name you give an object must begin with a letter, and the name can't be longer than 40 characters. Unique and intuitive object names will help you identify objects on the form and in the program code. Because object names are included in event procedure names and property settings in the program code, you should set an object's Name property immediately after creating the object.

The following illustration shows the MyButtons program with its original object names and a set that I think are more intuitive and easier to use. I began each object name with the img prefix (an abbreviation for the Image control) and described the function of each button in the name.

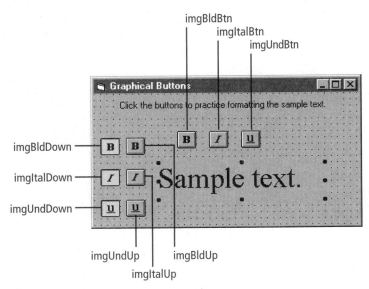

## Object Naming Conventions

The Visual Basic community has agreed on a set of three-character prefixes that everyone can use in their object names. Using these standard prefixes helps programmers identify which control created an object. You can use these naming conventions for the objects you create to make your program code more descriptive and more easily understood by other Visual Basic developers. Learning the naming conventions will also help you understand the sample programs that are included with Visual Basic. In addition, the naming conventions cause objects to be listed alphabetically in groups in the Object list box in the Code window.

 **IP** By convention, Visual Basic programmers use three-character prefixes to identify objects.

The following table lists the object naming conventions and includes an example of each. You'll get a chance to practice using the conventions in the next exercise.

| Object | Prefix | Example |
|---|---|---|
| combo box | cbo | cboEnglish |
| check box | chk | chkReadOnly |
| command button | cmd | cmdCancel |
| common dialog | dlg | dlgOpen |
| Data | dat | datBiblio |
| data-bound combo box | dbc | dbcEnglish |
| data-bound list box | dbl | dblPolicyCode |
| directory list box | dir | dirSource |
| drive list box | drv | drvTarget |
| file list box | fil | filSource |
| Frame | fra | fraLanguage |
| Form | frm | frmPrintForm |
| horizontal scroll bar | hsb | hsbVolume |
| Image | img | imgEmptyBarrel |

*(continued)*

*(continued)*

| Object | Prefix | Example |
|--------|--------|---------|
| Label | lbl | lblInstructions |
| Line | lin | linUnderline |
| list box | lst | lstPeripherals |
| Menu | mnu | mnuFileOpen |
| OLE | ole | oleObject1 |
| option button | opt | optFrench |
| picture box | pic | picSmokeCloud |
| Shape | shp | shpWireScreen |
| text box | txt | txtGetName |
| Timer | tmr | tmrRunAnimation |
| Vertical scroll bar | vsb | vsbTemperature |

 **IP** Some Visual Basic programmers also use naming conventions to describe the variable types they are using or the source of external objects and constants, such as third-party ActiveX controls or Microsoft Office applications. For example, the variable name strFileName contains a str prefix that by convention identifies the variable type as String, and the constant name wdPaperLegal contains a wd prefix that by convention identifies the value as a constant supplied by Microsoft Word. Feel free to use these naming conventions in your programs as well.

## Using the Name Property to Change Object Names

1. On the File menu, click the New Project command, and then click OK.

*Label control*

*Properties Window button*

2. Use the Label control to create two label objects in the center of the form, one near the top edge of the form and one in the middle.

3. Click the Properties Window button on the toolbar, and then set the following properties for the label and form objects. Use the naming conventions as indicated.

| Object | Property | Setting |
|--------|----------|---------|
| Label1 | Caption | "Welcome to the program!" |
|        | Name    | lblWelcome |
| Label2 | Caption | "To exit the program, click Quit." |
|        | Name    | lblInstructions |
| Form1  | Caption | "Naming Conventions" |
|        | Name    | frmMainForm |

When you set the Name properties, the names of the objects change both in the Properties window and internally in the program. The *lbl* or *frm* prefix identifies each object as a label or a form, and the rest of each object name identifies the object's purpose in the program.

*CommandButton control*

4. Use the CommandButton control to create a command button below the lblInstructions object.

5. Click the Properties Window button on the toolbar, and then set the properties for the command button:

| Object | Property | Setting |
|--------|----------|---------|
| Command1 | Caption | "Quit" |
|          | Name    | cmdQuit |

The *cmd* prefix identifies the object as a command button, and *Quit* describes the purpose of the button in the program.

6. Double-click the cmdQuit button to open the object's event procedure.

The event procedure cmdQuit_Click appears in the Code window. Visual Basic is using the name you entered as the official name of the object.

7. Open the Object drop-down list box in the Code window.

The list of object names appears in the list box, as shown at the top of the next page.

Here, the value of the object naming you've done becomes immediately apparent. It's easy to recognize which object does what in the program. Other programmers will benefit from your new names, too.

8. Press Esc to close the Object list box, and then type **End** in the cmdQuit_Click event procedure.

*Start button*

9. Close the Code window, and then click the Start button on the toolbar to run the program.

---

 **IP** The complete NameConv program is available in the \LearnVb6\Less09 folder.

---

Your screen should look similar to the following:

10. Click the Quit button to stop the program.

    The program stops, and the programming environment returns.

*Save Project
button*

11. Click the Save Project button on the toolbar, and then save the form as **MyNameConv.frm** in the \LearnVb6\Less09 folder. Save the project file as **MyNameConv.vbp**.

---

**MPORTANT**   Assigning intuitive names to objects will really pay off when you start to write longer programs or work in a group with other program-mers. In general, it's a good idea to use the naming conventions if you have more than two objects of the same type on a form.

---

### If You Want to Boost Your Productivity

Take a few minutes to explore the Browser utility (browser.vbp) in the \LearnVb6\Extras folder on your hard disk. I wrote this program as an extension of the Magnify program to give you a little more practice with the printing, form, and drag-and-drop concepts in this lesson and Lesson 8. The application is a bitmap browser that lets you evaluate up to three bitmaps at a time on your system and print them. I find it a useful tool for evaluating the dozens of bitmap (.bmp) files I routinely use in my programming projects for toolbars and other artwork. (Look in your \Windows folder for a few good examples.) If you like, you can try to expand the program yourself or simply use it as is for your daily work.

# Managing
# Corporate Data

# Using Modules and Procedures

After studying the programs and completing the exercises in Lessons 1 through 9, you can safely call yourself an intermediate Visual Basic programmer. You've learned the basics of programming in Microsoft Visual Basic, and you have the skills necessary to create a variety of useful utilities. In Part 4, you'll learn what it takes to write more complex programs in Visual Basic. You'll start by learning how to create standard modules.

A standard module is a separate container in a program that contains global, or *public,* variables and Function and Sub procedures. In this lesson, you'll learn how to create your own public variables and procedures and how to call them from event procedures. The skills you'll learn will be especially applicable to larger programming projects and team development efforts.

# Working with Standard Modules

As you write longer programs, you're likely to have several forms and event procedures that use some of the same variables and routines. By default, variables are *local* to an event procedure, meaning that they can be read or changed only in the event procedure in which they were created. Likewise, event procedures are local to the form in which they were created—you can't, for example, call the cmdQuit_Click event procedure from Form2 if the event procedure is associated with Form1.

To share variables and procedures among all the forms and event procedures in a project, you need to declare them in one or more *standard modules* for that project. A standard module, or code module, is a special file that has the filename extension *.bas* and contains variables and procedures that can be used anywhere in the program. Just like forms, standard modules are listed separately in the Project window, and a standard module can be saved to disk by using the Save Module1 As command on the File menu. Unlike forms, however, standard modules contain no objects or property settings—only code that can be displayed and edited in the Code window.

The illustration at the top of the next page shows how a public variable declared in a standard module can be used in other event procedures in a Visual Basic project.

 **IP**    By contrast to those in standard modules, the objects and event procedures associated with a form are stored in a *form module,* and a new object is created in a *class module.*

First declare the variable as public.

Then assign it a value.

Then use it to perform useful work.

## Creating a Standard Module

To create a new standard module in a program, you click the Down arrow on the Add Form button on the toolbar and click Module, or you click the Add Module command on the Project menu. When you create a new standard module, it appears immediately in the Code window. The first standard module in a program is named Module1 by default, but you can change the name when you save the module to disk. Try creating an empty standard module in your project now.

### Creating and saving a standard module

1. Start Visual Basic and open a new standard project, and then click the Add Module command on the Project menu and click Open.

   Visual Basic adds a standard module named Module1 to your project. The module appears in the Code window, as shown in the figure at the top of the next page.

The Object and Procedure list boxes indicate that the general declarations section of the standard module is open. Variables and procedures declared here will be available to the entire program. (You'll try declaring variables and procedures later.)

2. Double-click the Project window title bar to see the entire Project window.

The Project window appears, as shown here:

Module object name

Module filename

The Project window lists the standard module you added to the program in a new folder. The name Module1 in parentheses shows the default filename of the module. The Module object name (the name of the module in the program) appears to the left of the parentheses. You'll change both settings in the next steps.

3. On the File menu, click the Save Module1 As command to save the empty standard module to disk.

4. Select the \LearnVb6\Less10 folder if it's not already selected. Type **MyTestMod.bas** and press Enter.

---

 **IP**  Standard modules have the filename extension .bas.

---

The standard module is saved to disk as a .bas file, and the module filename in the Project window is updated.

---

 **IP**  You can also load this .bas file by name in a different project by using the Add File command on the Project menu.

---

5. Double-click the Properties window title bar.

   The Properties window appears full size, as shown in the following illustration:

Because a standard module has no objects, its only property is Name. The Name property lets you specify an object name for the module, which you can use to distinguish one module from another if you create more than one. By convention, module names are given the prefix *mod*.

6. Change the Name property to **modVariables** and press Enter.

   The object name of the standard module is updated in the Properties window, the Project window, and the Code window.

As you can see, working with standard modules in a project is a lot like working with forms. In the next exercise, you'll add a public variable to the standard module you've created.

> **TIP** To remove a standard module from a project, click the module in the Project window, and then click the Remove command on the Project menu. Remove does not delete the module from your hard disk, but it does remove the link between the specified module and the current project.

# Working with Public Variables

Declaring a global, or public, variable in a standard module is simple—you type the keyword *Public* followed by the variable name. After you declare the variable, you can read it, change it, or display it in any procedure in your program. For example, the program statement

```
Public RunningTotal
```

declares a public variable named RunningTotal in a standard module.

By default, public variables are declared as variant types in modules, but you can specify a fundamental type name by using the *As* keyword and indicating the type. For example, the statement

```
Public LastName As String
```

declares a public string variable named LastName in your program.

The following exercises demonstrate how you can use a public variable named Wins in a standard module. You'll revisit Lucky Seven, the first program you wrote in this book, and you'll use the Wins variable to record how many spins you win as the slot machine runs.

## Revisiting the Lucky Seven Project

1. Click the Open Project button on the toolbar, click No to discard your changes, and then open the project Lucky.vbp in the \LearnVb6\Less02 folder.

2. If the Lucky form is not visible, select Lucky.frm in the Project window and click the View Object button. (Resize the form window, if necessary.)

   You'll see the following user interface shown at the top of the next page.

*Start button*

3. Click the Start button on the toolbar to run the program.

4. Click the Spin button six or seven times, and then click the End button.

   You win the first five spins (a seven appears each time), and then your luck goes sour. As you might recall, the program uses the Rnd function to generate three random numbers each time you click the Spin button. If one of the numbers is a seven, the event procedure for the Spin button (Command1_Click) displays a stack of coins and sounds a beep.

   In your revision to the program, you'll add a new label to the form and you'll add a public variable that tracks the number of times you win.

5. On the File menu, click the Save Lucky.frm As command. Specify the \LearnVb6\Less10 folder, and then save the form to disk with the name **MyWins.frm**.

6. On the File menu, click the Save Project As command. Specify the \LearnVb6\Less10 folder, and then save the project to disk with the name **MyWins.vbp**.

Now you'll edit the Wins form and add a standard module to create a new program.

## Adding a Standard Module

1. Resize the Lucky Seven label so that it takes up less space on the form. The object currently extends far below the label text.

*Label control*

2. Click the Label control, and then create a new rectangular label below the Lucky Seven label.

3. Set the properties shown in the following table for the new label and the form. To help identify the new label in the program code, you'll change the new label object's name to lblWins.

| Object | Property | Setting |
|--------|----------|---------|
| Label5 | Alignment | 2 – Center |
|        | Caption | "Wins: 0" |
|        | Font | Arial, Bold Italic, 12-point |
|        | ForeColor | Green |
|        | Name | lblWins |
| Form1  | Caption | "Lucky Seven" |

When you've finished, your form should look similar to the following:

New lblWins label ——

Now you'll add a new standard module to the project.

4. Click the Add Module command on the Project menu, and then click Open.

   A module named Module1 appears in the Code window.

5. Type **Public Wins** in the standard module, and then press Enter.

   This program statement declares a public variable of the variant type in your program. When your program runs, each event procedure in the program will have access to this variable. Your standard module should look like the following:

6. On the File menu, click the Save Module1 As command, type **MyWins.bas**, and then press Enter to save the module to disk.

7. In the Project window, click Form1 (MyWins.frm), click the View Object button, and then double-click the Spin button.

   The Command1_Click event procedure for the Spin button appears in the Code window.

8. Type the following statements below the Beep statement in the event procedure:

```
Wins = Wins + 1
lblWins.Caption = "Wins: " & Wins
```

   This is the part of the program code that increments the Wins public variable if a seven appears in a spin. The second statement uses the concatenation (&) operator to assign a string to the lblWins object in the format *Wins: X*, where *X* is the number of wins. The completed event procedure should look like this:

```
Project1 - Form1                                    _ □ ×
Command1                    ▼    Click                        ▼
    Private Sub Command1_Click()
        Image1.Visible = False          ' hide coins
        Label1.Caption = Int(Rnd * 10)  ' pick numbers
        Label2.Caption = Int(Rnd * 10)
        Label3.Caption = Int(Rnd * 10)
        'if any caption is 7 display coin stack and beep
        If (Label1.Caption = 7) Or (Label2.Caption = 7) _
          Or (Label3.Caption = 7) Then
            Image1.Visible = True
            Beep
            Wins = Wins + 1
            lblWins.Caption = "Wins: " & Wins
        End If
    End Sub
```

These two statements use the Wins public variable.

9. Close the Code window, and then click the Save Project button to save the project to disk.

10. Click the Start button to run the program.

11. Click the Spin button 10 times.

   The Wins label keeps track of your jackpots. Each time you win, it increments the total by 1. After 10 spins, you'll have won 6 times, as shown in the following illustration:

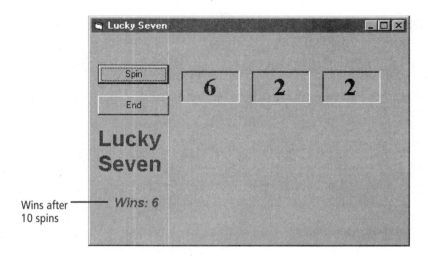

Wins after 10 spins

12. Click End to quit the program.

The public variable Wins was useful here because it maintained its value through 10 calls to the Command1_Click event procedure. If you had declared Wins locally in the Command1_Click event procedure, the variable would have reset each time, just as the trip odometer in your car does when you reset it. Using a public variable in a standard module lets you avoid "hitting the reset." Public variables have more in common with the main odometer in your car.

# Creating General-Purpose Procedures

In addition to containing public variables, standard modules can contain general-purpose procedures that can be called from anywhere in the program. A general-purpose procedure isn't like an event procedure because it's not associated with a runtime event or with an object you created by using a toolbox control. General-purpose procedures are similar to built-in Visual Basic statements and functions—they're called by name, they can receive arguments, and each performs a specific task.

For example, imagine a program that has three mechanisms for printing a bitmap: a menu command named Print, a Print toolbar button, and a drag-and-drop printer icon. You could place the same printing routine in each of the three event procedures, or you could handle printing requests from all three sources by using one procedure in a standard module. General-purpose procedures save you typing time, reduce the possibility of errors, make programs smaller and easier to handle, and make event procedures easier to read.

You can create three types of general-purpose procedures in a standard module:

■ **Function procedures.** Function procedures are called by name from event procedures or other procedures. They can receive arguments, and they always return a value in the function name. They are typically used for calculations.

---

**TIP** Function and Sub procedures in a standard module let you create general-purpose routines.

---

- **Sub procedures.** Sub procedures are called by name from event procedures or other procedures. They can receive arguments, and they also can be used to perform tasks in the procedure and to return values. Unlike functions, however, Subs do not return values associated with their particular Sub names (although they can return values through variable names). Sub procedures are typically used to receive or process input, display output, or set properties.

- **Property procedures.** Property procedures are used to create and manipulate user-defined properties in a program. This is a useful, if somewhat advanced, feature that lets you customize existing Visual Basic controls and extend the Visual Basic language by creating new objects, properties, and methods.

## Advantages of General-Purpose Procedures

General-purpose procedures allow you to associate an often-used routine with a familiar name in a standard module. General-purpose procedures

- Eliminate repeated lines. You can define a procedure once and have your program execute it any number of times.

- Make programs easier to read. A program divided into a collection of small parts is easier to take apart and understand than a program made up of one large part.

- Simplify program development. Programs separated into logical units are easier to design, write, and debug. Plus, if you're writing a program in a group setting, you can exchange procedures and modules instead of entire programs.

- Can be reused in other programs. You can easily incorporate standard-module procedures into other programming projects.

- Extend the Visual Basic language. Procedures often can perform tasks that can't be accomplished by individual Visual Basic keywords.

# Writing Function Procedures

A *Function procedure* is a group of statements located between a Function statement and an End Function statement in a standard module. The statements in the function do the meaningful work—typically processing text, handling input, or calculating a numeric value. You execute, or *call,* a function in a program by placing the function name in a program statement along with any required arguments. (*Arguments* are the data used to make functions work.) In other words, using a Function procedure is exactly like using a built-in function such as Time, Int, or Str.

---

 **IP**   Functions declared in standard modules are public by default; they can be used in any event procedure.

---

## Function Syntax

The basic syntax of a function is as follows:

```
Function FunctionName([arguments]) [As Type]
    function statements
End Function
```

The following syntax items are important:

- **FunctionName** is the name of the function you are creating in the standard module.

- **arguments** is a list of optional arguments (separated by commas) to be used in the function.

- **As Type** is an option that specifies the function return type (the default is Variant).

- **function statements** is a block of statements that accomplish the work of the function.

Optional syntax items are enclosed by brackets ( [] ). Syntax items *not* enclosed by brackets are *required* by Visual Basic.

Functions always return a value to the calling procedure in the function's name (*FunctionName*). For this reason, the last statement in a function is often an assignment statement that places the final calculation of the function in *FunctionName*. For example, the Function procedure TotalTax shown below computes the state and city taxes for an item and then assigns the result to the TotalTax name:

```
Function TotalTax(Cost)
    StateTax = Cost * 0.05   'State tax is 5%
    CityTax = Cost * 0.015   'City tax is 1.5%
    TotalTax = StateTax + CityTax
End Function
```

 **IMPORTANT**   I recommend that you assign a value to the function's name each time you write a function. That way, you'll always be sure of the result you're returning to the program.

## Calling a Function Procedure

To call the TotalTax function in an event procedure, you would use a statement similar to the following:

```
lblTaxes.Caption = TotalTax(500)
```

This statement computes the total taxes required for a $500 item and then assigns the result to the Caption property of the lblTaxes object. (Functions are typically assigned to variables or properties like this.)

The TotalTax function can also take a variable as an argument, as shown in the following statement:

```
TotalCost = SalesPrice + TotalTax(SalesPrice)
```

This line uses the TotalTax function to determine the taxes for the number in the SalesPrice variable and then adds them to SalesPrice to get the total cost of an item. See how much clearer the code is when a function is used?

## Using a Function to Perform a Calculation

In the following exercise, you'll add a function to the Lucky Seven program to calculate the win rate in the game (the percentage of spins in which one or more sevens appear). To do this, you'll add a function named Rate and a public variable named Spins to the standard module.

Then you'll call the Rate function every time the Spin button is clicked. You'll display the results in a new label you'll create on the form.

### Creating a win rate function

1. Open the Project window.

   The components of the MyWins.vbp project appear in the Project window. You'll save the components of the project as MyRate to preserve the MyWins program.

2. Click the MyWins.frm form. On the File menu, click the Save MyWins.frm As command. Save the form to disk as **MyRate.frm** in the \LearnVb6\Less10 folder.

3. Click the MyWins.bas standard module in the Project window. On the File menu, click the Save MyWins.bas As command. Save the module to disk as **MyRate.bas**.

4. On the File menu, click the Save Project As command. Save the project as **MyRate.vbp**.

*View Object button*

5. If the form is not visible, click the MyRate.frm form in the Project window and then click the View Object button.

   The user interface for the Lucky Seven program appears.

6. Move the Wins label closer to the Lucky Seven label to make room for a new label. You might need to resize one or both labels to make enough room.

*Label control*

7. Use the Label control to create a new label below the Wins label. Set the following properties for the label:

| Object | Property | Setting |
|--------|----------|---------|
| Label5 | Alignment | 2 – Center |
|        | Caption | "0.0%" |
|        | Font | Arial, Bold Italic, 12-point |
|        | ForeColor | Red |
|        | Name | lblRate |

Your form should look similar to the figure that follows.

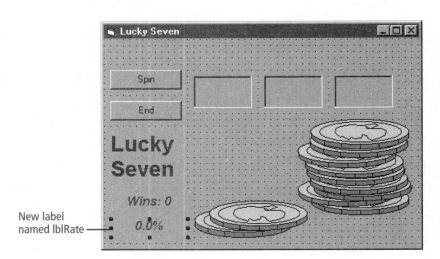

New label
named lblRate

8. In the Project window, click the MyRate.bas module, and then click the View Code button in the Project window.

   The Module1 standard module appears in the Code window.

9. Type the following public variable declaration below the Public Wins statement:

   ```
   Public Spins
   ```

   The standard module now includes two public variables (Wins and Spins) that will be available to all the procedures in the program. You'll use Spins as a counter to keep track of the number of spins you make.

10. Now type the following function declaration:

    ```
    Function Rate(Hits, Attempts) As String
        Percent = Hits / Attempts
        Rate = Format(Percent, "0.0%")
    End Function
    ```

    After you type the first line of the function code, Visual Basic opens a new procedure in the standard module to hold the function declaration. After you type the remainder of the function's code, your screen should look like the figure shown at the top of the next page.

Procedure drop-down list.

The Rate function determines the percentage of wins by dividing the Hits argument by the Attempts argument and then adjusting the appearance of the result by using the Format function. The Rate function is declared as a string because the Format function returns a string. The Hits argument and the Attempts argument are placeholders for the two variables that will be passed to the function during the function call. The Rate function is general-purpose enough to be used with any numbers or variables, not only with Wins and Spins.

11. Close the Code window, and then double-click the Spin button on the Lucky Seven form to bring up the Command1_Click event procedure.

12. Below the fourth line of the event procedure (the third statement containing the Rnd function), type the following statement:

```
Spins = Spins + 1
```

This statement increments the Spins variable each time the user clicks Spin and new numbers are placed in the spin windows.

13. Scroll down in the Code window, and then type the following statement as the last line in the Command1_Click event procedure, between the End If and the End Sub statements:

```
lblRate.Caption = Rate(Wins, Spins)
```

As you type the Rate function, notice how Visual Basic automatically displays the names of the arguments for the Rate function you just built (a nice touch).

The purpose of this statement is to call the Rate function, using the Wins and Spins variables as arguments. The result returned is a percentage in string format, and this value is assigned to the Caption property of the lblRate label on the form after each spin. That's all there is to it!

*Save Project button*

14. Close the Code window, and then click the Save Project button to update your project files.

Now you'll run the program.

### Running the MyRate program

*Start button*

1. Click the Start button to run the program.

---

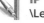 **IP**  The complete Rate.vbp program is available on disk in the \LearnVb6 \Less10 folder.

---

2. Click the Spin button 10 times.

   The first 5 times you click Spin, the win rate stays at 100.0%. You're hitting the jackpot every time. As you continue to click, however, the win rate adjusts to 83.3%, 71.4%, 75.0% (another win), 66.7%, and 60.0% (a total of 6 for 10). After 10 spins, your screen looks like the figure shown on the next page.

   If you continue to spin, you'll notice that the win rate drops to about 28%. The Rate function shows you that you were really pretty lucky when you started spinning, but after a while reality set in.

3. When you're finished with the program, click the End button.

   The program stops, and the programming environment returns.

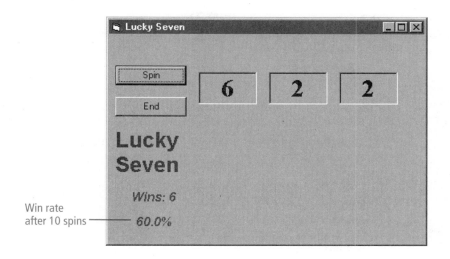

> **TIP** To revise this program so that it displays a random series of spins each time you run the program, put a Randomize statement in the Form_Load event procedure. For instructions, see the section in Lesson 2 entitled "Adding to a Program."

# Writing Sub Procedures

A *Sub procedure* is similar to a Function procedure, except that a Sub doesn't return a value associated with its name. Subs are typically used to get input from the user, display or print information, or manipulate several properties associated with a condition. Subs are also used to process and return several variables during a procedure call. Most functions can return only one value, but Sub procedures can return many.

## Sub Procedure Syntax

The basic syntax for a Sub procedure is

```
Sub ProcedureName([arguments])
    procedure statements
End Sub
```

The following syntax items are important:

- **ProcedureName** is the name of the Sub procedure you're creating.

- **arguments** is a list of optional arguments (separated by commas, if there's more than one) to be used in the Sub.

- *procedure statements* is a block of statements that accomplish the work of the procedure.

In the procedure call, the number and type of arguments sent to the Sub procedure must match the number and type of arguments in the Sub declaration. If variables passed to a Sub are modified during the procedure, the updated variables are returned to the program. By default, Sub procedures declared in a standard module are public, so they can be called by any event procedure.

---

**IMPORTANT** Passing a variable to a procedure is called passing an argument *by reference,* because a variable can be modified by a procedure and returned to the program. Passing a literal value (such as a string in quotation marks) to a procedure is called passing an argument *by value,* because a value cannot be modified by a procedure. You can pass variables by value if you use a special notation. You'll learn how to do this in the section entitled "Passing a Variable by Value" later in this lesson.

---

You can use the Sub procedure below to add names to a list box on a form at runtime. The procedure receives one string variable passed by reference.

If this Sub procedure is declared in a standard module, it can be called from any event procedure in the program.

```
Sub AddNameToListBox(person$)
    If person$ <> "" Then
        Form1.List1.AddItem person$
        Msg$ = person$ & " added to list box."
    Else
        Msg$ = "Name not specified."
    End If
    MsgBox (Msg$), , "Add Name"
End Sub
```

The AddNameToListBox procedure receives the name to be added by using the person$ argument, a string variable received by reference during the procedure call. If the value of person$ is not empty, or *null,* the specified name is added to the List1 list box object by using the AddItem method, and a confirming message is displayed by the MsgBox function.

If the argument *is* null, the procedure skips the AddItem method and displays the message "Name not specified."

---

 **TIP** When you set properties from a procedure in a standard module, you need to prefix each object name with the form name and a period (Form1., in this example). This lets Visual Basic know which form you're referencing.

---

## Calling a Sub Procedure

To call a Sub procedure in a program, you specify the name of the procedure and then list the arguments required by the Sub. For example, to call the AddNameToListBox procedure by using a literal string (to call it *by value*), you could type the following statement:

```
AddNameToListBox "Kimberly"
```

Similarly, you could call the procedure by using a variable (call it *by reference*) by typing this statement:

```
AddNameToListBox NewName$
```

In both cases, the AddNameToListBox procedure would add the specified name to the list box. In this Sub procedure, calls by value and calls by reference produce similar results because the argument is not modified in the procedure.

The space-saving advantages of a Sub procedure become clear when you call the procedure many times, as shown in the example below.

```
AddNameToListBox "Kimberly"   'always add two names
AddNameToListBox "Rachel"
Do                            'then let user add extra names
    NewName$ = InputBox("Enter a list box name.", "Add Name")
    AddNameToListBox NewName$
Loop Until NewName$ = ""
```

Here the user is allowed to enter as many names to the list box as he or she likes. The next exercise gives you a chance to practice using a Sub procedure to handle another type of input in a program.

## Using a Sub Procedure to Manage Input

Sub procedures are often used to handle input in a program when information comes from two or more sources and needs to be in the same format. In the following exercise, you'll create a Sub procedure named AddName that prompts the user for input and formats the text so that it can be displayed on multiple lines in a text box. The procedure will save you programming time because you'll use it in two event procedures, each associated with a different text box. Because the procedure will be declared in a standard module, you need to type it in only one place.

## Creating a Text Box Sub Procedure

1. On the File menu, click the New Project command, and then click OK.

   A new, empty form appears.

*TextBox control*

2. Use the TextBox control to create two text boxes, side by side, in the middle of the form.

   You'll use these text boxes to hold the names of employees you'll be assigning to two departments. You get to make your own personnel decisions today.

*Label control*

3. Use the Label control to create two labels above the text boxes.

   These labels will hold the names of the departments.

*CommandButton control*

4. Use the CommandButton control to create a command button under each text box and a separate command button at the bottom of the form.

   You'll use the first two command buttons to add employees to their departments. You'll use the last command button to quit the program.

5. Set the properties shown in the table on the next page for the objects in the program.

Because the text boxes will contain more than one line, you'll set their MultiLine properties to True and their ScrollBars properties to Vertical. You'll also set their TabStop properties to False and their Locked properties to True so that the information can't be modified. These settings are typically used when multiple lines are displayed in text boxes.

| Object | Property | Setting |
| --- | --- | --- |
| Text1 | Text | (Empty) |
| | MultiLine | True |
| | ScrollBars | 2 – Vertical |
| | TabStop | False |
| | Locked | True |
| | Name | txtSales |
| Text2 | Text | (Empty) |
| | MultiLine | True |
| | ScrollBars | 2 – Vertical |
| | TabStop | False |
| | Locked | True |
| | Name | txtMkt |
| Label1 | Caption | "Sales" |
| | Font | Bold |
| | Name | lblSales |
| Label2 | Caption | "Marketing" |
| | Font | Bold |
| | Name | lblMkt |
| Command1 | Caption | "Add Name" |
| | Name | cmdSales |
| Command2 | Caption | "Add Name" |
| | Name | cmdMkt |
| Command3 | Caption | "Quit" |
| | Name | cmdQuit |
| Form1 | Caption | "Assign Department Teams" |

When you've finished, your form should look similar to the following:

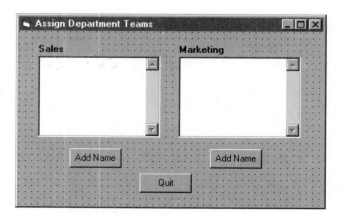

Now you'll add a standard module and create the general-purpose AddName Sub procedure.

6. On the Project menu, click the Add Module command, and then click Open.

   A new standard module appears in the Code window.

7. Type the AddName procedure into the standard module:

```
Sub AddName(Team$, ReturnString$)
    Prompt$ = "Enter a " & Team$ & " employee."
    Nm$ = InputBox(Prompt$, "Input Box")
    WrapCharacter$ = Chr(13) + Chr(10)
    ReturnString$ = Nm$ & WrapCharacter$
End Sub
```

This general-purpose Sub procedure uses the InputBox function to prompt the user for an employee name. It receives two arguments during the procedure call: Team$, a string containing the department name; and ReturnString$, an empty string variable that will return the formatted employee name to the calling event procedure.

---

 **IP**    Use Chr(13) and Chr(10) to create a new line in a text box.

---

Before the employee name is returned, carriage return and linefeed characters are appended to the string so that each name in the text box will appear on its own line. This is a general technique that you can use in any text box.

Your Code window should look like the following:

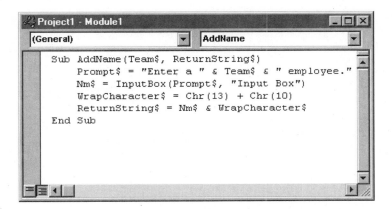

8. Close the Code window, and then double-click the first Add Name button on the form (the button below the Sales text box). Type the following statements in the cmdSales_Click event procedure:

```
AddName "Sales", SalesPosition$
txtSales.Text = txtSales.Text & SalesPosition$
```

The call to the AddName Sub procedure includes one argument passed by value ("Sales") and one argument passed by reference (SalesPosition$). The second line uses the argument passed by reference to add text to the txtSales text box. The concatenation operator (&) adds the new name to the end of the text in the text box.

9. Open the Object drop-down list box in the Code window and click the cmdMkt object. Type the following statements in the cmdMkt_Click event procedure:

```
AddName "Marketing", MktPosition$
txtMkt.Text = txtMkt.Text & MktPosition$
```

This event procedure is identical to cmdSales_Click, except that it sends "Marketing" to the AddName procedure and updates the txtMkt text box. The name of the local return variable was changed to make it more intuitive.

10. Open the Object drop-down list box and click the cmdQuit object. Type **End** in the cmdQuit_Click event procedure, and then close the Code window.

*Save Project button*

11. Click the Save Project button on the toolbar. Specify the \LearnVb6\Less10 folder, and then save the standard module as **MyTeams.bas**. Save your form as **MyTeams.frm**, and then save the project as **MyTeams.vbp**.

That's it! Now you'll run the MyTeams program.

### Running the MyTeams program

*Start button*

1. Click the Start button on the toolbar to run the program.

**TIP** The complete Teams.vbp program is available on disk in the \LearnVb6 \Less10 folder.

2. Click the Add Name button under the Sales text box, and then type **Maria Palermo** in the Input Box.

Your input box should look like the following:

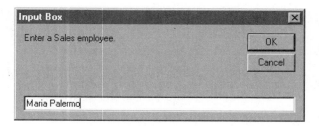

3. Click the OK button to add the name to the Sales text box.

The name appears in the text box.

4. Click the Add Name button under the Marketing text box, type
**Henry James** in the Marketing Input Box, and then press Enter.

The name appears in the Marketing text box. Your screen should
look like the following:

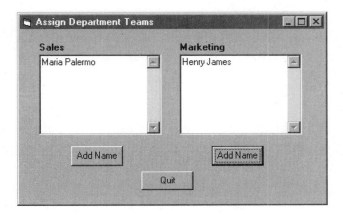

5. Enter four or five more names in each of the text boxes. This is your
chance to create your own dream departments.

Each name should appear on its own line in the text boxes. The text
boxes don't scroll automatically, so you won't see every name
you've entered if you enter more names than can fit in a text box.
You can use the scroll bars to access names that are not visible.

6. When you've finished, click the Quit button to stop the program.

## Passing Arguments by Reference

In this discussion of Sub procedures, you learned that arguments are
passed to procedures by reference or by value. When a variable is passed
by reference (the default), any changes made to the variable are passed
back to the calling procedure. You took advantage of this feature in the
MyTeams program when you used a variable passed by reference to add
names to a text box. Passing by reference can have significant advantages,
as long as you're careful not to change a variable unintentionally in a

procedure. For example, consider the following Sub procedure declaration and call:

```
Sub CostPlusInterest(Cost, Total)
    Cost = Cost * 1.05  'add 5% to cost...
    Total = Int(Cost)    'then make integer and return
End Sub
.
.
.
Price = 100
Total = 0
CostPlusInterest Price, Total
Print Price; "at 5% interest is"; Total
```

In this example, the programmer passes two variables by reference to the CostPlusInterest procedure: Price and Total. The programmer plans to use the updated Total variable in the subsequent Print method but has unfortunately forgotten that the Price variable was also updated in an intermediate step in the procedure. (Because Price was passed by reference, changes to Cost automatically result in the same changes to Price.) This produces the following erroneous result when the program is run:

```
105 at 5% interest is 105
```

 **IMPORTANT**   Beware the pitfalls of passing variables by reference!

## The ByVal Keyword

An obvious way to avoid the preceding problem is never to modify a variable passed in a procedure. But this solution can add program code and can prove unreliable if you're working as part of a group of several programmers. A better method is to use the ByVal keyword in the argument list when you declare a procedure. This tells Visual Basic to keep a copy of the original argument and to return it unchanged when the procedure ends—even if the variable was modified in the procedure. ByVal is used in an argument list in the following manner:

```
Sub CostPlusInterest(ByVal Cost, Total)
```

When the Cost argument is declared by using ByVal, the program produces the correct output:

```
100 at 5% interest is 105
```

## Passing a Variable by Value

If you don't want to rely on the ByVal keyword, you can use an alternative method to prevent a passed variable from being modified: you can convert it to a literal value by enclosing it in parentheses. This seldom-used trick always works in Visual Basic, and it makes your procedure calls more intuitive. If you specifically pass the variable by value, everyone will know what you mean. It's also an efficient way to pass a variable by value *sometimes*. The syntax for calling the CostPlusInterest procedure and passing the Price variable by value is

```
CostPlusInterest (Price), Total
```

If the example program is called in this way, the correct result is produced:

```
100 at 5% interest is 105
```

In this lesson, you've learned to use public variables, functions, and Sub procedures to manage information in a program. Do take advantage of these constructions as your programs get larger. You'll find that they save you considerable time and that they can be used again in future projects.

# Working with Collections and Arrays

In this lesson, you will learn about groups of objects called *collections* in a Microsoft Visual Basic program, and you'll see how you can process collections by using a special loop called For Each...Next. You'll also learn how to organize variables into containers called *arrays*. Arrays make data management in a program easy, and they provide a good introduction to the database programming techniques you'll use in Lesson 13.

# Working with Object Collections

You already know that objects on a form are stored together in the same file. But did you also know that Visual Basic considers the objects to be members of the same group? In Visual Basic terminology, the entire set of objects on a form is called the *Controls collection*. The Controls collection is created automatically when you open a new form and expands when you add objects to the form. In fact, Visual Basic maintains several standard collections of objects that you can use when you write your programs. In the first section of this lesson, you'll learn the basic skills you need to work with any collection you encounter.

## Collection Notation

Each collection in a program has its own name so that you can reference it as a distinct unit in the program code. For example, as you just learned, the collection containing all the objects on a form is called the Controls collection. However, because you can have more than one form in a program (and therefore more than one Controls collection), you need to include the form name when you use the Controls collection in a program that contains more than one form. For example, to refer to the Controls collection on Form1, you would use the following name in your code:

```
Form1.Controls
```

The period between the Form1 object name and the Controls keyword makes Controls look like a property in this notation, but Visual Basic programmers describe the Controls collection as an object *contained by* the Form1 object. The relationship, or *hierarchy*, between objects is a little like that between folders in a pathname; you'll see this notation again when you start working with application objects in Lesson 14.

---

 **IMPORTANT**    Each form has a Controls collection.

---

In addition to letting you work with objects and collections in your own programs, Visual Basic lets you browse your system for other application objects and use them in your programs. We'll pick up this topic again in Lesson 14 when you learn how to use the Visual Basic Object Browser.

## Referencing Objects in a Collection

You can reference the objects in a collection, or the individual members of the collection, in several ways. The first way is to specify the objects by using their names directly in an assignment statement. For example, the statement

```
Form1.Controls!Label1.Caption = "Employees"
```

singles out the Label1 object in the Controls collection and sets its Caption property to "Employees". An exclamation point (!) is used to link the Label1 object to the Controls collection. Although this statement might seem like a mouthful for the compiler, it gives a precise description of the hierarchy within the collection.

The second way to address an object in a collection is to specify the *index position* of the object in the group. Visual Basic stores collection objects in the reverse order of that in which they were created, so you can use an object's "birth order" to reference the object individually, or you can use a loop to step through several objects. For example, to identify the last object created on a form, you would specify the 0 (zero) index, as shown in this example:

```
Form1.Controls(0).Caption = "Business"
```

This statement sets the Caption property of the last object on the form to "Business". (The second to the last object created has an index of 1, the third to the last object created has an index of 2, and so on.)

## Writing For Each...Next Loops

Although you can reference individual members of a collection, the most useful way to work with objects in a collection is to process them as a group. In fact, the reason collections exist is so that you can process groups of objects efficiently. For example, you might want to display, move, sort, rename, or resize an entire collection of objects at once.

To handle one of these tasks, you can use a special loop called For Each...Next to cycle through objects in a collection one at a time. A For Each...Next loop is similar to a For...Next loop, which you learned about in Lesson 7. When a For Each…Next loop is used with the Controls collection, it looks like this:

```
For Each Control in FormName.Controls
    process object
Next Control
```

*Control* is a special variable representing the current object in the collection, and *FormName* is the name of the form. The body of the loop is used to process the individual objects of the collection. For example, you might want to change the Enabled, Left, Top, Caption, or Visible properties of the objects in the collection, or you might want to list the name of each object in a list box.

## Moving a Collection of Objects

In the following exercise, you'll use the Controls collection to move a group of objects from left to right across the form at the same time. The program uses a For Each…Next loop to move the objects every time the user clicks a command button named Move Objects. Sometimes certain objects in a collection require special treatment, so in the exercise that follows this one you'll learn how to modify the program so that it moves every object except the command button.

### Using a For Each…Next loop to process the Controls collection

1. Start Visual Basic.

   The New Project dialog box appears.

2. Click on the Existing tab, and open the project Move.vbp in the \LearnVb6\Less11 folder.

3. If the Working with Collections form does not appear, select Move.frm in the Project window, and then click the View Object button.

   This form contains five objects that are part of the Controls collection. The Picture, Name, and Caption properties for the objects have been set, but you need to add the code to move the collection across the screen.

The Controls collection contains all the objects on a form.

4. Double-click the Move Objects button on the form.

   The cmdButton_Click event procedure appears in the Code window.

5. Type the following program statements:

```
For Each Ctrl In Controls
    Ctrl.Left = Ctrl.Left + 200
Next Ctrl
```

> **TIP** Using a For Each...Next loop to adjust the Left property of each object makes the objects move as a group.

   Each time the user clicks the Move Objects button, this For Each...Next loop steps through the objects in the Controls collection one by one and moves them 200 twips to the right. (To move objects 200 twips to the left, you would subtract 200 instead.) The Ctrl variable is a "stand-in" for the current object in the collection and contains the same property settings as the object it represents. In this loop, you're adjusting the Left property, which determines an object's position relative to the left side of the form.

6. On the File menu, click the Save Move.frm As command. Save the form as **MyMove.frm**.

7. On the File menu, click the Save Project As command. Save the project as **MyMove.vbp**.

*Start button*

8. Close the Code window, and then click the Start button on the toolbar.

   The program runs, and four icons appear on the left side of the form. A command button appears at the bottom of the form.

9. Click the Move Objects button several times.

   Each time you click the button, the objects on the form move to the right. The Move Objects button marches right along with the images because it's part of the Controls collection.

*End button*

10. Click the End button on the toolbar to stop the program.

Moving all the objects together isn't a requirement. Visual Basic allows you to process collection members individually if you want to. In the next exercise, you'll learn how to keep the Move Objects button in one place while the image objects move to the right.

## Using the Tag Property in a For Each...Next Loop

If you want to process one or more members of a collection differently than you want to process the other members, you can use the Tag property. You set the Tag property of objects that you want to process differently. Your program reads each object's Tag property while it's processing the items in a For Each...Next loop; based on the value of the Tag property, the program either processes the object as usual or gives it special treatment.

For example, let's say you placed the word *Slow* in the Tag property of the imgBanana object in the MyMove program. You could use an If...Then statement to spot the Slow tag when the loop evaluated the imgBanana object, and then you could move the banana a shorter distance than the other objects.

---

 **IP**　If you plan to give several objects special treatment in a For Each...Next loop, you can use ElseIf statements with the If...Then statement, or you can use a Select Case decision structure.

---

In the following exercise, you'll set the cmdButton Tag property to "Button" to stop the For Each...Next loop from moving the command button to the right.

### Using a tag to give a collection object special treatment

1. On the File menu, click the Save MyMove.frm As command. Save the form as **MyTag.frm**.

   Before you make changes to the program, you save it under a new name to preserve the original MyMove project.

2. On the File menu, click the Save Project As command. Save the project as **MyTag.vbp**.

3. Click the Move Objects button on the form, and then open the Properties window.

4. Set the Tag property of the cmdButton object to "Button".

5. Double-click the Move Objects button on the form.

   The cmdButton_Click event procedure appears in the Code window, as shown in the following illustration:

6. Modify your event procedure so that it looks like the code on the following page. (The third and fifth lines are new, and the fourth line has been further indented.)

```
Private Sub cmdButton_Click()
For Each Ctrl In Controls
    If Ctrl.Tag <> "Button" Then
        Ctrl.Left = Ctrl.Left + 200
    End If
Next Ctrl
End Sub
```

The new feature of this For Each...Next loop is the If...Then statement that checks each collection member to see if it has a Tag property containing "Button". If the loop encounters this marker, it passes over the object without moving it. The tag "Button" has no special meaning to Visual Basic—it's simply a word I decided to use to identify the command button object in the program. I could just as easily have used a tag such as "Don't Move" or "Leave It".

7. Close the Code window, and then click the Start button.

*Start button*

✎ **TIP** The complete Tag.vbp program is available in the \LearnVb6\Less11 folder.

The program runs, and the five interface objects appear on the form.

8. Click the Move Objects button seven or eight times.

As you click the button, the icons on the form move across the screen. The Move Objects button stays in the same place, however:

The Tag property lets you give this object special treatment.

318

Giving one object in a collection special treatment can be very useful. In this case, using a tag in the For Each...Next loop improved the usability of the user interface. As you use other types of collections in Visual Basic, be sure to keep the Tag property in mind.

9. Click the End button on the toolbar to stop the program.

*End button*

10. Click the Save Project button on the toolbar to save your changes to **MyTag.vbp.**

## Visual Basic for Applications Collections

If you decide to write Visual Basic macros for Microsoft Office applications in the future, you'll find that collections play a big role in the object models of Microsoft Word, Microsoft Excel, Microsoft Access, Microsoft PowerPoint, and several other applications that support the Visual Basic for Applications programming language. In Word, for example, all the

---

### Useful Visual Basic Collections

Visual Basic provides built-in support for the following collections in your programs, in addition to the Controls collection.

| Collection | Description |
| --- | --- |
| Forms collection | A collection of all the loaded forms in a program. By using a For Each...Next loop, you can set the characteristics of one or more of these forms or one or more of the objects contained in them. |
| Printers collection | A collection of all the available printers on your system. By using a For Each...Next loop and the AddItem method, you can display the names of all the available printers in a list box and let the user pick the printer to use for output. |
| Database collections | A variety of collections related to data access and database management. Especially useful database collections include Columns, Containers, Indexes, and Databases. You'll learn more about databases in the next lesson. |

open documents in the word processor are stored in the Documents collection, and each paragraph in the current document is stored in the Paragraphs collection. You can manipulate these collections with the For...Each loop just as you did in the preceding exercise.

For example, the following sample code comes from a Word macro that uses a For...Each loop to check each open document in the Documents collection for a file named MyLetter.doc. If the file is found in the collection, the macro makes MyLetter the active document in Word with the Activate method. If the file isn't found in the collection, the macro loads the file from the Samples folder on drive C.

```
Dim aDoc, docFound, docLocation
docLocation = "c:\samples\myletter.doc"
For Each aDoc In Documents
    If InStr(1, aDoc.Name, "myletter.doc", 1) Then
        aDoc.Activate
        Exit For
    Else
        docFound = False
    End If
Next aDoc
If docFound = False Then Documents.Open FileName:=docLocation
```

**TIP** I've included this sample Word macro to show you how you can use collections in Visual Basic for Applications, but the source code is designed for Word, not the Visual Basic compiler. To try it you'll need to open up Word 97 or later and enter the code in Word's special macro editor. (If you're not in Word, the Documents collection won't have any meaning to the compiler.) You can learn more about Word macros in my book *Microsoft Word 97 Visual Basic Step by Step*, by Michael Halvorson and Chris Kinata (Microsoft Press, 1997).

The macro begins by declaring three variables, all of type Variant. The aDoc variable will represent the current collection element in the For...Each loop. The variable docFound will be assigned a Boolean value of False if the document isn't found in the Documents collection. The variable docLocation will contain the pathname of the MyLetter.doc file on disk. (This routine assumes that the MyLetter.doc file is in a hypothetical folder named Samples on drive C.)

The For…Each loop cycles through each document in the Documents collection searching for the MyLetter file. If the file is detected by the InStr function (which detects one string in another), the file is made the active document. If the file isn't found, the macro opens it by using the Open method of the Documents object.

Also note the Exit For statement, which I use to exit the For…Each loop when the MyLetter file has been found and activated. Exit For is a special program statement you can use to exit a For…Next loop or For…Each loop when continuing will cause unwanted results. In our example, if the MyLetter.doc file has been located in the collection, continuing the search would be fruitless. Here, the Exit For statement affords a graceful way to stop the loop as soon as its task is completed.

# Working with Arrays of Variables

In Lesson 7, you used cut-and-paste techniques to create a control array to store more than one picture box under the same object name. In the control array you used, each object in the group shared the same object name, so you were able to process the entire set of picture boxes by using one For…Next loop.

In this section, you'll learn how to use similar techniques to store variables in an array. Just like control arrays and collections, variable arrays (simply called *arrays*) allow you to refer to an entire group of values by using one name and then to process the values individually or as a group by using a For…Next or Do loop.

Arrays are useful because they help you track large amounts of data in ways that would be impractical using traditional variables. For example, imagine creating a nine-inning baseball scoreboard in a program. To save the scores for each inning of the game, you might be tempted to create two groups of 9 variables (a total of 18 variables) in the program. You'd probably name them something like Inning1HomeTeam, Inning1Away Team, and so on, to keep them straight. Working with the variables individually would take considerable time and real estate in your program. Fortunately, Visual Basic lets you organize groups of variables like these in an array that has one common name and an easy-to-use index. For example, you could create a two-dimensional (2-by-9) array named Scoreboard to contain the scores for the baseball game. Let's see how this works.

## Creating an Array

You create, or *declare,* arrays in program code just as you declare variables. However, the place in which you declare the array determines where it can be used, or its *scope,* in the program. If an array is declared locally, it can be used only in the procedure in which it's declared. If an array is declared publicly in a standard module, it can be used anywhere in the program. When you declare an array, you need to include the following information in your declaration statement.

| Information in an array declaration statement | Description |
| --- | --- |
| Array name | The name you will use to represent your array in the program. In general, array names follow the same rules as variable names. (See Lesson 5 for more information on variables.) |
| Data type | The type of data you will store in the array. In most cases, all the variables in an array will be of the same type. You can specify one of the fundamental data types, or, if you're not yet sure which type of data will be stored in the array or whether you will store more than one type, you can specify the Variant type. |
| Number of dimensions | The number of dimensions your array will contain. Most arrays are one-dimensional (a list of values) or two-dimensional (a table of values), but you can add dimensions if you're working with a complex mathematical model such as a three-dimensional shape. |
| Number of elements | The number of elements your array will contain. The elements in your array correspond directly to the array index. By default, the first array index is 0 (zero), as it is with control arrays. |

**IP** Arrays that contain a set number of elements are called *fixed-size* arrays. Arrays that contain a variable number of elements (arrays that can expand during the execution of the program) are called *dynamic* arrays.

## Declaring a Fixed-Size Array

The basic syntax for a public fixed-size array is

```
Public ArrayName(Dim1Elements, Dim2Elements, ...) As DataType
```

The following arguments are important:

- **Public** is the keyword that creates a global array.

- *ArrayName* is the variable name of the array.

- *Dim1Elements* is the number of elements in the first dimension of the array.

- *Dim2Elements* is the number of elements in the second dimension of the array (additional dimensions can be included).

- *DataType* is a keyword corresponding to the type of data that will be included in the array.

Because the array is public, you need to place the declaration in a standard module in the project (along with other public, or global, variables).

 **IP** To declare arrays locally in an event procedure, replace the Public keyword with the Static keyword and place the declaration inside an event procedure. Local arrays can be used only inside the procedure in which they are declared.

For example, to declare a public one-dimensional string array named Employees that has room for 10 employee names, you would type the following in a standard module:

```
Public Employees(9) As String
```

When you create the array, Visual Basic sets aside room for it in memory. The illustration below shows conceptually how the array is organized. The 10 array elements are numbered 0 through 9 rather than 1 through

10, because array indexes start with 0 unless you use the Option Base statement. (See "The Option Base Statement" sidebar later in this lesson for more information.)

---

 **IP**   By default, the first element in an array has an array index of 0.

---

Employees

| 0 | |
|---|---|
| 1 | |
| 2 | |
| 3 | |
| 4 | |
| 5 | |
| 6 | |
| 7 | |
| 8 | |
| 9 | |

To declare a public two-dimensional array named Scoreboard that has room for two rows and nine columns of variant data, you would type the following statement in a standard module. (This array would be suitable for the baseball scoreboard discussed earlier in this lesson and will be used in an exercise later in this lesson.)

```
Public Scoreboard(1, 8) As Variant
```

When you declare a two-dimensional array, Visual Basic sets aside room for it in memory. You can then use the array in your program as if it were a table of values, as shown in the illustration at the top of the next page: (In this case, the array elements are numbered 0 through 1 and 0 through 8.)

Scoreboard

Columns

|       | 0 | 1 | 2 | 3 | 4 | 5 | 6 | 7 | 8 |
|-------|---|---|---|---|---|---|---|---|---|
| Rows  |   |   |   |   |   |   |   |   |   |
| 0     |   |   |   |   |   |   |   |   |   |
| 1     |   |   |   |   |   |   |   |   |   |

## Working with Array Elements

After you've declared an array by using the Static or Public keyword, you're ready to use the array in the program. To refer to an element of an array, you use the array name and an array index enclosed in parentheses. The index must be an integer value; for example, it can be a simple number or an integer variable. (The counter variable of a For...Next loop is often used.) The following statement would assign the value "Leslie" to element 5 in the Employees array example in the previous section:

```
Employees(5) = "Leslie"
```

This would produce the result shown in the following illustration in our Employees array.

Employees

| 0 |        |
|---|--------|
| 1 |        |
| 2 |        |
| 3 |        |
| 4 |        |
| 5 | Leslie |
| 6 |        |
| 7 |        |
| 8 |        |
| 9 |        |

> ## The Option Base Statement
>
> If you think your program would be clearer conceptually if the index of the first element in each array were 1 instead of 0, you can place the following Option Base statement in a standard module:
>
> ```
> Option Base 1
> ```
>
> This statement associates the first element—or base—of all the arrays in a program with the number 1. The program you'll create in the following section will use Option Base in this way.

---

> **TIP** Arrays are maintained in system memory, or RAM, while the program is running.

---

Similarly, the following statement would assign the number 4 to row 0, column 2 (the top of the third inning) in the Scoreboard array example in the previous section:

```
Scoreboard(0, 2) = 4
```

This would produce the following result in our Scoreboard array:

Scoreboard

Columns

| | 0 | 1 | 2 | 3 | 4 | 5 | 6 | 7 | 8 |
|---|---|---|---|---|---|---|---|---|---|
| Rows 0 | | | 4 | | | | | | |
| 1 | | | | | | | | | |

You can use these indexing techniques to assign or retrieve any array element.

## Creating a Fixed-Size Array to Hold Temperatures

The following exercise uses a one-dimensional public array named Temperatures to record the daily high temperatures for a seven-day week. The program demonstrates how you can use an array to store and process a collection of related values in a program. Temperatures are assigned to the array by using an InputBox function and a For...Next loop. The loop counter in the loop is used to reference each element in the array. The array contents are then displayed on the form by using a For...Next loop and the Print method, and the average high temperature is calculated and displayed.

### Using a fixed-size array

1. On the File menu, click the New Project command, and click OK.

2. Use the CommandButton control to create three command buttons at the bottom of the form.

3. Set the following properties for the command button and form objects:

| Object | Property | Setting |
|--------|----------|---------|
| Command1 | Caption | "Enter Temperatures" |
| | Name | cmdEnterTemps |
| Command2 | Caption | "Display Temperatures" |
| | Name | cmdDisplayTemps |
| Command3 | Caption | "Quit" |
| | Name | cmdQuit |
| Form1 | Caption | "Temperatures" |
| | AutoRedraw | True |

4. Your form should look like the following:

> **IMPORTANT**  Always set a form's AutoRedraw property to True when you're using the Print method to display information on the form. This will cause Visual Basic to redraw the screen if the form gets covered by another window.

5. On the Project menu, click the Add Module command, and then click Open to create a standard module for the array declaration.

   A standard module appears in the Code window.

6. Type the following statements in the standard module:

```
Option Base 1
Public Temperatures(7) As Variant
```

   The Option Base statement changes the index of the first array element from 0 to 1 for all arrays in the program. The second statement creates a public array named Temperatures (of the type *Variant*) that has seven elements. Because the array has been declared publicly, it will be available throughout the program.

7. Close the standard module Code window, and then double-click the Enter Temperatures button.

   The cmdEnterTemps_Click event procedure appears in the Code window.

8. Type the following program statements to prompt the user for temperatures and to load the input into the array:

```
Cls
Prompt$ = "Enter the high temperature."
For i% = 1 To 7
    Title$ = "Day " & i%
    Temperatures(i%) = InputBox(Prompt$, Title$)
Next i%
```

> **TIP**  The Cls method at the top of the event procedure clears any previous Print statements from the form so that you can enter more than one set of temperatures.

The For...Next loop uses the counter variable i% as an array index to load temperatures into array elements 1 through 7. The input is received by the InputBox function, which uses the Prompt$ and Title$ variables as arguments.

9. Open the Object drop-down list box in the Code window, and then click the cmdDisplayTemps object. Type the following statements in the cmdDisplayTemps_Click event procedure:

```
Print "High temperatures for the week:"
Print
For i% = 1 To 7
    Print "Day "; i%, Temperatures(i%)
    Total! = Total! + Temperatures(i%)
Next i%
Print
Print "Average high temperature:  "; Total! / 7
```

This event procedure uses the Print method to display the information stored in the Temperatures array on the form. It uses a For... Next loop to cycle through the elements in the array, and it calculates the total of all the temperatures by using the statement

```
Total! = Total! + Temperatures(i%)
```

The last line in the event procedure displays the average high temperature of the week, the result of dividing the temperature total by the number of days.

10. Open the Object drop-down list box in the Code window, and then click the cmdQuit object. Type the following statement in the cmdQuit_Click event procedure:

```
End
```

*Save Project button*

11. Click the Save Project button on the toolbar to save the standard module, the form, and the project to disk. Select the \LearnVb6 \Less11 folder, and save each file using the name **MyFixArray**.

*Start button*

12. Click the Start button to run the program.

> **TIP** The complete FixArray.vbp project can be found in the \Vb6Sbs\Less11 folder.

13. Click the Enter Temperatures button, and then enter seven different temperatures as you are prompted to by the InputBox function. (How about the temperatures during your last vacation?)

The InputBox function dialog box should look similar to this:

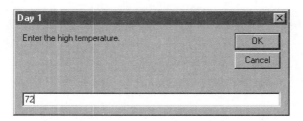

14. After you've entered the temperatures, click the Display Temperatures button.

Visual Basic uses the Print method to display each of the temperatures on the form and prints an average at the bottom. Your screen should look similar to the following:

15. Click the Quit button to end the program.

## Creating a Dynamic Array

As you can see, arrays are quite handy for working with lists of numbers, especially if you process them by using For...Next loops. But what if you're not sure how much array space you'll need before you run your program? For example, what if you want to let the user choose how many temperatures are entered into the MyFixArray program?

Visual Basic handles this problem efficiently with a special elastic container called a *dynamic array*. Dynamic arrays are dimensioned at runtime, either when the user specifies the size of the array or when logic you add to the program determines an array size based on specific conditions. Dimensioning a dynamic array takes several steps because although the size of the array isn't specified until the program is running, you need to make "reservations" for the array at design time. To create a dynamic array, you follow these basic steps:

- Specify the name and type of the array in the program at design time, omitting the number of elements in the array. For example, to create a public dynamic array named Temperatures, you type

```
Public Temperatures() as Variant
```

- Add code to determine the number of elements that should be in the array at runtime. You can prompt the user by using an InputBox function, or you can calculate the storage needs of the program by using properties or other logic. For example, the following statement gets the array size from the user and assigns it to the Days variable:

```
Days = InputBox("How many days?", "Create Array")
```

- Use the variable in a ReDim statement to dimension the array. For example, the following statement sets the size of the Temperatures array at runtime by using the Days variable:

```
ReDim Temperatures(Days)
```

- Use the number as the upper bound in a For...Next loop to process the array element, if necessary. For example, the following For...Next loop uses the Days variable as the upper bound of the loop:

```
For i% = 1 to Days
    Temperatures(i%) = InputBox(Prompt$, Title$)
Next i%
```

In the following exercise, you'll use these four steps to revise the MyFixArray program so that it can process any number of temperatures by using a dynamic array.

### Using a dynamic array to hold temperatures

1. Open the Project window and click MyFixArray.frm. You'll save each of the files in the MyFixArray project under a new name to preserve the originals.

2. On the File menu, click the Save MyFixArray.frm As command. Type **MyDynArray.frm** in the Save File As dialog box, and then click Save.

3. Click the MyFixArray.bas module in the Project window. Then, on the File menu, click the Save MyFixArray.bas As command. Next type **MyDynArray.bas** in the Save File As dialog box, and then click Save.

4. On the File menu, click the Save Project As command, and then type **MyDynArray.vbp**. Click Save when you're finished.

*View Code button*

5. Click Module1 in the Project window, and then click the View Code button to open it in the Code window.

6. Remove the number 7 from the array declaration statement to make Temperatures a dynamic array.

   The statement should look like the following:

   ```
   Public Temperatures() As Variant
   ```

7. Add the following public variable declaration to the standard module as the third line:

   ```
   Public Days As Integer
   ```

   The public integer variable Days will be used to receive input from the user and to dimension the dynamic array at runtime.

*View Object button*

8. Close the standard module. Click Form1 in the Project window, click the View Object button, and then double-click the Enter Temperatures button. Replace the current cmdEnterTemps_Click event procedure with the code at the top of the next page.

```
Cls
  Days = InputBox("How many days?", "Create Array")
  If Days > 0 Then
    ReDim Temperatures(Days)
    Prompt$ = "Enter the high temperature."
    For i% = 1 To Days
      Title$ = "Day " & i%
      Temperatures(i%) = InputBox(Prompt$, Title$)
    Next i%
  End If
```

The second and third lines prompt the user for the number of temperatures he or she wants to save, and then the lines use the input to dimension a dynamic array. The If...Then statement is used to verify that the number of days is greater than 0. (Dimensioning an array with the number 0 or a number less than 0 will cause a runtime error.) The Days variable is also used as the upper bound of the For...Next loop.

9. Open the Object drop-down list box, and then click the cmdDisplay-Temps object. Replace the current cmdDisplayTemps_Click event procedure with the following code:

```
If Days > 0 Then
  Print "High temperatures:"
  Print
  For i% = 1 To Days
    Print "Day "; i%, Temperatures(i%)
    Total! = Total! + Temperatures(i%)
  Next i%
  Print
  Print "Average high temperature:  "; Total! / Days
Else
  Print "No temperature data available."
End If
```

An If statement verifies that the Days variable contains temperature data, and replaces the number 7 twice in the event procedure.

*Save Project button*

10. Close the Code window, and then click the Save Project button to save your changes to disk.

*Start button*

11. Click the Start button on the toolbar to run the program.

**IP**   The complete DynArray.vbp program is available on disk in the \LearnVb6\Less11 folder.

12. Click the Enter Temperatures button and type **5** when you are prompted for the number of days you want to record.

13. Enter five temperatures as you are prompted to do so.

14. When you've finished entering temperatures, click the Display Temperatures button.

    The program displays the five temperatures on the form along with their average. Your screen should look similar to the following:

15. Click the End button on the toolbar to end the program.

*End button*

Congratulations! You've learned to store an unlimited number of values by using an array, and you've learned how to process them by using a For...Next loop. These skills will be useful whenever you need to store large amounts of information in memory while a program runs. In the next two lessons, you'll learn how to store this type of information in text files and databases.

# Using Multidimensional Arrays

In addition to one-dimensional arrays, which handle lists of information, Visual Basic lets you create *multidimensional arrays,* which handle one or more tables of information. Working with multidimensional arrays can be difficult until you get the hang of it, and many of the applications are beyond the scope of this book, but the results can save you considerable time and energy if you're working with large tables of data.

In the following exercise, you'll use a two-dimensional array called Scoreboard to record the runs in an imaginary baseball game between the Seattle Mariners and the New York Yankees. The array you'll use will be a 2-by-9 array similar to the one you dimensioned earlier. After you master two-dimensional arrays, you might wish to experiment with three-dimensional or four-dimensional arrays to push your brain to its conceptual limits. (These sophisticated arrays are often used for computer graphics or scientific applications.)

## Creating a Baseball Scoreboard by Using a Two-Dimensional Array

*Open Project button*

*View Object button*

1. Click the Open Project button on the toolbar.

2. Open the Baseball.vbp project in the \LearnVb6\Less11 folder.

   The program loads, and the project files appear in the Project window.

3. If the Baseball.frm form does not appear, click it and then click the View Object button.

   The Scoreboard form appears, as shown here:

The Scoreboard form uses two text boxes and two command buttons to display the runs scored in a nine-inning baseball game.

The Mariners are listed as the home team on the scoreboard, and the Yankees are listed as the away team, but you can change these names to those of your own favorite teams. The information is displayed on the scoreboard by using the Print method and is stored in the program by using a two-dimensional public array named Scoreboard.

*Start button*

4. Click the Start button on the toolbar to run the program.

   The program starts, and the cursor blinks in the Yankees text box at the bottom of the form.

   The label above the text box indicates that the program is ready to record the first inning of the game. You get to create your own dream game.

5. Type **0** and then press Tab.

   The cursor moves to the Mariners text box.

6. Type **0**, and then click the Next Inning button.

   A 0–0 tie is recorded in the scoreboard on the form.

7. Continue to enter baseball scores inning by inning until you finish with the ninth inning.

   If you want, you can click the Next Inning button more than once to record the same score for multiple innings.

   When you've finished, your screen should look similar to the one at the top of the following page. I've chosen my scoreboard to replay Game 1 of the 1995 American League Division Series, in which New York beat Seattle (the Mariners had trouble with relief pitching).

8. Click the Quit button to end the program.

   Now you'll look at the program code to see how the Scoreboard array was created and used.

*View Code button*

9. Click the Baseball.bas standard module in the Project window, and then click the View Code button.

The Code window appears, containing the declarations section of the standard module and the first part of the AddUpScores procedure, as shown below.

Scoreboard is a public two-dimensional array

```
Option Base 1           'set array base to 1
Public Scoreboard(2, 9) As Variant
Public Inning As Integer

Sub AddUpScores()
'AddUpScores is a public procedure that totals and
'displays the runs in the Scoreboard array.

    For i% = 1 To 9    'use loop to add scores
        AwayScore% = AwayScore% + Scoreboard(1, i%)
        HomeScore% = HomeScore% + Scoreboard(2, i%)
    Next i%            'then display scores in box
    Form1.CurrentX = 5000
    Form1.CurrentY = 1050
```

There are four critical components here: an Option Base statement, the declaration statement for a public two-dimensional (2-by-9) array named Scoreboard, the declaration for a public variable named Inning, and a general-purpose public procedure named AddUpScores. The Scoreboard array is declared as a table of values in memory, with rows representing the two teams and columns representing the nine innings. The organization is similar to that of a basic spreadsheet. The Inning variable is used to reference the column (or inning) values in the array.

10. Spend a few moments examining the code in the AddUpScores procedure.

    AddUpScores is used to sum the scores in the array and to display them. Because this public procedure is declared in a standard module, it's available throughout the program.

11. Now close the standard module, and then double-click the Next Inning button on the Baseball.frm form.

    The event procedure associated with this button handles the task of moving baseball scores from the team text boxes to the Scoreboard array and finally to the scoreboard on the form. Each Scoreboard array assignment requires two index values, one for the row and one for the column. Considerable care was taken to place the cursor in the correct *x, y* location on the scoreboard to display the information. CurrentX and CurrentY are properties that determine the coordinates of the cursor on the form, and they require values in twips, an effective measurement system to use when you get the hang of it. Because there are 1440 twips in an inch, the coordinate system is granular enough to place the cursor anywhere you want on the form.

12. Scroll down to the Form_Load event procedure in the Code window.

    The Form_Load event procedure initializes the Inning variable to 1 and displays the header on the scoreboard. The Show method is required in this procedure before the Print method is used. Normally, the Print method displays information without help, but because the form is still loading, the Show method is required to print while the Form_Load event is in progress.

13. Continue to explore the Baseball program for ideas you can use in your own programs and run it again if you like.

# Exploring Text Files and String Processing

In this lesson, you'll learn how to work with information stored in text files on your system. You'll learn how to open a text file and display its contents by using a text box object, and you'll learn how to create a new text file on disk. You'll also learn how to manage textual elements called *strings* in your programs and to use strings to combine, sort, encrypt, and display words, paragraphs, and entire text files.

# Displaying Text Files by Using a Text Box Object

The simplest way to display a text file in a program is to use a text box object. You can create text box objects in a variety of sizes. If the contents of the text file don't fit neatly in the text box, you can also add scroll bars to the text box so the user can examine the entire file. To load the contents of a text file into a text box, you need to use three statements and one function. Their corresponding keywords are described in the following table and will be demonstrated in the first exercise in this lesson.

| Keyword | Description |
|---------|-------------|
| Open | Opens a text file for input or output |
| Line Input | Reads a line of input from the text file |
| EOF | Checks for the end of the text file |
| Close | Closes the text file |

## Opening a Text File for Input

A *text file* consists of one or more lines of numbers, words, or characters. Text files are distinct from *document files,* which contain formatting codes, and from *executable files,* which contain instructions for the operating system. Typical text files on your system will be identified by Windows Explorer as "Text Documents" or will have the extension .txt, .ini, .log, .inf, .dat, or .bat. Because text files contain only ordinary, recognizable characters, you can display them easily by using text box objects.

You can let the user decide which text file to open in a program by using a common dialog object to prompt the user for the file's pathname. Common dialog objects support the ShowOpen method, which displays the Open common dialog box on the screen. After the user selects the file in the dialog box, its pathname is returned to the program in the FileName property, and you can use this name to open the file. The common dialog object doesn't open the file; it just gets the pathname.

## The Open statement

After you get the pathname from the user, you open the file in the program by using the Open statement. The syntax for the Open statement is

```
Open pathname For mode As #filenumber
```

The following arguments are important:

- **pathname** is a valid Windows pathname.

- **mode** is a keyword indicating how the file will be used. (You'll use the Input and Output modes in this lesson.)

- **filenumber** is an integer from 1 through 255.

The file number will be associated with the file when it's opened. You then use this file number in your code whenever you need to refer to the open file. Aside from this association, there's nothing special about file numbers; Microsoft Visual Basic simply uses them to keep track of the different files you open in your program.

A typical Open statement using a common dialog object looks like this:

```
Open CommonDialog1.FileName For Input As #1
```

Here the CommonDialog1.FileName property represents the pathname, Input is the mode, and 1 is the file number.

 **IP** Text files that are opened by using this syntax are called *sequential files*, because their contents must be worked with in sequential order. By contrast, you can access the information in a database file in any order. (You'll learn more about databases in Lesson 13.)

The following exercise demonstrates how you can use a common dialog object and the Open statement to open a text file. The exercise also demonstrates how you can use the Line Input and EOF keywords to display the contents of a text file in a text box and how you can use the Close keyword to close a file.

### Running the Text Browser program

1. Start Visual Basic if it's not already running.

*Open Project button*

2. Click the Existing tab in the New Project dialog box, or click the Open Project button on the toolbar.

3. Select the \LearnVb6\Less12 folder, and then double-click the filename ShowText.

   The ShowText program loads into the programming environment.

4. If the form isn't already visible, select the ShowText form in the Project window, and then click the View Object button.

   The ShowText form appears, as shown in the following illustration:

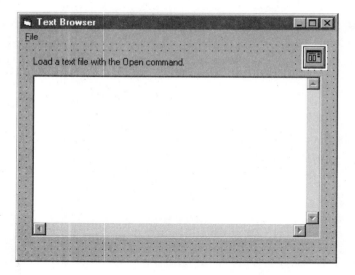

The form contains a large text box object that has scroll bars. It also contains a common dialog object, a label that provides operating instructions for the program, and a File menu containing Open, Close, and Exit commands. I also created the property settings shown in the table at the top of the next page. (Note especially the text box settings.)

| Object | Property | Setting |
|--------|----------|---------|
| txtFile | Enabled | False |
| | Multiline | True |
| | Name | txtFile |
| | ScrollBars | 3 – Both |
| | Text | (Empty) |
| mnuItemClose | Enabled | False |
| | Name | mnuItemClose |
| lblFile | Caption | "Load a text file with the Open command." |
| | Name | lblFile |
| Form1 | Caption | "Text Browser" |

*Start button*

5. Click the Start button on the toolbar.

   The Text Browser program starts to run.

6. On the Text Browser's File menu, click the Open command.

   The Open dialog box appears, as shown in the following illustration:

7. Select the \LearnVb6\Less12 folder, and then double-click the filename Badbills.txt in the Open dialog box.

343

Badbills, a text file containing an article written in 1951 about the dangers of counterfeit money, appears in the text box:

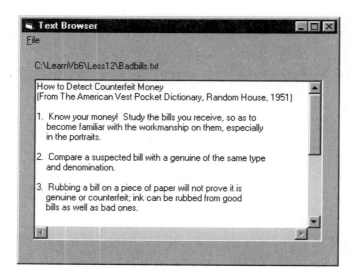

8.  Use the scroll bars to view the entire document. Memorize number 5.

9.  When you've finished, click the Close command on the File menu to close the file, and then click the Exit command to quit the program.

    The program stops, and the programming environment returns. Now you'll take a look at two important event procedures in the program.

### Examining the ShowText program code

1.  On the Text Browser form's File menu, click the Open command.

    The mnuItemOpen_Click event procedure appears in the Code window.

2.  Resize the Code window to see more of the program code.

    Your screen should look similar to the illustration shown at the top of the next page.

```
Project1 - Form1 [Code]

mnuItemOpen                          Click

Private Sub mnuItemOpen_Click()
    Wrap$ = Chr$(13) + Chr$(10)    'create wrap character
    CommonDialog1.Filter = "Text files (*.TXT)|*.TXT"
    CommonDialog1.ShowOpen          'display Open dialog box
    If CommonDialog1.FileName <> "" Then
        Form1.MousePointer = 11 'display hourglass
        Open CommonDialog1.FileName For Input As #1
        On Error GoTo TooBig:       'set error handler
        Do Until EOF(1)             'then read lines from file
            Line Input #1, LineOfText$
            AllText$ = AllText$ & LineOfText$ & Wrap$
        Loop
        lblFile.Caption = CommonDialog1.FileName
        txtFile.Text = AllText$  'display file
        txtFile.Enabled = True
        mnuItemClose.Enabled = True
        mnuItemOpen.Enabled = False
CleanUp:
```

This event procedure performs the following actions. The Visual Basic statements used are shown in parentheses.

- Prompts the user for a pathname by using a common dialog object.

- Opens the specified file for input (Open...For Input).

- Copies the file one line at a time into a string named AllText$ (Line Input).

- Copies lines until the end of the file is reached (EOF) or until there is no more room in the string. The AllText$ string has room for 64 KB of characters.

- Displays the AllText$ string in the text box and enables the scroll bars.

- Handles any errors that occur (On Error GoTo).

- Updates the File menu commands and the mouse pointer and closes the file (Close).

3. Take a moment to see how the statements in the mnuItemOpen_Click event procedure work—especially the Open, Line Input, EOF, and Close keywords.

The TooBig: error handler in the procedure displays a message and aborts the loading process if the user selects a file bigger than 64 KB. This error handler is necessary because of the 64 KB string size limitation of the text box object. (For files bigger than 64 KB in size, you'll want to use the Rich Textbox control—see Lesson 15.)

If you select a file that's several pages long, Visual Basic will take a few moments to load it. For this reason, I use the MousePointer property to change the pointer to an hourglass shape until the file is displayed on the screen. It's always a good idea to give users some visual feedback if they have to wait more than a second or so for an action to occur.

4. Open the Object drop-down list box, and then click mnuItemClose to display the mnuItemClose_Click event procedure.

This procedure runs when the Close menu command is executed. The procedure clears the text box, disables the Close command, enables the Open command, and disables the text box.

5. When you've finished looking at the ShowText program code, close the Code window.

Now you can use this simple program as a template for more advanced utilities that process text files. In the next exercise, you'll learn how to type your own text into a text box and how to save the text and text box to disk in a file.

## Creating a New Text File on Disk

To create a new text file on disk by using Visual Basic, you'll use many of the objects and keywords you used in the last example. Creating new files on disk and saving data to them will be useful if you plan to generate custom reports or logs, save important calculations or values, or create a special-purpose word processor or text editor. Here's an overview of the steps you'll need to follow in the program:

1. Get input from the user or perform mathematical calculations, or do both.

2. Assign the results of your processing to one or more variables. For example, you could assign the contents of a text box to a variable named InputForFile$.

3. Prompt the user for a pathname by using a Save As common dialog box. You use the ShowSave method of a common dialog object to display the dialog box.

4. Use the pathname received in the dialog box to open the file for output (Open...For Output).

5. Use the Print # statement to save one or more values to the open file (Print #).

6. Close the file when you've finished (Close).

The following exercise demonstrates how you can use text box and common dialog objects and the Open, Print #, and Close statements to create a simple note-taking utility. You can use this tool to take notes at home or at work and then to stamp them with the current date.

## Running the QNote Program

*Open Project button*

1. Click the Open Project button on the toolbar.

2. Select the \LearnVb6\Less12 folder, and then double-click the project QNote.

   The QNote program loads into the programming environment.

3. If the form isn't visible, click the QNote form in the Project window, and then click the View Object button.

   The QNote form appears, as shown in the illustration at the top of the next page.

   The form contains a large text box object that has scroll bars. It also contains a common dialog object, a label that provides operating instructions for the program, and a File menu containing Save As, Insert Date, and Exit commands. I set the properties as shown in the table on the next page.

| Object | Property | Setting |
|--------|----------|---------|
| txtNote | Multiline | True |
| | Name | txtNote |
| | ScrollBars | 3 – Both |
| | Text | (Empty) |
| Label1 | Caption | "Type your note and then save it to disk." |
| Form1 | Caption | "Quick Note" |

*Start button*

4. Click the Start button on the toolbar.

5. Type the following text, or some text of your own, in the text box:

**How to Detect Counterfeit Coins**

1. **Drop coins on a hard surface. Genuine coins have a bell-like ring; most counterfeit coins sound dull.**

2. **Feel all coins. Most counterfeit coins feel greasy.**

3. **Cut edges of questionable coins. Genuine coins are not easily cut.**

When you've finished, your screen should look similar to the illustration shown at the top of the next page.

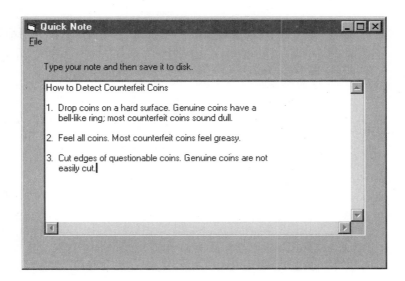

**TIP** To copy text from the Windows Clipboard into the text box, press Shift+Ins. To copy text from the text box to the Windows Clipboard, select the text by using the mouse and then press Ctrl+C.

Now try using the commands on the File menu.

6. On the File menu, click the Insert Date command.

The current date appears as the first line in the text box:

Current date

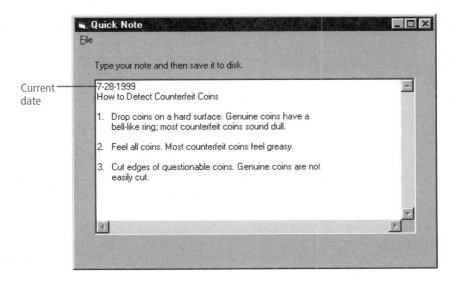

The Insert Date command provides a handy way to include the current date in a file. This is useful if you're creating a diary or a logbook.

7. On the File menu, click the Save As command.

8. In the Save As dialog box, select the \LearnVb6\Less12 folder if it's not already selected. Then type **Badcoins.txt** in the File Name text box and click Save.

   The text of your document is saved in the new text file Badcoins.txt.

9. On the File menu, click the Exit command.

   The program stops, and the programming environment returns.

Now you'll take a look at the event procedures in the program.

## Examining the QNote Program Code

1. On the QNote form File menu, click the Insert Date command.

   The mnuItemDate_Click event procedure appears in the Code window, as shown in the following illustration:

```
Project1 - Form1 (Code)                                    _ □ X
mnuItemDate                    ▼   Click                      ▼
    Private Sub mnuItemDate_Click()
        Wrap$ = Chr$(13) & Chr$(10)   'add date to string
        txtNote.Text = Date$ & Wrap$ & txtNote.Text
    End Sub

    Private Sub mnuItemExit_Click()
        End                          'quit program
    End Sub

    Private Sub mnuItemSave_Click()
    'note: the entire file is stored in a string
        CommonDialog1.Filter = "Text files (*.TXT)|*.TXT"
        CommonDialog1.ShowSave       'display Save dialog
        If CommonDialog1.FileName <> "" Then
            Open CommonDialog1.FileName For Output As #1
            Print #1, txtNote.Text  'save string to file
            Close #1                'close file
        End If
    End Sub
```

This event procedure adds the current date to the text box by linking together, or *concatenating*, the current date (generated by the Date$ function), a carriage return, and the Text property. You could use a similar technique to add the current time or any other information to the text in the text box.

2. Take a moment to see how the concatenation statements work, and then examine the mnuItemSave_Click event procedure in the Code window.

This block of statements uses a common dialog object to display a Save As common dialog box, opens the file for output as file number 1, writes the value in the txtNote.Text property to disk by using the Print # statement, and then closes the text file. Note especially the statement

```
Print #1, txtNote.Text
```

which assigns the entire contents of the text box to the open file. Print # is similar to the Print method, except that it directs the output to the specified file rather than to the screen or the printer. The important thing to note here is that the entire file is stored in the txtNote.Text string.

3. Review the Open, Print #, and Close statements, and then close the Code window.

You've finished with the QNote program.

# Processing Text Strings with Program Code

As you learned in the preceding exercises, you can quickly open, edit, and save text files to disk with the TextBox control and a handful of well-chosen program statements. Visual Basic also provides a number of powerful statements and functions specifically designed for processing the textual elements in your programs. In this section, you'll learn how to extract useful information from a text string, copy a group of strings into a string array, sort a text box by comparing string expressions, and protect sensitive information by encrypting strings.

## Sorting Text

An extremely useful skill to develop when working with textual elements is the ability to sort a list of strings. The basic concepts in sorting are simple. You draw up a list of items to sort, and then compare the items one by one until the list is sorted in ascending or descending alphabetical or numeric order. In Visual Basic, you compare one item to another using the same relational operators that you use to compare numeric values. The tricky part (which sometimes provokes long-winded discussion among computer scientists) is the specific sorting algorithm you use to compare elements in a list. We won't get into the advantages and disadvantages of different sorting algorithms in this lesson. (The bone of contention is usually speed, which only makes a difference when several thousand items are sorted.) Instead, we'll explore how the basic string comparisons are made in a sort. Along the way, you'll learn the skills necessary to sort your own text boxes, list boxes, files, and databases.

## What Is ASCII?

Before Visual Basic can compare one character to another in a sort, it must convert each character into a number by using a translation table called the *ASCII character set* (also called the ANSI character set). ASCII is an acronym standing for American Standard Code (for) Information

---

### Processing Strings with Statements and Functions

The most common task you'll do with strings is concatenating them by using the & (concatenation) operator. For example, the following program statement concatenates three literal string expressions and assigns the result (*Bring on the circus!*) to the string variable slogan$:

```
slogan$ = "Bring" & " on the " & "circus!"
```

You can also modify string expressions by using several special statements, functions, and operators in your program code. The following table lists the most useful keywords; I'll introduce several in subsequent exercises.

---

*(continued)*

**Processing Strings with Statements and Functions** *continued*

| Keyword | Description | Example |
|---------|-------------|---------|
| Ucase | Changes a string's letters to uppercase | `Ucase("Kim")` *returns* `KIM` |
| Lcase | Changes a string's letters to lowercase | `Lcase("Kim")` *returns* `kim` |
| Len | Determines the length (in characters) of a string | `Len("Mississippi")` *returns* 11 |
| Right | Returns a fixed number of characters from the right side of a string | `Right("Budapest", 4)` *returns* `pest` |
| Left | Returns a fixed number of characters from the left side of a string | `Left("Budapest", 4)` *returns* `Buda` |
| Mid | Returns a fixed number of characters in the middle of a string from a given starting point | `Mid("Sommers", 4, 3)` *returns* `mer` |
| InStr | Finds starting point of one string within a larger string | `start% = InStr("bob", "bobby")` *returns* 1 to start% variable |
| String | Repeats a string of characters | `String(8,"*")` *returns* `********` |
| Asc | Returns the ASCII code of the specified letter | `Asc("A")` *returns* 65 |
| Chr | Returns the character for the specified ASCII code | `Chr$(65)` *returns* A |
| Xor | Performs an "exclusive or" operation on two numbers, returning a value that can be used to encrypt and decrypt text | `65 Xor 50` *returns* 115 `115 Xor 50` *returns* 65 |

Interchange. Every symbol that you can display on your computer has a different ASCII code. The ASCII character set includes the basic set of "typewriter" characters (codes 32 through 127); special "control" characters, such as tab, linefeed, and carriage return (codes 0 through 31); and the foreign-language and drawing characters in the *IBM extended character set* (codes 128 through 255). For example, the lowercase letter "a" corresponds to the ASCII code 97, and the uppercase letter "A" corresponds to the ASCII code 65. (This fact explains why Visual Basic treats these two characters quite differently when sorting or performing other comparisons.)

---

 **IP**  In older versions of the BASIC language, string processing functions that returned string values typically had a $ symbol at the end of their name. Thus Chr was named Chr$ and Mid was named Mid$. You can still use these older names in Visual Basic if you like. Both forms call the same function. (Now and then you'll see me use them interchangeably.)

---

To determine the ASCII code of a particular letter, you can use the Asc function. For example, the following program statement assigns the number 122 (the ASCII code for the lowercase letter "z") to the AscCode% integer variable:

```
AscCode% = Asc("z")
```

Conversely, you can convert an ASCII code to a letter with the Chr function. For example, this program statement assigns the letter "z" to the letter$ string variable:

```
letter$ = Chr(122)
```

The same result could also be achieved if you used the AscCode% variable, defined above:

```
letter$ = Chr(AscCode%)
```

How can you compare one text string or ASCII code with another? You simply use one of the six relational operators Visual Basic supplies for working with textual and numeric elements. These relational operators are shown in the table at the top of the next page.

| Operator | Meaning |
|----------|---------|
| <> | Not equal |
| = | Equal |
| < | Less than |
| > | Greater than |
| <= | Less than or equal to |
| >= | Greater than or equal to |

A character is "greater than" another character if its ASCII code is higher. For example, the ASCII value of the letter "B" is greater than the ASCII value of the letter "A", so the expression

```
"A" < "B"
```

is true, and the expression

```
"A" > "B"
```

is false.

When comparing two strings that each contain more than one character, Visual Basic begins by comparing the first character in the first string to the first character in the second string and then proceeds through the strings character by character until it finds a difference. For example, the strings Mike and Michael are the same up to the third characters ("k" and "c"). Because the ASCII value of "k" is greater than that of "c," the expression

```
"Mike" > "Michael"
```

is true.

If no differences are found between the strings, they are equal. If two strings are equal through several characters but one of the strings continues and the other one ends, the longer string is greater than the shorter string. For example, the expression

```
"AAAAA" > "AAA"
```

is true.

## Sorting Strings in a Text Box

The following exercise demonstrates how you can use relational operators and several string functions to sort lines of text in a Visual Basic text
box. The program is a revision of the QNote utility and features an Open
command that allows you to open an existing file. There is also a Sort
Text command on the File menu that lets you sort the text currently displayed in the text box.

Because the entire contents of a Visual Basic text box are stored in one
string, the program must first break that long string into smaller individual strings. These strings can then be sorted by using the *ShellSort
subprogram,* a sorting routine based on an algorithm created by Donald
Shell in 1959. To simplify these tasks, I created a standard module that
defines a dynamic string array to hold each of the lines in the text box. I
also placed the ShellSort subprogram in the standard module so that I
could call it from any event procedure in the project. (For more about
standard modules, see Lesson 10.)

One interesting part of this program is the routine that determines the
number of lines in the text box object. No existing Visual Basic function
computes this value automatically. I wanted the program to be able to sort
a text box of any size line by line. To accomplish this, I created the code
shown below. It uses the Chr function to detect the carriage return character at the end of each line.

```
'determine number of lines in text box object (txtNote)
lineCount% = 0  'this variable holds the total number of lines
charsInFile% = Len(txtNote.Text)  'get total characters in box
For i% = 1 To charsInFile%  'move one char at a time through box
    letter$ = Mid(txtNote.Text, i%, 1) 'put next char in letter$
    If letter$ = Chr(13) Then 'if carriage ret found (end of line!)
        lineCount% = lineCount% + 1 'go to next line (add to count)
        i% = i% + 1   'skip linefeed char (which always follows cr)
    End If
Next i%
```

This routine returns the number of lines in the text box to the
lineCount% variable. I can use this value to dimension a dynamic array
in the program to hold each individual text string. The resulting array of
strings then gets passed to the ShellSort subprogram for sorting, and

ShellSort returns the string array in alphabetical order. Once the string array is sorted, I can simply copy it back to the text box by using a For loop.

## Running the SortDemo Program

1. Click the Open Project button on the toolbar and open the SortDemo project in the \LearnVb6\Less12 folder.

2. Click the Start button on the toolbar to run the program.

*Start button*

3. Type the following text, or some text of your own, in the text box:

   **Zebra**
   **Gorilla**
   **Moon**
   **Banana**
   **Apple**
   **Turtle**

   Be sure to press Enter after "Turtle" when you enter text in the text box, so that Visual Basic will calculate the number of lines correctly.

4. On the File menu, click the Sort Text command.

   The text you typed is sorted and redisplayed in the text box as follows:

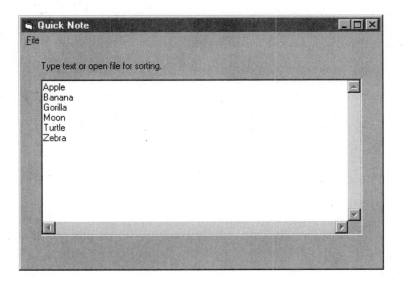

5. On the File menu, click the Open command and open the file abc.txt in the \LearnVb6\Less12 folder.

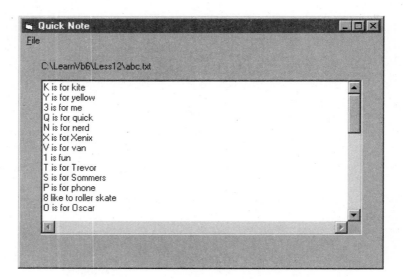

The abc.txt file contains 36 lines of text. Each line begins with either a letter or a number (1–10).

6. On the File menu, click the Sort Text command to sort the contents of the abc.txt file.

The SortDemo program sorts the file in ascending order and displays the sorted list of lines in the text box shown on the next page.

7. Scroll through the file to see the results of the alphabetical sort.

Notice that although the alphabetical portion of the sort ran perfectly, the sort did produce a strange result for one of the numeric entries—the line beginning with the number 10 appears second in the list rather than tenth. What's happening here is that Visual Basic is reading the 1 and the 0 in the number 10 as two independent characters, not as a number. Because we're comparing the ASCII codes of these strings from left to right, the program produces a purely alphabetical sort. If you want to sort numbers with this program, you'll need to store the numbers in numeric variables and compare them without using string functions.

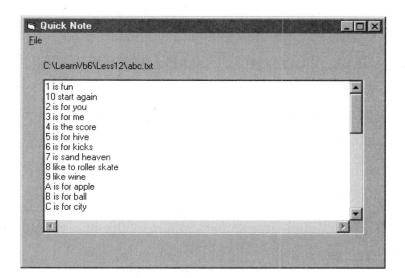

## Examining the SortDemo Program Code

1. On the SortDemo program's File menu, click the Exit command to stop the program.

2. Open the Code window (if it's not already open), and display the code for the mnuItemSortText event procedure.

   We've already discussed the first routine in this event procedure, which counts the number of lines in the text box by using the Mid function to search for carriage return codes. The remainder of the event procedure dimensions a string array, copies each line of text into the array, calls a subprogram to sort the array, and displays the reordered list in the text box.

3. Scroll down to the second routine in the event procedure.

   Your screen should look similar to the illustration shown on the next page.

```
Project1 - Form1 (Code)                                    _□×
mnuItemSortText                     ▼    Click                     ▼
    'build an array to hold the text in the text box
    ReDim strArray$(lineCount%) 'create array of proper size
    curline% = 1
    ln$ = ""  'use ln$ to build lines one character at a time
    For i% = 1 To charsInFile%        'loop through text again
        letter$ = Mid(txtNote.Text, i%, 1)
        If letter$ = Chr$(13) Then 'if carriage return found
            curline% = curline% + 1     'increment line count
            i% = i% + 1                 'skip linefeed char
            ln$ = ""                    'clear line and go to next
        Else
            ln$ = ln$ & letter$      'add letter to line
            strArray$(curline%) = ln$ 'and put in array
        End If
    Next i%

    'sort array
    ShellSort strArray$(), lineCount%
```

The array strArray$ was declared in a standard module (SortDemo.bas) that is also part of this program. By using the Redim statement, I am dimensioning strArray$ as a dynamic array with the lineCount% variable. This statement creates an array that has the same number of elements as the text box has lines of text (a requirement for the ShellSort subprogram). Using a For loop and the ln$ variable, I scan through the text box again, looking for carriage return characters and copying each complete line found to strArray$. After the array is full of text, I call the ShellSort subprogram I created previously in the SortDemo.bas standard module.

The ShellSort subprogram uses the <= relational operator to compare array elements and swap any that are out of order. The subprogram looks like this:

```
Sub ShellSort(sort$(), numOfElements%)
'The ShellSort subprogram sorts the elements of sort$()
'array in descending order and returns it to the calling
'procedure.
span% = numOfElements% \ 2
 Do While span% > 0
    For i% = span% To numOfElements% - 1
        j% = i% - span% + 1
        For j% = (i% - span% + 1) To 1 Step -span%
            If sort$(j%) <= sort$(j% + span%) Then Exit For
```

```
                    'swap array elements that are out of order
                    temp$ = sort$(j%)
                    sort$(j%) = sort$(j% + span%)
                    sort$(j% + span%) = temp$
            Next j%
        Next i%
        span% = span% \ 2
    Loop
    End Sub
```

The method of the sort is to continually divide the main list of elements into sublists that are smaller by half. The sort then compares the tops and the bottoms of the sublists to see if the elements are out of order. If the top and bottom are out of order, they are exchanged. The end result is an array (sort$) that is sorted alphabetically in descending order. To change the direction of the sort, simply reverse the relational operator (change <= to >=).

# Protecting Text with Encryption

Now that you've had some experience with ASCII codes, you can begin to write simple encryption routines that shift the ASCII codes in your documents and "scramble" the text to hide it from intruding eyes. This process, known as *encryption*, mathematically alters the characters in a file, making them unreadable to the casual observer. Of course, to use encryption successfully you also need to be able to reverse the process—otherwise, you'd simply be "trashing" your files rather than protecting them. The following exercises show you how to encrypt and decrypt text strings safely. You'll run the Encrypt program now to see a simple encryption scheme in action.

## Encrypting Text by Changing ASCII Codes

1. Click the Open Project button on the toolbar and open the Encrypt project in the \LearnVb6\Less12 folder.

2. Click the Start button on the toolbar to run the program.

3. Type the following text, or some text of your own, in the text box:

   **Here at last, my friend, you have the little book long since expected and promised, a little book on vast matter, namely, "On my own ignorance and that of many others."**
   **Francesco Petrarca, c. 1368**

4. On the File menu, click the Save Encrypted File command and save the file in the \LearnVb6\Less12 folder with the name **padua.txt**.

   As you save the text file; the program scrambles the ASCII code and displays the results in the text box shown below.

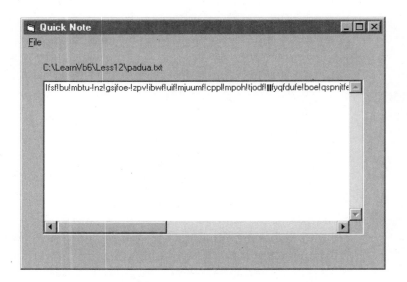

If you open this file in Microsoft Word or another text editor, you'll see the same result—the characters in the file have been encrypted to prevent unauthorized reading.

5. To restore the file to its original form, choose the Open Encrypted File command on the File menu, and open the padua.txt file in the \LearnVb6\Less12 folder.

   The file appears again in its original form, as shown in the figure at the top of the next page.

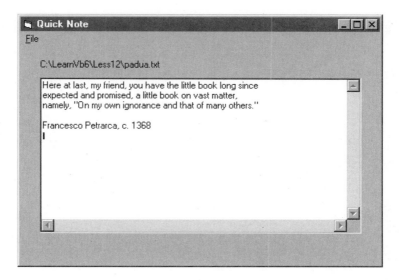

6. On the File menu, click the Exit command to end the program.

## Examining the Encrypt Program Code

1. Open the mnuItemSave event procedure in the Code window to see the program code that produces the encryption you observed when you ran the program.

   Although the effect you saw might have looked mysterious, it was a very straightforward encryption scheme. Using the Asc and Chr functions and a For loop, I simply added one number to the ASCII code for each character in the text box, and then saved the encrypted string to the specified text file.

```
'save text with encryption scheme (ASCII code + 1)
encrypt$ = ""   'initialize encryption string
charsInFile% = Len(txtNote.Text) 'find string length
For i% = 1 To charsInFile%   'for each character in file
    letter$ = Mid(txtNote.Text, i%, 1) 'read next char
    'determine ASCII code of char and add one to it
    encrypt$ = encrypt$ & Chr(Asc(letter$) + 1)
Next i%
Open CommonDialog1.FileName For Output As #1 'open file
Print #1, encrypt$            'save encrypted text to file
txtNote.Text = encrypt$       'display encrypted text
```

The crucial statement is

```
encrypt$ = encrypt$ & Chr(Asc(letter$) + 1)
```

This statement determines the ASCII code of the current letter, adds 1 to it, converts the ASCII code back to a letter, and adds it to the encrypt$ string. In the last two statements of this routine, the encrypt$ string is used to pass the encrypted text to a file and display it in the text box.

2. Now open the mnuOpenItem event procedure in the Code window to see how the program reverses the encryption.

This program code is nearly identical to that of the Save command, but rather than adding 1 to the ASCII code for each letter, it subtracts 1:

```
'now, decrypt string by subtracting 1 from ASCII code
decrypt$ = ""    'initialize string for decryption
charsInFile = Len(AllText$) 'get length of string
For i% = 1 To charsInFile    'loop once for each char
    letter$ = Mid(AllText$, i%, 1) 'get char with Mid
    decrypt$ = decrypt$ & Chr(Asc(letter) - 1) 'subtract 1
Next i%                       'and build new string
txtNote.Text = decrypt$       'then display converted string
```

This type of simple encryption may be all you need to conceal the information in your text files. However, files encrypted in this way can easily be decoded. By searching for possible equivalents of common characters such as the space character, determining the ASCII shift required to restore the common character, and running the conversion for the entire text file, a person experienced in encryption could readily decipher the file's content. Also, this sort of encryption doesn't prevent a malicious user from physically tampering with the file—for example, simply by deleting it if it's unprotected on your system or by modifying it in significant ways. But if you're just looking to hide information quickly, this simple encryption scheme could do the trick.

## Using the Xor Operator

The encryption scheme demonstrated above is quite "safe" for text files, because it only shifts the ASCII character code value up by one. However, you'll want to be careful about shifting ASCII codes more than a few characters if you store the result as text in a text file. Keep in mind that dramatic shifts in ASCII codes (such as adding 500 to each character code) will not produce actual ASCII characters that can be decrypted later. For example, adding 500 to the ASCII code for the letter "A" (65) would give a result of 565. This value could not be translated into a character by the Chr function. Instead, Chr would return a Null value, which you could not decrypt later. In other words, you couldn't recover the encrypted text—it would be lost forever.

A safe way around this problem is to convert the letters in your file to numbers when you encrypt the file, so that you can reverse the encryption no matter how large (or small) the numbers get. If you followed this line of thought, you could then apply mathematical functions—multiplication, logarithms, and so on—to the numbers as long as you knew how to reverse the results.

One of the best tools for encrypting numeric values is already built into Visual Basic. This tool is the *Xor operator*, which performs the "exclusive or" operation, a function carried out on the bits that make up the number itself. The Xor operator can be best observed by using the Immediate Window tool, which executes program code immediately when it's entered. You can open the Immediate Window in Visual Basic by choosing the Immediate Window command from the View menu. If you type

```
print asc("A") Xor 50
```

in the Immediate window and press Enter, Visual Basic displays a numeric result of 115 directly below the program statement. If you type

```
print 115 Xor 50
```

in the Immediate window, Visual Basic displays a result of 65, the ASCII code for the letter A (our original value). In other words, the Xor operator produces a result that can be reversed—if the original Xor code is used again on the result of the first operation. This interesting behavior of the Xor function is used in many popular encryption algorithms. It can make your secret files much more difficult to decode.

### Encrypting text with the Xor operator

Run the Encrypt2 program now to see how the Xor operator works.

1. Click the Open Project button on the toolbar and open the Encrypt2 project in the \LearnVb6\Less12 folder.

2. Click the Start button on the toolbar to run the program.

3. Type the following text (or some of your own) for the encrypted text file:

   **Rothair's Edict (Lombard Italy, c. 643)**
   **296. On Stealing Grapes. He who takes more than three grapes from another man's vine shall pay six soldi as composition. He who takes less than three shall bear no guilt.**

4. On the File menu, click the Save Encrypted File command and save the file in the \LearnVb6\Less12 folder with the name **oldlaws.txt**.

   The program prompts you for a secret encryption code that will be used to encrypt the file and decrypt it later. (Take note—you'll need to remember this code to decode the file.)

5. Type **500**, or another numeric code, and press Enter.

Visual Basic encrypts the text by using the Xor operator and stores it on disk as a series of numbers. You won't see any change on your screen, but rest assured that the program created an encrypted file on disk. (You can verify this with a word processor or text editor.)

6. Delete the text in the text box by selecting it with the mouse and pressing the Del key.

Now you'll restore the encrypted file.

7. On the File menu, click the Open Encrypted File command.

8. Double-click the oldlaws.txt file, type **500** in the encryption code dialog box when it appears, and click OK. (If you specified a different encryption code, enter that instead.)

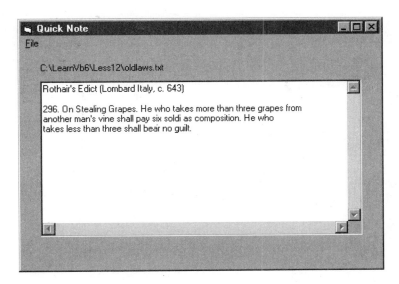

The program opens the file and restores the text by using the Xor operator and the encryption code you specified.

9. On the File menu, click the Exit command to end the program.

### Examining the encryption code

The Xor operator is used in both the mnuOpenItem and the mnuItemSave event procedures. By now, these generic menu processing routines will be quite familiar to you. Specifically, this mnuItemSave event procedure uses the statements at the top of the next page to prompt the user for an encryption code and to encrypt the file based on that code.

```
code = InputBox("Enter Encryption Code", , 1)
If code = "" Then Exit Sub   'if Cancel chosen, exit sub
Form1.MousePointer = 11      'display hourglass
charsInFile% = Len(txtNote.Text) 'find string length
Open CommonDialog1.FileName For Output As #1 'open file
For i% = 1 To charsInFile%   'for each character in file
    letter$ = Mid(txtNote.Text, i%, 1) 'read next char
    'convert to number w/ Asc, then use Xor to encrypt
    Print #1, Asc(letter$) Xor code; 'and save in file
Next i%
Close #1                     'close file when finished
```

In the Print #1 statement, the Xor operator is used to convert each letter in the open text box to a numeric code, which is then saved to disk. (To see how this process is reversed, you can open and review the code for the mnuOpenItem event procedure.) As I mentioned earlier, the look of these encrypted files is no longer textual, but numeric—guaranteed to bewilder even the nosiest snooper. For example, the following illustration shows the encrypted file produced by the preceding encryption routine, displayed in Windows Notepad. (I've enabled Word Wrap so that you can see all of the codes.) Although the file's contents might look like gibberish, you now have the skills to decrypt codes like these. Just be sure not to lose your encryption key!

# 13

# Managing Access Databases

In this lesson, you'll learn how to work with information stored in Microsoft Access databases on your system. You'll learn how to open existing databases by using a data object, how to search for specific items, and how to add and delete database records. Microsoft Visual Basic was specifically designed to create custom interfaces, or *front ends,* for existing databases, so if you'd like to customize or dress up data that you've already created with another application, such as Access, you can get started immediately.

# Working with Databases in Visual Basic

As you learned in Lesson 3, a database is an organized collection of information stored electronically in a file. You can create powerful databases by using a variety of database products, including Access, Microsoft FoxPro, Btrieve, Paradox, and dBASE. You can also use Open Database Connectivity (ODBC) client-server databases, such as Microsoft SQL Server.

If you regularly work with databases—especially the databases listed above—you should consider using Visual Basic as a powerful tool to enhance and display your data. Because Visual Basic implements the same database technology that's included with Access (a database engine called Microsoft Jet), you can create basic custom database applications with just a few dozen lines of program code.

In this section, you'll learn how to use a Visual Basic data object to manage a database named Students.mdb that I created in Access. Students.mdb contains various tables of academic information that would be useful for a teacher who is tracking student coursework or for a school administrator who is scheduling rooms, assigning classes, or building a time schedule. You'll learn how to display several fields of information from this database and how to write program code that performs useful tasks, such as searching for records, adding new records, deleting unwanted records, and backing up files. When you've finished, you'll be able to put these skills to work in your own database projects.

## Creating Customized Database Applications

A *customized database application* is a program that takes the fields and records of a database and displays them in a way that is meaningful to a specific group of users. For example, a public library might create a customized version of its card catalog for a group of scientific researchers. Customized database applications typically present a variety of commands to their users. The commands allow users to use viewing filters; to search for, print, add, and delete records; and to make backup copies of the database. Because of the peculiarities of their design or subsequent evolution, some databases are organized in a way that makes them difficult to use in their original form or database environment. With Visual Basic, you can build a custom database application that displays just the information your users want, and you can supply just the commands they need to process the data.

## Using Bound Controls to Display Database Information

Most objects you create by using the Visual Basic toolbox controls have the built-in ability to display database information. In database terminology, these objects are called *bound controls*. An object is bound to a database when its DataSource property is set to a valid database name and its DataField property is set to a valid table in the database. A *table* is a group of fields and records that you or someone else defined when the database was created. As you learned in Lesson 3, you can link your Visual Basic program to a database by using a data object. After the connection has been established, you can display database information by using objects created with any of the standard controls shown in the following table:

| Control | Description |
| --- | --- |
| ☑ | CheckBox |
| | ComboBox |
| | Image |
| A | Label |
| | ListBox |
| | PictureBox |
| abl | TextBox |

## Using Text Box Objects to Display Data

The following program uses one data object and four text box objects to display four database fields from the Students.mdb database. This program demonstrates how you can create a custom database application to view only the information you want. In this application, the ReadOnly property of the data object is set to True, so the information in the database can be viewed but not changed. To allow users to make changes to the Students.mdb database, you set the ReadOnly property to False by using the Properties window.

---

 **TIP** To keep the original Students.mdb database unchanged, use Microsoft Windows Explorer to make a backup copy of it before you complete the following exercises.

---

## Running the Courses Program

1. Start Visual Basic, and then open the Courses.vbp project in the \LearnVb6\Less13 folder.

   The Courses program loads into the programming environment.

*View Object button*

2. If the form isn't visible, click the Courses form in the Project window, and then click the View Object button.

   The Courses form appears, as shown in the illustration at the top of the next page.

   The form contains information about the program, artwork, a data object, several labels and text boxes, and a command button. The property settings listed on the next page have been made for the data object and the text box objects, which are the objects involved with data transfer. To examine the property settings for the other objects, use the Properties window.

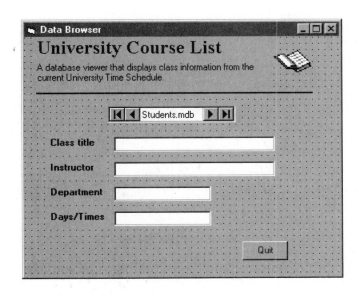

| Object | Property | Setting |
|--------|----------|---------|
| datStudent | Caption | "Students.mdb" |
| | Connect | Access |
| | DatabaseName | "c:\learnvb6\less03\students.mdb" |
| | Name | datStudent |
| | ReadOnly | True |
| | RecordsetType | 0 – Table |
| | RecordSource | Classes |
| txtTitle | DataField | ClassName |
| | DataSource | datStudent |
| | Name | txtTitle |
| | Text | (Empty) |
| txtProf | DataField | Prof |
| | DataSource | datStudent |
| | Name | txtProf |
| | Text | (Empty) |
| txtDept | DataField | Department |
| | DataSource | datStudent |
| | Name | txtDept |
| | Text | (Empty) |
| txtTime | DataField | DaysAndTimes |
| | DataSource | datStudent |
| | Name | txtTime |
| | Text | (Empty) |

The data object has its RecordSource property set to Classes and its DatabaseName property set to "c:\learnvb6\less03\students.mdb" (the same file you first used in Lesson 3). The four text boxes have the same DataSource property (datStudent), but different field settings for the DataField property. These settings establish the basic link between the school database on disk, the data object in the program, and the individual text fields on the form. The other properties fine-tune these basic settings.

*Start button*

3. Click the Start button on the toolbar.

The Courses program starts, and the first record of the Classes table in the Students.mdb database appears on the form.

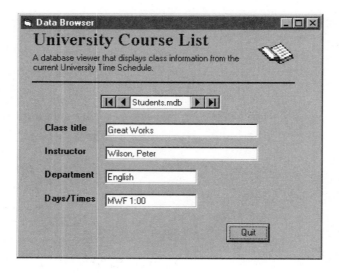

4. Click the inside right arrow on the data control to view the second record in the Classes table.

The record for the course *Relational Database Design* appears on the form. Each time you scroll in the database, all four text boxes are updated.

5. Click the outside right arrow to view the last record in the Classes table.

The record for the psychology course *Deviant Behavior* appears.

6. Click the Quit button to stop the program.

> The Courses program ends.

This program contains only one line of program code (the End statement), but it still gives you quite a bit of information. The nice thing about it is that it displays only the database fields *you* want to see. By using a data object and several data-bound text boxes, you can create an effective window into your data.

# Using a Recordset Object

In the Courses program, you used a data property named RecordsetType to identify your database information as a table. In Visual Basic, a *Recordset* is an object representing the part of the database you're working with in the program.

The Recordset object includes special properties and methods that let you search for, sort, add, and delete records. In the following exercise, you'll use a Recordset object to search for course titles in the Students.mdb database and display them.

## Searching for Data in Students.mdb

Before you modify the program, you'll save it under a new name to protect the original.

1. On the File menu, click the Save Courses.frm As command. Save the Courses form in the \LearnVb6\Less13 folder as **MyFindRec.frm**.

2. On the File menu, click the Save Project As command. Save the project as **MyFindRec.vbp**.

3. Click the CommandButton control, and then create a command button object on the lower-left side of the form.

*CommandButton control*

4. Set the following properties for the command button object:

| Object | Property | Setting |
|--------|----------|---------|
| Command1 | Caption | "Find" |
|  | Name | cmdFind |

5. Double-click the Find command button to open the cmdFind_Click event procedure in the Code window.

6. Type the following program statements in the event procedure:

```
prompt$ = "Enter the full (complete) course title."
'get string to be used in the ClassName field search
SearchStr$ = InputBox(prompt$, "Course Search")
datStudent.Recordset.Index = "ClassName"   'use ClassName
datStudent.Recordset.Seek "=", SearchStr$  'and search
If datStudent.Recordset.NoMatch Then        'if no match
    datStudent.Recordset.MoveFirst          'go to first record
End If
```

This event procedure displays a search dialog box to get a course name (SearchStr$) from the user. Next it uses the Seek method to search the database ClassName field from beginning to end until it finds a match or reaches the end of the list. If no match is found, Visual Basic displays a message, and the first record in the Recordset appears in the first text box. The Recordset properties and methods shown below are used in the event procedure.

| Recordset property or method | Description |
| --- | --- |
| Index | A property used to define the database field that will be used for the search and for future sorting. |
| Seek | A method used to search for the record. In addition to =, the relational operators >=, >, <=, and < can be used to compare the search string to text in the database. |
| NoMatch | A property set to True if no match is found in the search. |
| MoveFirst | A method that makes the first record in the Recordset the current record. |

*Save Project button*

7. Close the Code window and click the Save Project button to save your changes to disk.

Now you'll run the program.

## Running the MyFindRec Program

*Start button*

1. Click the Start button on the toolbar.

---

 **IP** The complete FindRec program is available in the \LearnVb6\Less13 folder.

---

Information from the Classes table in the Students.mdb database appears in the text boxes, as before.

2. Click the Find button.

   The Course Search dialog box appears, as shown here:

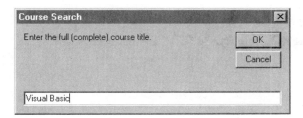

3. Type **Visual Basic** in the dialog box, and then press Enter.

   The cmdFind_Click event procedure searches the ClassName field of the database and stops on the record shown here:

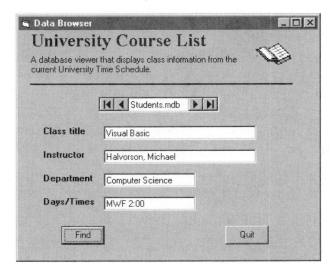

4. Click the Find button again, type **Norwegian 101**, and press Enter.

   The event procedure doesn't find a course named *Norwegian 101,* so the following dialog box appears:

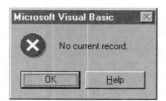

5. Click OK to close the dialog box.

   The program uses the MoveFirst method to display the first record in the table. However, take a close look at this record—does it look like the one you saw when the program first ran? Actually, it's not. A side effect of setting the Index property as shown for the search operation is that it changes the field to be sorted in the table. Originally, this program used the default CourseID field to sort records in the table. CourseID is an internal field in the Students database that tracks the order in which records were created. However, by changing the Index field to ClassName, we directed the Data object to use the ClassName field as the key for the alphabetical sort.

   In this demonstration program, the particular order in which records are listed isn't significant. However, if you find that a consistent sorting order is important to you, be sure to use the Index property consistently in your code.

6. Click the Quit button to end the program.

   The program stops, and the programming environment returns.

# Adding Records to the Students.mdb Database

To add a new record to a database, you set the data object's ReadOnly property to False in design mode, and then you use the AddNew method in an event procedure to open a new record in the database. When the blank record appears on the form, the user fills in the necessary fields and, when finished, moves to a different record in the database. The easiest way for the user to move to a different record is to click one of the buttons on the data object. When the user moves to a different record, the new record is inserted into the database in alphabetical order.

The following exercise demonstrates how the ReadOnly property and the AddNew method can be used to insert new records in a database. An InputBox function gives the user some visual feedback during the process.

## Letting Users Add Records to the Database

Before you modify the program, you'll save it under a new name to protect the original.

1. On the File menu, click the Save MyFindRec.frm As command. Save the MyFindRec form as **MyAddRec.frm**. Use the Save Project As command to save the project as **MyAddRec.vbp**.

2. Click the datStudent object (the data object) on the form, and then open the Properties window.

3. Set the datStudent object's ReadOnly property to False.

   The ReadOnly property determines how the Students.mdb database will be opened. Setting this property to False lets the user make changes to the database and insert new records.

*CommandButton control*

4. Click the CommandButton control, and then create a command button object to the right of the Find button on the form.

5. Set the following properties for the command button object:

| Object | Property | Setting |
|--------|----------|---------|
| Command1 | Caption | "Add" |
| | Name | cmdAdd |

Your form should look similar to the following illustration:

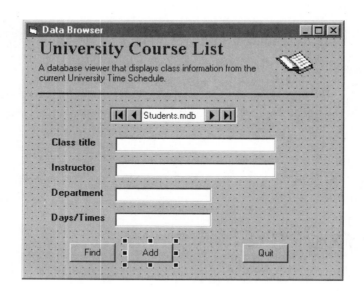

6. Double-click the Add button to open the cmdAdd_Click event procedure in the Code window.

7. Type the following program statements in the event procedure:

```
prompt$ = "Enter the new record, and then click" & _
    "the left arrow button."
reply = MsgBox(prompt$, vbOKCancel, "Add Record")
If reply = vbOK Then                'if the user clicks OK
    txtTitle.SetFocus               'move cursor to Title box
    datStudent.Recordset.AddNew     'and get new record
End If
```

The procedure first displays a dialog box containing data entry instructions for the user. The MsgBox function uses the vbOKCancel argument (a numeric constant defined by Visual Basic) to display a dialog box that has OK and Cancel buttons. If the user clicks OK, the AddNew method creates a new record. If the user clicks Cancel, the operation is skipped. The event procedure also uses the SetFocus method to place the cursor in the Title text box. The SetFocus method can be used to activate any object that can receive the focus.

*Save Project
button*

8. Close the Code window, and then click the Save Project button on the toolbar to save your changes.

Now you'll use the Add button to add a record to the database.

## Running the MyAddRec Program

*Start button*

1. Click the Start button on the toolbar.

---

 **IP** The complete AddRec program is available in the \LearnVb6\Less13 folder.

---

Information from the Titles table in the Students.mdb database appears in the text boxes.

2. Click the Add button.

The Add Record dialog box appears, as shown in the following illustration:

3. Click the OK button.

A new, blank record appears on the form. Enter the information shown in the following illustration for the new record; press Tab to move between fields. (See the illustration at the top of the next page.)

4. When you've finished entering the fictitious record, click the outside-left arrow button on the data object.

The record for a new Basic Chemistry course is inserted in the database as the last record. The program then displays the first record in the database (if you clicked the outside-left arrow on the data object).

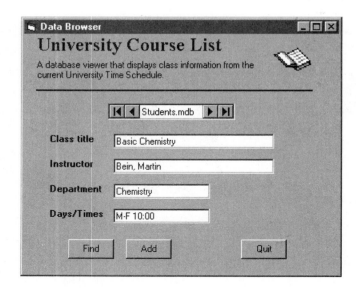

5. Click the Find button, type **Basic Chemistry**, and press Enter.

   The record for Basic Chemistry appears on the form. After the search, the record is first in the alphabetically sorted course list.

6. Click the Quit button to end the program.

   The program stops, and the programming environment returns. You can use the Add button to add any number of records to the Students.mdb database.

# Deleting Records from the Students.mdb Database

To delete a record from a database, you display the record you want to delete and then use the Delete method with the Recordset object to remove the record. Before you open the database in the program, you must set the data object's ReadOnly property to False. (You did this earlier when you used the AddNew method to add a record.) After deleting the record, your code should display another record in the database, because the data object doesn't do this automatically. Usually, the best technique is to use the MoveNext method to display the next record in the database.

The following exercise shows how you can use Visual Basic to delete records from the Students.mdb database. Pay particular attention to the use of the MsgBox function in the program. Because the data object doesn't provide an "undo" feature, it's important that the program verify the user's intentions before it permanently deletes a record from the database.

---

**MPORTANT** The Delete method permanently deletes a record from the database. Don't give your users access to this method unless you want them to be able to delete records.

---

## Letting Users Delete Records from the Database

Before you modify the MyAddRec program, you'll save it under a new name to protect the original.

1. On the File menu, click the Save MyAddRec.frm As command. Save the MyAddRec form as **MyDelRec.frm**. Use the Save Project As command to save the project as **MyDelRec.vbp**.

2. Click the datStudent object (the data object) on the form, and then open the Properties window.

3. Verify that the datStudent object's ReadOnly property is set to False.

*CommandButton control*

4. Click the CommandButton control, and then create a command button object to the right of the Add button on the form.

5. Set the following properties for the command button object:

| Object | Property | Setting |
|--------|----------|---------|
| Command1 | Caption | "Delete" |
|  | Name | cmdDelete |

Your form should look like the illustration shown at the top of the next page.

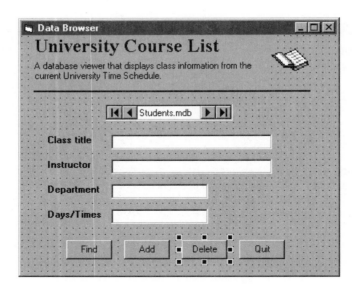

6. Double-click the Delete command button to open the cmdDelete_Click event procedure in the Code window.

7. Type the following program statements in the event procedure:

```
prompt$ = "Do you really want to delete this course?"
reply = MsgBox(prompt$, vbOKCancel, "Delete Record")
If reply = vbOK Then              'if the user clicks OK
    datStudent.Recordset.Delete   'delete current record
    datStudent.Recordset.MoveNext 'move to next record
End If
```

---

 **ARNING**   The Delete method deletes a record from the database!

---

This procedure first displays a dialog box asking whether the user wants to delete the current record. Again, the MsgBox function is used with the vbOKCancel argument to let the user back out of the delete operation if he or she decides not to go through with it. If the user clicks OK, the Delete method deletes the current record, and the MoveNext method displays the next record. If the user clicks Cancel, the delete operation is skipped.

*Save Project
button*

8. Close the Code window, and then click the Save Project button to save your changes.

Now you'll use the Delete button to delete the record for the new Chemistry course from the database.

## Running the MyDelRec Program

*Start button*

1. Click the Start button on the toolbar.

---

**IP** The complete DelRec program is available in the \LearnVb6\Less13 folder.

---

Information from the Classes table in the Students.mdb database appears in the text boxes.

2. Use the Find button to display the record for the course entitled Basic Chemistry.

The record you added in the last exercise appears on the form.

---

**MPORTANT** The following steps will delete this record permanently from the Students.mdb database.

---

3. Click the Delete button on the form.

The Delete Record dialog box appears, as shown here:

4. Click the OK button to delete the record.

The record for Basic Chemistry is deleted from the database.

5. Click the Quit button to end the program.

You've finished working with the data object in this lesson. To learn more about writing database applications, read Lessons 18 and 19.

# Making a Backup Copy of a File

If you're like most people, the information you keep in databases is very important, and you'd be in a bind if something happened to it. For this reason, you should always make a backup copy of each database you use before making changes to it. If anything goes wrong when you're working with the copy, you can simply replace the copy with the original database. Your backup routine might include using a commercial backup program, Windows Explorer, or a special backup feature of your own in your database program. As an additional safeguard, you can create a backup copy of one or more files from within a Visual Basic program by using the FileCopy statement. FileCopy makes a separate copy of the file (as Windows Explorer's Edit Copy command does) when you use the statement with the following syntax:

```
FileCopy sourcepath destinationpath
```

where *sourcepath* is the pathname of the file you want to copy and *destinationpath* is the pathname of the file you want to create.

---

 **IP**   FileCopy does not work if the file specified by *sourcepath* is currently open.

---

In the following exercise, you'll add a backup feature to the MyDelRec program by placing a FileCopy statement in the Form_Load event procedure.

## Using FileCopy to Make a Backup of Students.mdb

First you'll save the MyDelRec program under a new name to protect the original. If MyDelRec isn't open, load DelRec.vbp from disk and display its form.

1. On the File menu, click the Save MyDelRec.frm As command. Save the MyDelRec form as **MyBackup.frm**. Use the Save Project As command to save the project as **MyBackup.vbp**.

2. If the form isn't already visible, select the form in the Project window and click the View Object button.

3. Double-click the form (not an object) to open the Form_Load event procedure in the Code window.

Placing the FileCopy statement in the startup procedure gets the user to back up the database before making any changes to it.

4. Type these program statements in the Form_Load event procedure:

```
prompt$ = _
    "Would you like to create a backup copy of the database?"
reply = MsgBox(prompt$, vbOKCancel, datStudent.DatabaseName)
If reply = vbOK Then   'copy the database if the user clicks OK
    FileNm$ = InputBox$ _
        ("Enter the pathname for the backup copy.")
    If FileNm$ <> "" Then _
        FileCopy datStudent.DatabaseName, FileNm$
End If
```

This routine displays a message box when the program starts, asking the user if he or she would like to make a backup copy of the database. The MsgBox function is used with the vbOKCancel argument to give the user a chance to cancel. This time the DatabaseName property is also used in the MsgBox function to display the name of the database in the dialog box title bar. If the user clicks OK, another message box gets the pathname of the backup file from the user. When the user clicks OK again, the FileCopy statement copies the file.

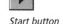

*Save Project button*

5. Close the Code window, and then click the Save Project button to save your changes.

Now you'll run the program to see how the backup feature works.

## Running the MyBackup Program

*Start button*

1. Click the Start button on the toolbar.

>  **IP**  The complete Backup program is available in the \LearnVb6\Less13 folder.

The dialog box shown at the top of the next page appears on the screen, asking whether you want to make a backup copy of the database.

2. Click OK to make a backup copy.

   A dialog box appears asking for the pathname of your backup file.

3. Type **c:\learnvb6\less13\mystudents.mdb,** and then click OK.

   Visual Basic copies the Students.mdb database to the Lesson 13 folder and gives it the name MyStudents.mdb. Now, if you make any mistakes in the Students.mdb file, you have a backup.

4. Click the Quit button to end the program.

---

### If You Want to Boost Your Productivity

Take a few minutes to explore the BookInfo utility (bookinfo.vbp) in the \LearnVb6\Extras folder on your hard disk. I wrote this program to give you a little more practice with the database concepts in this lesson. The application is an interface for the Biblio.mdb database that is supplied with the Visual Basic Working Model. If you selected the default installation, Visual Basic Setup put Biblio.mdb in the \Program Files\Microsoft Visual Studio\Vb98 folder. The Name property of the Data control in the BookInfo utility automatically looks in the Vb98 folder for the Biblio.mdb database. If you chose a non-standard location for your Visual Basic files, adjust the Name property of the Data object to the correct path before you run the program.

Biblio.mdb contains information about database programming books and techniques available from a variety of publishers—I sometimes use it to find a special book I need on new terms and concepts or to practice my database programming. (The database contains over 10,000 records.) The utility displays a selection of fields and records from the database; you can use the program now to search for your favorite books or expand it to practice working with databases.

---

# Connecting to Microsoft Office

In Lesson 3 you learned how to use the OLE control to launch Microsoft Windows-based applications in your programs. In this lesson, you'll learn how to control Office applications programmatically with an ActiveX technology known as Automation—the glue that binds Microsoft Visual Basic to Microsoft Office. You'll start by using the Visual Basic Object Browser to examine the application objects in Office applications, and then you'll use Automation to incorporate features of Microsoft Word, Microsoft Excel, and Microsoft Outlook into your projects.

# Programming Application Objects by Using Automation

Automation is a technology that allows Visual Basic programmers to rapidly incorporate the functionality of certain Windows-based applications into their projects. The applications that support Automation make available, or *expose,* their application features as a collection of objects with associated properties and methods. The Windows-based applications that expose their objects are called *object* or *server* applications, and the programs that use the objects are called *controlling* or *client* applications. Currently, the following Microsoft applications can be used as either object or controlling applications:

- Microsoft Visual Basic

- Microsoft Word 2000, Microsoft Word 97

- Microsoft Excel 2000, Microsoft Excel 97, Microsoft Excel 95, Microsoft Excel 5.0

- Microsoft PowerPoint 2000, Microsoft PowerPoint 97

- Microsoft Project 97, Microsoft Project 95

- Microsoft Outlook 2000, Microsoft Outlook 98, Microsoft Outlook 97

---

 **IP**  Microsoft is currently licensing the Visual Basic for Applications programming language, so you'll soon find other applications for Windows that support object Automation and Visual Basic programming techniques.

---

## Using Automation in Visual Basic

In Visual Basic, you can create both object and controlling applications that support Automation. Creating object applications that expose their functionality requires that you have Visual Basic Professional Edition or Enterprise Edition and is beyond the scope of this lesson. Creating controlling applications that use the features of object applications is a straightforward process in all editions of Visual Basic, including the Visual Basic Working Model.

**IP** The main applications in Office 2000 and Office 97 (Excel, Word, Microsoft Access, PowerPoint, and Outlook) are all capable of exposing their functionality through Automation. Because the features and objects provided by each of these applications are unique, you'll need to review the product documentation or online Help for each program before you move beyond the examples I show you here. If you have Office installed on your system now, the Visual Basic Object Browser will let you explore the objects, properties, and methods available.

In the next few sections, you'll learn how to write Visual Basic programs that work with each of the applications in Microsoft Office. First, you'll perform an especially useful task—you'll use a Word object to check the spelling in a text box. As you work through the exercises, note that the objects, properties, and methods exposed by an object application typically correspond to the menu commands and dialog box options provided by the object application.

## The Visual Basic Object Browser

The Visual Basic Object Browser is a viewing utility that has two uses. First, it can display the objects, properties, and methods used by the program you're working on in the Visual Basic programming environment. Second, the Object Browser can display the objects, properties, and methods available to you from object applications installed on your system. In the following exercise, you'll use the Object Browser to view the Automation objects exposed by Word.

 **IP** The illustrations show the Word 9.0 Object Library included in Word 2000. If you don't have a version of Word, use the Object Browser to examine other application objects on your system.

### Using the Object Browser to view Word objects

1. On the File menu, click the New Project command, and then click OK.

   A new form appears. You'll add a reference to the Word Object Library to this new project.

2. On the Project menu, click the References command.

The References dialog box appears. In the References dialog box, you can include in your project references to any object libraries that are available on your system. However, Visual Basic adds references to Automation object libraries only if you ask it to.

3. Select the check box by the reference titled Microsoft Word 9.0 Object Library. (Or a different object library, if you don't have this one.)

   You might have to scroll through a long list to find the library. (The references are listed in alphabetical order.) Your screen should look like the following:

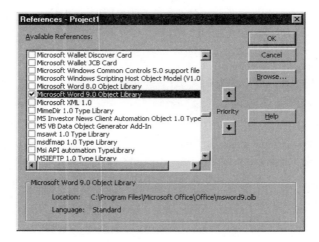

4. Click OK to close the dialog box and add the reference to your project.

   Now you're ready to use the Object Browser.

5. On the View menu, click the Object Browser command.

   The Object Browser appears, as shown in the illustration on the next page.

   The Object Browser contains a Project/Library drop-down list box that you can use to display the object libraries included in your project. It also contains a Search Text drop-down list box for creating keyword searches and a Classes list box that you can use to select a particular object to examine. When you select an object in the Classes list box, the methods, properties, and events featured in the object are listed in the Members list box.

6. Click the Down arrow to open the Project/Library drop-down list box, and then click the Word object library.

   A list of the Automation objects exposed by Word fills the Classes list box.

7. Scroll down the list in the Classes list box, and then click the Application object.

   A list of the methods and properties associated with the Application object appears in the Members list box. These are the commands Word provides for manipulating information in worksheets.

8. Click the CheckSpelling method in the Members list box.

   The syntax for the CheckSpelling method appears at the bottom of the Object Browser. This method invokes Word's spelling checker, a feature available to you from within Visual Basic. The method syntax shows you the options available if you want to customize the command. Your screen should look like the illustration shown at the top of the next page.

9. Click the question mark button at the top of the Object Browser.

If you installed the Visual Basic for Applications Help file when you ran the Office 2000 Setup program, a Help file for the CheckSpelling method will open in the programming environment. Maximize the window, so it looks like the one below:

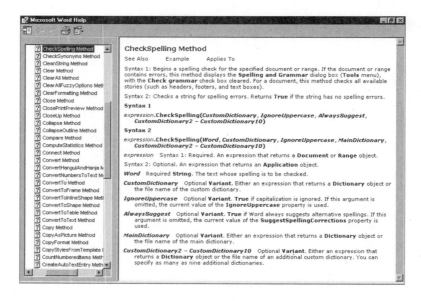

This Help file gives you detailed information about how to use the properties and methods in the Word object library. (If the file doesn't appear, you can run the Office Setup program again to copy it to your system. In certain Office 2000 installations, it may also be an "install on first use" feature, which means you'll need to locate your Office 2000 CDs.) Many object applications provide this information along with their object libraries so that Automation programmers can take full advantage of the programmable features the application provides. Using the object library Help system is a great way to learn more about Automation programming.

10. Review the article on the CheckSpelling method, and then close the Help file.

11. Click the Close button in the Object Browser.

You've finished exploring Automation objects for the time being. Now it's time to put the Word CheckSpelling method to work.

## Automating Word from Visual Basic

To use the Word CheckSpelling method in a Visual Basic program, you need to complete the following programming steps. Because the techniques apply to most application objects, you'll be able to use these guidelines to incorporate the functionality of most applications that support Automation into your programs.

---

 IP    Word's Visual Basic language is so useful and powerful that I wrote a
*Step by Step* book describing its features and capabilities with Chris Kinata,
a respected Word expert. If you're interested in learning more after reading this book, I recommend that you consult *Microsoft Word 97/Visual Basic Step by Step* (Microsoft Press, 1997), by Michael Halvorson and Chris Kinata.

---

■ **Step 1**  Add references to the necessary object libraries to your project by using the References command.

■ **Step 2**  Write your Visual Basic program. In the event procedure in which you plan to use Automation, create an object variable by using the Dim statement and then load an Automation object into the object variable by using the CreateObject function:

```
Dim X As Object                    'use X as variable name
Set X = CreateObject("Word.Application")
```

- **Step 3** Use the methods and properties of the Automation object in the event procedure, consulting the Help files in the Object Browser or the object application documentation for the proper syntax:

```
X.Visible = False              'hide Word
X.Documents.Add                'open a new document
X.Selection.Text = Text1.Text  'copy text box to document
X.ActiveDocument.CheckSpelling 'run spell check
Text1.Text = X.Selection.Text  'copy results back
```

- **Step 4** When you've finished using the object application, quit the application and release the object variable to conserve memory:

```
X.Quit             'quit Word
Set X = Nothing    'release object variable
```

In the following exercise, you'll create an application that uses the Word spelling checker to verify the spelling of text in a Visual Basic text box. The program will be built entirely in Visual Basic, using the functionality of Word remotely through Automation.

---

 **IP** The following steps require that you have Word 2000 or Word 97 installed on your system.

---

## Creating a Personal Spelling Checker

1. On the Project menu, click the References command. If you have Word 2000 on your system, verify that the reference to Microsoft Word 9.0 Object Library has a check mark next to it, and then click OK. If you have Word 97, place a check mark next to the Microsoft Word 8.0 Object Library reference instead.

   The Word object libraries give you access to the objects, methods, and properties exposed by the Word object application. This is the object library reference you added earlier in this lesson.

**IP** Object library references must be added to each new project by using the References command.

Now you'll create the form for the spelling checker and add the program code.

2. Resize the form until it appears as a medium-size rectangular window.

*Label control*

3. Use the Label control to create a long label across the top of the form.

The label will contain the instructions for the program.

*TextBox control*

4. Use the TextBox control to create a wide text box, four lines deep, in the middle of the form.

The text box will hold the text that the user wants to check.

*CommandButton control*

5. Use the CommandButton control to add two command buttons below the text box object.

The first command button will be used to start Word and to use the CheckSpelling method to check the spelling of the text in the text box. The second command button will be used to exit the program.

6. Set the following properties for the objects in the program:

| Object | Property | Setting |
|--------|----------|---------|
| Form1 | Caption | "Personal Spelling Checker" |
| Label1 | Caption | "Enter one or more words in the text box, and then click Check Spelling." |
| Text1 | MultiLine | True |
| | ScrollBars | 2 – Vertical |
| | Text | (Empty) |
| Command1 | Caption | "Check Spelling" |
| Command2 | Caption | "Done" |

After you set the properties, your form should look like this:

7. Double-click the Check Spelling command button to open the Command1_Click event procedure. Type the code as shown below in the event procedure.

```
Dim X As Object                    'create Word object variable
Set X = CreateObject("Word.Application")
X.Visible = False                  'hide Word
X.Documents.Add                    'open a new document
X.Selection.Text = Text1.Text      'copy text box to document
X.ActiveDocument.CheckSpelling     'run spell check
Text1.Text = X.Selection.Text      'copy results back
X.ActiveDocument.Close  SaveChanges:=wdDoNotSaveChanges
X.Quit                             'quit Word
Set X = Nothing                    'release object variable
```

These statements create a Word Automation object in the event procedure, start Word, set some of the Word object's properties, call some of the Word object's methods, and then release the memory used by the object. Word starts automatically when the first reference to the object variable is made. The Word Selection's Text property is then used to copy the contents of the text box to a Word document.

When the CheckSpelling method is executed, Word runs the spelling checker and checks the contents of the text for spelling errors. The Word Spelling And Grammar dialog box appears if a spelling mistake is found, and it gives the user a chance to make a correction. Word checks each of the words in the text box, even if the text box contains more than one line of text. When the check is finished, the corrected words are copied back into the Visual Basic text box and the Word application is closed. The Set statement at the end of the Command 1_Click event procedure releases the object variable's memory.

8. Close the Command1_Click event procedure, and then double-click the Done command button.

9. Type **End** in the event procedure, and then close the Code window.

You've finished building the Personal Spelling Checker program.

10. Use the Save Form1 As command to save the form to disk under the name **MyUseWord.frm**. Use the Save Project As command to save the project to disk under the name **MyUseWord.vbp**. (Use the \LearnVb6\Less14 folder for both files.)

Now you'll run the program to see how Automation works.

## Running the MyUseWord Program

1. Click the Start button on the toolbar.

 **IP**   The complete UseWord program is located on disk in the \LearnVb6 \Less14 folder.

The program runs in the programming environment, as shown in the following illustration:

 **OTE**   If you load and run this program on a system with Word 97 (and not Word 2000), you may see an error message suggesting that your object library is missing. Use the References command on the Project menu to change the object library from Word 9.0 to Word 8.0.

2. Type **workingg with objectss** in the text box.

   Be sure to intentionally misspell the words *working* and *objects*.

3. Click the Check Spelling button.

   Visual Basic creates an Automation object and starts Word. After a moment, the Word Spelling dialog box appears, identifying the first word that's not in its dictionary. Your screen should look like this:

4. Click Change to fix the first mistake. When Word highlights the second spelling error, click Change to fix it. (The Change button corrects a spelling mistake if Word has highlighted a suitable correction in the list box.)

   The Spelling dialog box closes, and after a moment the words in the text box are corrected.

5. Click Done to close the program.

Congratulations! Through Automation, you just used a handy feature of Word to fix your typing mistakes. Now you'll try running two more utilities that demonstrate Excel and Outlook objects.

# Automating Excel from Visual Basic

Excel contains several complex computation and data analysis tools that can powerfully enhance your Visual Basic programs. The following routine uses Excel's recursive Pmt function to calculate mortgage payments from the rate, term, and principal information you specify in a series of

Visual Basic text boxes. The event procedure that calls Excel to calculate the mortgage payment is shown here:

```
Private Sub Command1_Click()
Dim xl As Object    'create object for Excel
Dim loanpmt         'declare return value
                    'if all fields contain values
If Text1.Text <> "" And Text2.Text <> "" _
  And Text3.Text <> "" Then  'create object and call Pmt
    Set xl = CreateObject("Excel.Application")
    loanpmt = xl.WorksheetFunction.Pmt _
        (Text1.Text / 12, Text2.Text, Text3.Text)
    MsgBox "The monthly payment is " & _
        Format(Abs(loanpmt), "$#.##"), , "Mortgage"
    xl.quit
    Set xl = Nothing
Else
    MsgBox "All fields required", , "Mortgage"
End If
End Sub
```

First, this routine creates an object variable named xl and assigns it the Excel.Sheet object. Then the routine calls the Pmt function through Excel's WorksheetFunction object and converts the mortgage payment returned to a positive number with the Abs (absolute value) function. In Excel, loan payments are typically displayed as negative numbers (debits), but on a Visual Basic form, payments usually look best as positive values. If one of the required arguments for the Pmt function is missing, the procedure displays the message "All fields required."

---

 **IP** To complete the following steps, you'll need Excel 2000 installed on your computer, and your project will need a reference to the Excel 9.0 Object Library. Although earlier versions of Excel also support Automation, the code required to use the Excel object library has changed slightly, so you should test your code carefully with earlier versions. (Generally, I find it difficult to write one version of a program that effectively supports multiple versions of an application.) Use the online Help, if necessary.

---

## Running the Mortgage Program

You'll run the program now to see how Excel Automation works.

1. Open the Mortgage.vbp project in the \LearnVb6\Less14 folder on your hard disk.

2. From the Run menu, click the Start command.

   The mortgage payment calculator appears with a few default values specified.

3. Type **100000** in the Principal text box.

   Your form should look like the following:

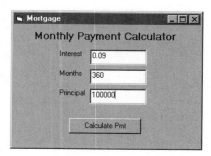

4. Click the Calculate Pmt button.

   The program uses Excel to calculate the mortgage payment for a $100,000 loan at 9% interest over 360 months (30 years). As shown in the following illustration, a result of $804.62 appears in a message box on the screen. (Remember that if this were a home mortgage payment, this amount would represent principal and interest only, not taxes, insurance, or other items that are typically included!)

5. Click the Close button, and then make a few more mortgage payment calculations using different values.

6. When you're finished, click the Close button on the form's title bar.

   You can also take a closer look at the program code in the Code window, if you like.

**TIP** If you're using this program to automate a localized version of Excel that uses a decimal separator other than the period, you should replace the decimal separator used in the Mortgage source code with the one employed in your locale. For example, the Dutch version of Excel uses a comma to separate decimal and integer values.

# Automating Microsoft Outlook from Visual Basic

Microsoft Outlook is the application in Microsoft Office that manages email, appointments, contact information, and other tasks related to scheduling and communicating in the workplace. I use Outlook as my primary email program, so it runs constantly on my Windows taskbar. Recently, I've found it useful to customize some of my Visual Basic programs so that they can send email messages to other people through the Outlook application. You might find this technique useful if you'd like to send data—the result of complex computations, status reports, database information, or simply a note that says "Happy Birthday" on a particular date each year—automatically to others. The nice thing about sending email messages with Outlook is that you can customize the To, Cc, Subject, and Message fields with just a few lines of program code, and you can also include one or more file attachments!

In the following exercise, you'll use the SendMail program to send an email message from a Visual Basic application by using Outlook. Before you run the program, you'll need to edit the code in the Command1_Click event procedure (shown on the following page) to use email names that fit your particular situation. Don't use the ones shown, because, with one exception, they're not real—you'll probably get an error back from your email service if you try them. (The exception is my email name, which I've included so you can send me a test message if you like. If I'm not on vacation when it arrives, I'll send you a response!)

```
Private Sub Command1_Click()
'This procedure uses Automation to place a test message in
'the Microsoft Outlook outbox. (If you are online and
'Outlook is open, Outlook will also send the message to
'your email service.) The Outlook program is required, and
```

```
'you'll find that the send operation is quicker and more
'memory efficient if Outlook is already running.

Dim out As Object           'create object variable
'assign Outlook.Application to object variable
Set out = CreateObject("Outlook.Application")

With out.CreateItem(olMailItem) 'using the Outlook object
    'insert recipients one at a time with the Add method
    '(these names are fictitious--replace with your own)
    .Recipients.Add "maria@384qn.com" 'To: field
    .Recipients.Add "casey@384qn.com" 'To: field
    'to place users in the CC: field, specify olCC type
    .Recipients.Add("mike_halvorson@msn.com").Type = olCC
    .Subject = "LVB Test Message"  'include subject field
    .Body = Text1.Text  'copy message text from text box
    'insert attachments one at a time with the Add method
    .Attachments.Add "c:\learnvb6\less14\smile.bmp"
    'finally, copy message to Outlook outbox with Send
    .Send
End With

End Sub
```

You'll run the program now to see how Outlook Automation works.

---

**IP** The With statement, introduced here for the first time, is a shorthand notation that allows you to use the methods and properties associated with an object without writing out the entire object notation every time you use it. Between With and End With statements, each method or property name that is preceded by a period (.) is considered a member of the original object listed after the With keyword. I'm using it here to save space and improve readability.

---

**OTE** To complete the following steps, you'll need Outlook 2000, Outlook 98, or Outlook 97 installed on your computer. The SendMail project also includes a reference to the Outlook 9.0 Object Library. (Change this to Outlook 8.0 Object Library if you're using Outlook 97 or to Outlook 98 Object Library if you're using Outlook 98.) In addition, note that I've designed the following exercise for "stand-alone" Outlook users who send and receive email by connecting to the Internet via a dial-up connection, not those who use Outlook in a workgroup setting. (A few commands are slightly different for workgroup users who send email through a corporate network.)

---

## Running the SendMail Program

1. Open the SendMail.vbp project in the \LearnVb6\Less14 folder on your hard disk.

2. Open the Code window and display the Command1_Click event procedure.

3. Change the three "dummy" email names used (maria@384qn.com, casey@384qn.com, and mike_halvorson@msn.com) to real names.

   If you don't want to use multiple email names, simply type a ' (comment) symbol before the lines you don't want to use now. (I included multiple lines so that you could see how items were added to the Recipients collections with the Add method.) However, at least one name in the To field is required for all Outlook mail messages.

4. Use the Windows Start menu to start Microsoft Outlook if it's not already running.

   You'll want to verify later that Visual Basic puts the email message in Outlook's Outbox folder.

*Start button*

5. From the Run menu, click the Start command to run the SendMail program.

   The simple user interface for the program appears:

Type your own email message content here.

6. Type a short (or long!) message in the text box.

   This text will be sent as the body of your email message. You could also assign this information inside your program. (No user interface is required to send mail from your Visual Basic program.)

7. Now click the Send Test message button to send your message.

   Visual Basic uses Automation to create a mail message in the Outlook Outbox folder. The message will remain in Outlook's Outbox folder until you connect to your email service and choose the Check For New Mail command from the Outlook Tools menu. (If you are currently online or connected to a corporate intranet, Outlook will send the message now.) After the message has been sent, Outlook moves the message from the Outbox folder and places a copy in the Sent Items folder so that you have a record of what you've sent.

8. Click the Close button on the SendMail program's title bar to close it.

9. Now restore Outlook and click the Outbox folder to see your message.

   You'll see a pending mail message, as shown in the following illustration:

Test message in Microsoft Outlook

10. Double-click the message in the Outbox.

Outlook opens the message and displays it on the screen. As you can see, Visual Basic created the message exactly as you directed, complete with a smiley face attachment (from the \LearnVb6 \Less14 folder) and all the necessary mail fields.

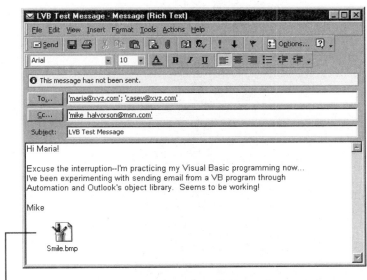

Double-click this bitmap attachment to view it in Microsoft Paint.

11. Click the Send button on the message toolbar to mark the message for mailing in the Outbox.

    Now you can either send or delete the message.

12. If you want to delete the test message, select the message and press Del. To send the message, choose the Check For New Mail command on the Tools menu.

That's it! You've learned the essential skills to automate three useful Office applications. The Object Browser will teach you more about the details of the application objects if you choose to explore Automation on your own. And, more importantly, you've mastered all the fundamental concepts in introductory Visual Basic programming. You are now ready to move on to more advanced topics. Congratulations on a job well done!

# Advanced Techniques

# Word Processing with the Rich Textbox Control

In Parts 1 through 4, you learned the fundamental programming skills that are essential to getting up and running with Microsoft Visual Basic. In Part 5, you'll start exploring more advanced Visual Basic programming concepts, including using "professional" ActiveX controls, working with the Internet, and using advanced database programming techniques.

In this lesson, you'll learn how to install and use the impressive collection of ActiveX controls included with the Visual Basic Working Model. You'll start off with the Rich Textbox control—a powerful tool that helps you add sophisticated word-processing support to your application. Rich Textbox, a more robust version of the standard Textbox control in the Visual Basic toolbox, allows you to include advanced formatting information with your text, streamlines file operations and searches, and stores its information in a sophisticated document format known as RTF (Rich Text Format). As you'll see in the RTFEdit utility I've created, you can quickly build a program with Rich Textbox that looks and operates just like WordPad, the RTF text editor included with Microsoft Windows.

# Exploring Professional ActiveX Controls

When you installed the Visual Basic Working Model software, part of the setup process included copying a large collection of .ocx files called *ActiveX controls* to your \Windows\System folder or System32 folder. The setup process also involved registering these controls in your system registry so that Visual Basic and other applications would know how to load the controls when you needed them. Most of the .ocx files that were installed represent individual ActiveX controls that you can add to the Visual Basic toolbox. However, a few .ocx files represent collections of controls that are organized around a particular theme. For example, the Windows Common Control (mscomctl.ocx) contains nine toolbox controls that you can use to add professional-looking interface options, such as toolbars, progress bars, and status windows, to your application.

The following table lists all the ActiveX controls that are included in the Visual Basic 6 Working Model. In the following lessons, I'll use several of these controls to create interesting and useful utilities.

| ActiveX control | Filename | Description |
| --- | --- | --- |
| ADO data | msadodc.ocx | Provides access to database information through the ActiveX Data Object (ADO) format. |
| Animation | mscomct2.ocx | Creates animation effects by playing .avi files (sound not supported). (In Windows Common Control-2.) |
| DTPicker | mscomct2.ocx | Provides a drop-down calendar for quick entry of dates and times. (In Windows Common Control-2.) |
| Flat scrollbar | mscomct2.ocx | Standard scroll bar functionality with a slick "flat" look. (In Windows Common Control-2.) |
| Flex grid | msflxgrd.ocx | Adds spreadsheet functionality to your application. Especially useful for displaying database information. |

*(continued)*

*continued*

| ActiveX control | Filename | Description |
|---|---|---|
| Hierarchical flex grid | mshflxgd.ocx | Enhanced version of the Flex grid control that can display hierarchical recordsets (recordsets created from several different tables). |
| Image combo | mscomctl.ocx | Similar to the standard combo box control, but with support for images. (In Windows Common Control.) |
| Image list | mscomctl.ocx | Holds a collection of images that can be used by other controls. (In Windows Common Control.) |
| List view | mscomctl.ocx | Displays data in "Windows Explorer" format using icons, small icons, list, or report views. (In Windows Common Control.) |
| MonthView | mscomct2.ocx | Allows the end user to pick dates and contiguous ranges of dates from a graphic representation of a calendar. (In Microsoft Common Control-2.) |
| Progress bar | mscomctl.ocx | Uses blocks to display the progress of an operation graphically. (In Windows Common Control.) |
| Rich text box | richtx32.ocx | Allows the user to type, edit, and format text in Rich Text Format (RTF). |
| Slider | mscomctl.ocx | Provides both an input device with "tick marks" and a method for displaying the progress of an operation. (In Windows Common Control.) |
| Status bar | mscomctl.ocx | Displays a status bar window with up to 16 panels for program information. (In Windows Common Control.) |
| Tab strip | mscomctl.ocx | Similar to the Tabbed dialog control. (In Windows Common Control.) |

*(continued)*

*continued*

| ActiveX control | Filename | Description |
|---|---|---|
| Tabbed dialog | tabctl32.ocx | Presents dialog box information through a series of "tabbed" windows. |
| Toolbar | mscomctl.ocx | Creates a toolbar with individual buttons. (In Windows Common Control.) |
| Tree view | mscomctl.ocx | Displays hierarchical information in nested "trees." (In Windows Common Control.) |
| UpDown | mscomct2.ocx | Displays a pair of arrow buttons that lets the user scroll through a list or set the value of an associated "buddy" control. (In Windows Common Control-2.) |

### Adding ActiveX Controls to the Toolbox

To add one of these ActiveX controls to the toolbox, you follow a three-step process.

1. On the Project menu, click the Components command, and then click the Controls tab.

   When you issue the Components command, Visual Basic will check the system registry and display all the ActiveX controls that are available on your system (not just the controls installed by Visual Basic).

2. Select the check box to the left of the control name you want to add to the toolbox.

3. Click OK to close the Components dialog box and add the ActiveX control.

   Visual Basic displays the control you specified in the toolbox.

## Introducing the Rich Textbox Control

One of the most useful ActiveX controls in the Working Model is the Rich Textbox control, which allows you to add advanced word-processing features to your application. Unlike the simple Textbox control included in the standard toolbox, the Rich Textbox control lets you format text by using a popular encoding standard called RTF. Like HTML (Hypertext Markup Language), RTF adds special formatting codes to your text to convey font information, point size, type style, paragraph style, alignment, and other common formatting options.

## Adding the Rich Textbox Control to the Toolbox

Before you work with the Rich Textbox control, you must add it to the toolbox.

1. On the Project menu, click the Components command, and then click the Controls tab.

   Visual Basic displays the ActiveX controls installed in your system.

2. Scroll down the list of controls until you see the name Microsoft Rich Textbox Control 6.0.

3. Click the check box next to the control name, and then click OK.

   Visual Basic adds the Rich Textbox control to your toolbox. Your toolbox will now look something like this:

 Rich Textbox control

Creating a text box with the Rich Textbox control is similar to creating a text box with the standard Textbox control. You simply click the Rich Textbox control in the toolbox, and then drag on your form to create a text box of the appropriate size for your application. However, the differences between the controls become obvious when you start manipulating the Rich Textbox control's properties and methods. The following demonstration program highlights the important differences.

## Running the RTFEdit Program

To explore the powerful capabilities of the Rich Textbox control, try running the RTFEdit program, a utility I created in Visual Basic that mimics much of the functionality of the Windows WordPad program.

1. Open the RTFEdit.vbp project, located in the C:\LearnVb6\Less15 folder.

   If you are prompted to save the changes in your empty project (which contains a reference to the Rich Textbox control), click No.

*Start button*

2. Click the Start button on the toolbar to run the program.

   The RTFEdit program appears on the screen, as shown in the illustration below:

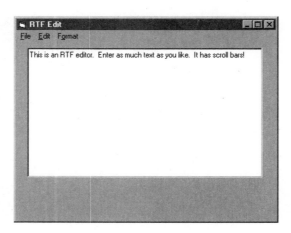

### Using the Format menu commands

First you'll experiment with the text formatting capabilities of the program.

1. Select the first sentence displayed in the text box (*This is an RTF editor.*), and then click the Format menu.

   The formatting commands provided by the RTF editor appear on the menu:

   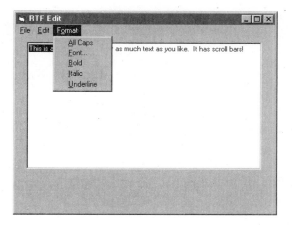

   I created each menu command in the Menu Editor and wrote an event procedure for each command in the Code window.

2. Click the All Caps command on the Format menu.

   The RTF editor changes the selected text to all capital letters.

3. Reselect the first sentence and click the Font command on the Format menu.

   The Font dialog box opens, as shown in the illustration at the top of the next page.

4. Specify a new font, the strikeout style, a larger point size, and a new color, and then click OK.

   The RTF editor formats the text as you requested.

5. Now practice using the Bold, Italic, and Underline commands on the Format menu.

   These commands are toggles—you can repeat them to reverse your formatting choice for the selected text. Just like WordPad, the RTF editor gives you full RTF formatting capabilities!

### Using the Edit menu commands

Now you'll try the four commands on the Edit menu.

1. Select the last sentence in the text box (*It has scroll bars!*).

2. On the Edit menu, click the Cut command.

   The text is copied to the Windows clipboard and removed from the text box.

3. Move the insertion point to the end of the paragraph, press Enter, and then click the Paste command on the Edit menu.

   The text is pasted from the clipboard into the text box.

4. Select the first sentence again (*This is an RTF editor.*), and then choose the Copy command from the Edit menu.

   The RTF editor copies the text with all of its formatting to the clipboard.

5. Press the Home key, and then click the Paste command on the Edit menu to paste the text into the text box.

   Next you'll try searching for text.

6. On the Edit menu, click the Find command.

7. Type the acronym **RTF** in the input box and click OK.

   The RTF editor highlights the first occurrence of the acronym in the text box.

 **TIP** If you select text in the text box before choosing the Find command, the RTF editor searches for the first occurrence of the word in the selection.

## Using the File menu commands

Now you'll try using the file-oriented commands in the RTF editor.

1. On the File menu, click the Save As command.

   The RTF editor displays a Save As dialog box prompting you for the name of the file.

2. Type **sample.rtf** and click Save. (You may also specify a different folder if you wish.)

   The program saves the file in RTF format in the location you specified.

 **IMPORTANT** Be sure to type the .rtf extension or click the Rich Text Format type in the Save As Type list box to register the file as an RTF file in Windows Explorer. If you don't, the file won't appear as an RTF file in the Open dialog box.

3. On the File menu, click the Close command.

   The RTF editor clears the text box. (If you have unsaved changes, you'll be prompted to save them.)

4. On the File menu, click the Open command.

The RTF editor displays an Open dialog box and lists the RTF files in the current folder.

5. Double-click the sample.rtf file to display it again.

6. If you have a printer attached to your system, turn it on, and then click the Print command on the File menu.

The RTF editor sends a copy of the document to the printer.

7. On the File menu, click the Exit command.

The program closes. If you have unsaved changes, the RTF editor will prompt you to save them.

# Event Procedures that Handle RTF Formatting

In most respects, the RTFEdit program is a fully functional word-processing application. If you need this kind of functionality in your Visual Basic programs, you can add it quickly with the Rich Textbox and Common Dialog controls. Let's take a look at the source code that produced these results, beginning with the menu commands on the Format menu. (Open each event procedure in the Code window as I discuss it in the text.)

## The All Caps Command

In the Rich Textbox control, the SelText property represents the text that is currently selected in the text box. One of the simplest formatting activities is to use one of Visual Basic's built-in functions to modify this text, such as UCase, which converts lowercase characters to uppercase. (If the text is already in uppercase, the function has no effect.) When the user clicks the All Caps command on the Format menu, Visual Basic executes the following event procedure to convert the text:

```
Private Sub mnuAllcapsItem_Click()
    RichTextBox1.SelText = UCase(RichTextBox1.SelText)
End Sub
```

To convert the text to lowercase, simply substitute the LCase command for the UCase command.

## The Font Command

The Font command uses the ShowFont method of the Common Dialog control to open a standard Font dialog box and return the selected information to the RTFEdit program. You learned how to use the Open, Save As, and Color standard dialog boxes provided by the Common Dialog control earlier in this book; opening the Font dialog box is a similar process. In the source code, notice that the properties returned by the CommonDialog1 object are immediately assigned to similar properties in the RichTextBox1 object (the text box in your program). The Rich Textbox control can produce any formatting style offered by the Font dialog box. The source code is shown below:

```
Private Sub mnuFontItem_Click()
    'Force an error if the user clicks Cancel
    CommonDialog1.CancelError = True
    On Error GoTo Errhandler:
    'Set flags for special effects and all available fonts
    CommonDialog1.Flags = cdlCFEffects Or cdlCFBoth
    'Display font dialog box
    CommonDialog1.ShowFont
    'Set formatting properties with user selections:
    RichTextBox1.SelFontName = CommonDialog1.FontName
    RichTextBox1.SelFontSize = CommonDialog1.FontSize
    RichTextBox1.SelColor = CommonDialog1.Color
    RichTextBox1.SelBold = CommonDialog1.FontBold
    RichTextBox1.SelItalic = CommonDialog1.FontItalic
    RichTextBox1.SelUnderline = CommonDialog1.FontUnderline
    RichTextBox1.SelStrikeThru = CommonDialog1.FontStrikethru
Errhandler:
    'exit procedure if the user clicks Cancel
End Sub
```

## The Bold, Italic, and Underline Commands

The Bold, Italic, and Underline commands on the Format menu are quite easy to manage in the Rich Textbox control. The only trick is to make sure that each command works as a *toggle,* a command that switches the current formatting state to the opposite state. For example, the Bold command should change bold text to regular text and regular text to bold text. This behavior is easily accomplished by using the Not logical operator in your program statements, which reverses the Boolean value stored in the SelBold, SelItalic, and SelUnderline properties. Use the following code:

```
Private Sub mnuBoldItem_Click()
    RichTextBox1.SelBold = Not RichTextBox1.SelBold
End Sub

Private Sub mnuItalicItem_Click()
    RichTextBox1.SelItalic = Not RichTextBox1.SelItalic
End Sub

Private Sub mnuUnderlineItem_Click()
    RichTextBox1.SelUnderline = Not RichTextBox1.SelUnderline
End Sub
```

# Editing Text with the Windows Clipboard

When you create a full-featured word-processing application, you'll need to give the user access to the standard text editing commands, such as Cut, Copy, and Paste, on the Edit menu. The most convenient way to accomplish this is to use the SetText and GetText methods of the Clipboard object, which connect your program to the data on the Windows clipboard. In this section, you'll examine the source code I used to cut, copy, and paste text with the Clipboard object. You'll also explore how to search for text with the Find method. (I recommend that you examine each event procedure in the Code window as you read this text.)

## The Cut, Copy, and Paste Commands

The Edit menu in the RTFEdit program contains four commands: Cut, Copy, Paste, and Find. The first three operations are facilitated by the SetText and GetText methods of the Clipboard object and the SelRTF property of the rich text box object. At runtime, the rich text box object's SelRTF property contains the complete text and formatting information stored in the text box. When you're working with the Windows clipboard, this is the property that holds your data during cut, copy, and paste operations. In addition, the Clipboard object's SetText and GetText methods are used to copy text to and from the clipboard, respectively. The only real difference between the Copy and Cut commands is that the Cut command deletes the selected text from the text box after the copy operation, and the Copy command does not. Here is the code you need to use:

```
Private Sub mnuCopyItem_Click()
    Clipboard.SetText RichTextBox1.SelRTF
End Sub

Private Sub mnuCutItem_Click()
    Clipboard.SetText RichTextBox1.SelRTF
    RichTextBox1.SelRTF = ""
End Sub

Private Sub mnuPasteItem_Click()
    RichTextBox1.SelRTF = Clipboard.GetText
End Sub
```

## The Find Command

Most word-processing applications provide basic text-searching functionality, and the RTFEdit program is no exception. The Find command is facilitated by the Find method of the rich text box object, which searches for a specified text string in the text box. The exact specifications of the search are controlled by the following options:

```
RichTextBox1.Find(string, start, end, options)
```

The *string* argument specifies the text that you want to find in the text box. The *start* argument is the starting position of the search (an integer from 1 to the number of characters in the document). The *end* argument is the ending position of the search. In the *options* argument is one of the following constants: rtfWholeWord (whole word search), rtfMatch Case (case-sensitive search), rtfNoHighlight (finds text string in document but does not highlight it).

The following event procedure demonstrates how you can search for the first matching word in a text box by prompting the user with an InputBox function. The Span method selects the word that is found.

```
Private Sub mnuFindItem_Click()
    Dim SearchStr As String  'text used for search
    Dim FoundPos As Integer  'location of found text
    SearchStr = InputBox("Enter search word", "Find")
```

```
        If SearchStr <> "" Then   'if search string not empty
            'find the first occurrence of the whole word
            FoundPos = RichTextBox1.Find(SearchStr, , , _
                rtfWholeWord)
            'if the word is found (if not -1)
            If FoundPos <> -1 Then
            'use Span method to select word (forward direction)
                RichTextBox1.Span " ", True, True
            Else
                MsgBox "Search string not found", , "Find"
            End If
        End If
End Sub
```

# Managing File Operations with the Rich Textbox Control

Finally, you'll probably want to add basic file management features to your RTF application. I accomplished this in my program by adding a File menu with Open, Close, Save As, Print, and Exit commands. Examine the following source code now in the Code window to see how the essential File management tasks are handled with the rich text box object. You'll find that the process is a little different from the procedure I recommended for managing text files with the TextBox control in Lesson 12.

## The Open Command

Opening files in a rich text box object is made easy by using the object's LoadFile method, which opens the specified file in the text box. Be sure to set the ScrollBars property to rtfVertical in the Properties window if you want to view documents longer than one page.

When you load a file in a text box, you should specify whether the file is in RTF or text format. This distinction is controlled by the rtfRTF and rtfText options in the LoadFile method. When a document is stored in RTF, it contains a number of formatting codes that instruct the loading application how to display the file's formatting information. If you load an RTF file as "text," the codes themselves are displayed in the text box. (For an example of this, see "Displaying the RTF Codes in a Document" at the end of this lesson.)

The Open command in the RTFEdit program sets the CancelError property of the common dialog object to True. If the user clicks the Cancel button in the Open dialog box, the event procedure will therefore skip the loading operation. The ShowOpen method displays the Open dialog box to allow the user to specify which file to load. The LoadFile method opens the file returned by the common dialog object. I also specified the rtfRTF argument so that the rich text box object will convert any RTF codes it sees to the proper formatting.

```
Private Sub mnuOpenItem_Click()
    CommonDialog1.CancelError = True
    On Error GoTo Errhandler:
    CommonDialog1.Flags = cdlOFNFileMustExist
    CommonDialog1.ShowOpen
    RichTextBox1.LoadFile CommonDialog1.FileName, rtfRTF
Errhandler:
    'if Cancel clicked, then exit procedure
End Sub
```

## The Close Command

The purpose of the Close command on the File menu is simply to close the open RTF file by clearing the contents of the text box with the Text method and an empty string argument (""). However, I also decided to add several lines of code to handle an important closing condition: determining if there are currently any unsaved changes in the document, and if so, prompting the user to save them. To handle this condition, I created a public variable named UnsavedChanges of type Boolean in the Declarations section:

```
Dim UnsavedChanges As Boolean
```

The variable is of type Boolean because I want it to maintain a True or False value to reflect the current state (saved or unsaved) of any changes to the document. UnsavedChanges will be set to True if there are unsaved changes in the document and False if there are not. The program manages this editorial state by using a handy Rich Textbox event called Change. Whenever the text is changed or the formatting is modified in the text box, the rich text box object triggers the Change event and executes the code in the RichTextBox1_Change event procedure. By placing a statement that sets the value of UnsavedChanges to True in this procedure, I'm able to check for unsaved changes—the problem I want to catch—when the user clicks the Close and Exit commands. (I could also check this variable in the Form_Unload procedure, to stop the user from closing the form without saving its contents.) The code for the RichTextBox1_Change event procedure is the following:

```
Private Sub RichTextBox1_Change()
    'Set public variable UnsavedChanges to True each time
    'the text in the Rich text box is modified.
    UnsavedChanges = True
End Sub
```

In the event procedure for the Close menu command, I check the value of the UnsavedChanges variable. If it evaluates to True (if there are unsaved changes), I prompt the user to save those changes by means of a message box. If the user decides to save the changes, the Save As dialog box requests a filename. The file is then saved with the SaveFile method:

```
Private Sub mnuCloseItem_Click()
    Dim Prompt As String
    Dim Reply As Integer
    'jump to error handler if the Cancel button is clicked
    CommonDialog1.CancelError = True
    On Error GoTo Errhandler:
    If UnsavedChanges = True Then
        Prompt = "Would you like to save your changes?"
        Reply = MsgBox(Prompt, vbYesNo)
        If Reply = vbYes Then
            CommonDialog1.ShowSave
            RichTextBox1.SaveFile CommonDialog1.FileName, _
                rtfRTF
        End If
    End If
    RichTextBox1.Text = ""   'clear text box
    UnsavedChanges = False
Errhandler:
    'Cancel button clicked.
    Exit Sub
End Sub
```

## The Save As Command

To save the RTF file that is currently loaded in a rich text box object, you call the SaveFile method with the name of the file and the argument rtfRTF. (Although I don't do it in this program, you could also save the file in plain text format by specifying the rtfText argument and changing the Filter property of the Common Dialog control to save the file with a .txt extension.) You'll typically want to specify the pathname for the saved file by using the FileName property of the common dialog object. In my program, I also allow the user to abort the save operation by clicking the Cancel button in the Save As dialog box.

```
Private Sub mnuSaveAsItem_Click()
    CommonDialog1.CancelError = True
    On Error GoTo Errhandler:
    CommonDialog1.ShowSave
    'save specified file in RTF format
    RichTextBox1.SaveFile CommonDialog1.FileName, rtfRTF
    UnsavedChanges = False
Errhandler:
    'Cancel button clicked
End Sub
```

## The Print Command

Printing is quite simple in a rich text box. You simply use the SelPrint method and specify the internal address or *device handle* of the printer that you want to use. In this program, printing is accomplished by using the Printer object and the hDC property, which contains the current device handle of the system printer:

```
Private Sub mnuPrintItem_Click()
    'Prints the current document using the device
    'handle of the current printer
    RichTextBox1.SelPrint (Printer.hDC)
End Sub
```

## The Exit Command

The basic purpose of the Exit command is to terminate the program by using the End statement. However, as in the Close command above, I have included program code on the next page that first checks to see if there are any unsaved changes in the document before I allow the program to exit and discard the user's data permanently. Again, I test for the current save state by using the public variable UnsavedChanges, and give the user an opportunity to save any unsaved changes. Notice that, like the Close command, the Exit command also sets the value of UnsavedChanges to False after it saves the file to disk.

```
Private Sub mnuExitItem_Click ()
    Dim Prompt As String
    Dim Reply As Integer
    CommonDialog1.CancelError = True
    On Error GoTo Errhandler:
    If UnsavedChanges = True Then
        Prompt = "Would you like to save your changes?"
        Reply = MsgBox(Prompt, vbYesNo)
        If Reply = vbYes Then
            CommonDialog1.ShowSave
            RichTextBox1.SaveFile CommonDialog1.FileName, _
                rtfRTF
            UnsavedChanges = False
        End If
    End If
    End 'after file has been saved, quit program
Errhandler:
    'Cancel button clicked (return to program)
End Sub
```

# Displaying the RTF Codes in a Document

As you've just learned, the Rich Textbox control lets you create advanced effects in your document by adding special codes to your file in a formatting scheme known as RTF. Because the Rich Textbox control also has the ability to display straight text files, you can examine the document's formatting codes up close if you want more information about RTF. To modify the RTFEdit program so that it opens files in *text mode* and displays the RTF formatting, complete the following steps.

## Viewing your RTF Code

1. Open the Code window and select the mnuOpenItem event procedure in the Object drop-down list box.

2. Change the program statement that loads the RTF file in the event procedure to the following:

```
RichTextBox1.LoadFile CommonDialog1.FileName, rtfText
```

Note that the final argument in the statement has been changed from rtfRTF to rtfText.

*Start button*

3. Click the Start button on the toolbar, and then click the Open command on the File menu.

4. Open the sample.rtf file that you created earlier in this lesson.

   You may open a different RTF file if you like. Your form will look similar to the following:

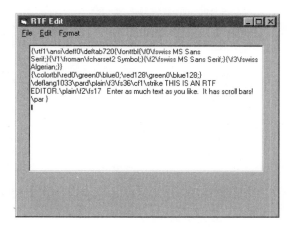

5. Take a few minutes to examine the RTF codes in the document.

   You'll see information about the font, color, text style, alignment, and so on. Somewhere in the middle, you'll also see your text. (So this explains why word-processing files get so big!)

6. On the File menu, choose the Exit command to close the program. Click No when you are asked to save your changes.

7. In the mnuOpenItem_Click event procedure, change the rtfText argument back to rtfRTF.

Congratulations! You're now ready to create your own RTF documents and (if you like) a full-featured word-processing application.

# 16

# Displaying Progress and Status Information

In Lesson 15, you learned how to add word-processing features to your application with the Rich Textbox control. In this lesson, you'll continue your work with ActiveX controls by integrating the Progress Bar, Slider, and Status Bar controls into your application. The Progress Bar is designed to give the user some visual feedback during lengthy operations, such as complex sorting or saving a file. The Slider provides a mechanism both for receiving input and for displaying output: you can either drag the slider tab across a horizontal bar with tick marks, or you can have your program move the slider tab to show the progress of a task. Finally, the Status Bar displays information about your program and keyboard states in up to 16 panes at the bottom of your application. These boxes are typically used to display the time and date, font information, spreadsheet data, facts about the operating system, and the status of toggle keys on your keyboard. As a group, these three ActiveX controls allow you to create handsome and effective graphical user interfaces.

# Displaying Task Progress with the Progress Bar Control

In this age of the World Wide Web, most software professionals spend a little time each day downloading files or other information from the Internet. As a result, one of the regular players in our computing experience is the *progress bar*, a horizontal status indicator that shows us graphically how long a particular operation is taking. A typical progress bar in Microsoft Internet Explorer looks like this:

A progress bar doesn't always indicate how many minutes or seconds it will take the computer to perform a given task, but it does provide the visual feedback necessary to convince the user that his or her transaction hasn't ground to a halt or locked up the computer. In psychological terms, a progress bar eases the tension associated with waiting for the results of complex calculations and provides a tangible measure of the progress of a particular computing task.

In this section you'll learn how to add a progress bar to your application's user interface. I use a progress bar whenever the task my application is tackling causes a delay of five or more seconds for the user of a typical computer. The following list shows a few activities that can cause this type of delay:

- Downloading files from the Internet
- Opening and saving files
- Sorting long lists
- Playing songs or other media on a multimedia device

- Tracking time-intensive computations, such as complex financial calculations

- Copying disks or setting up software

## Installing the Progress Bar Control

Before you can use the Progress Bar control, you must add it to your toolbox. The Progress Bar ActiveX control and all the other ActiveX controls you'll use in this lesson are stored in a master file called the Microsoft Windows Common Control (mscomctl.ocx). When you add the Windows Common Control to your toolbox, you get a set of nine ActiveX controls that you can use to customize your program's user interface.

---

 **TIP** For more information about the ActiveX controls included with the Visual Basic Working Model, see "Exploring Professional ActiveX Controls" in Lesson 15, "Word Processing with the Rich Textbox Control."

---

## Add the Windows Common Control to your Toolbox

The sample project you'll use in this lesson already has the Windows Common Control included in the toolbox. When you create your own projects in the future, however, you'll need to add it manually. The following steps show you how. (You can either practice them now or keep them handy for future reference.)

1. On the Project menu, click the Components command, and then click the Controls tab.

   Microsoft Visual Basic displays the ActiveX controls installed in your system.

2. Scroll through the list of controls until you see the name Microsoft Windows Common Controls 6.0.

3. Click the check box next to the control name, and then click OK.

   Don't pick Microsoft Windows Common Controls-2. This master file contains other useful ActiveX controls, including Month View, Date and Time Picker, and Flat ScrollBar (see Lesson 15 for the details).

After you click OK, Visual Basic adds nine Windows user interface controls to your toolbox. Your toolbox will look something like the following figure:

Status Bar control — Progress Bar control — Slider control

# The Progress Program

I created the Progress program in the \LearnVb6\Less16 folder to demonstrate how you can use a progress bar to provide appropriate feedback during lengthy computations. The Progress program is a revision of the SortDemo program in Lesson 12, which uses the Shell sort algorithm to sort a text box. Because the sort takes several seconds to reorganize a lengthy list, I thought it might be nice to give the user something to look at while the sort algorithm runs through its paces. You'll run the Progress program now to see how it works.

## Running the Progress Program

1. Open the Progress.vbp project in the \LearnVb6\Less16 folder.

   If you are prompted to save your changes (the Windows Common Control you practiced adding above), click No.

*Start button*

2. Click the Start button on the toolbar to run the program.

   Visual Basic displays the user interface of the Progress program.

3. On the File menu of the Progress program, click the Open command, and then open the sorttest.txt file in the \LearnVb6\Less16 folder.

   Visual Basic displays the contents of the text file in the text box. (The file contains five copies of an ABCs text—a total of 180 lines.)

4. On the File menu, click the Sort Text command to sort the text box alphabetically.

   Visual Basic begins the sort, and, as shown in the following figure, displays a progress bar at the bottom of the form to track the progress of the calculation.

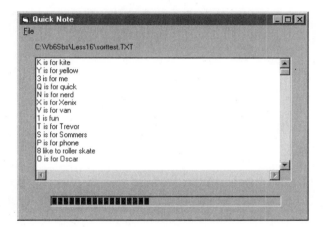

Watch closely: you'll see the progress bar fill two times. The first pass is a measure of the data prep process, in which the file is scanned to determine the number of lines; the second pass tracks the progress of the actual sort. I like showing a lengthy computation like this in individual phases; it makes the user feel more involved.

After a moment, the program displays the sorted list in the text box, and the progress bar disappears.

5. On the File menu, click the Exit command to quit the program.

## Examining the Progress Program Code

The program code that manipulates the progress bar is located in the mnuItemSortText_Click event procedure, a routine that runs each time the user clicks the Sort Text command on the File menu. You'll take a look at the code now.

→ Display the Code window and open the mnuItemSortText_Click event procedure.

You've seen this source code before—in Lesson 12 you used it to sort the contents of a text box with the Shell sort algorithm. The actual contents of the Shell sort are located in the progress.bas code module of this project. The event procedure handles several important tasks before and after the sort is calculated. These include determining the number of lines in the text box, loading each line into a string array named strArray, calling the ShellSort procedure, and displaying the results in the text box. In this lesson I'll only discuss the program code that controls the progress bar.

In design mode, I set the progress bar's Visible property to False so it wouldn't appear on the screen until I needed it. Accordingly, my first task in the mnuItemSortText_Click event procedure is to make the progress bar visible and set its Max property to the number of characters in the file. I also set its Min property to 1 and its Value property to 1 (the starting square in the progress bar):

```
charsInFile% = Len(txtNote.Text)
...
ProgressBar1.Visible = True
ProgressBar1.Min = 1
ProgressBar1.Max = charsInFile%       'set max for progress bar
ProgressBar1.Value = 1                'set initial value
```

Next, I scan the contents of the text box character by character to determine the number of lines in the document, a value I need when I call the ShellSort procedure later in the routine. As I process each line, I update the progress bar's Value property with the current character, represented by the counter variable i% (shown in bold below):

```
'determine number of lines in the text box
For i% = 1 To charsInFile%
    letter$ = Mid(txtNote.Text, i%, 1)
    ProgressBar1.Value = i%      'move progress bar
    If letter$ = Chr$(13) Then 'if carriage ret found
        lineCount% = lineCount% + 1  'increment line count
        i% = i% + 1              'skip linefeed char
    End If
Next i%
```

After the first pass through the progress bar, I reset the Value property to the first square and set the Max property to the number of lines in the document (this amount is currently held in the lineCount% variable):

```
'reset progress bar for next phase of sort
ProgressBar1.Value = 1
ProgressBar1.Max = lineCount%
```

As I add each line to the strArray in preparation for the sort, I update the progress bar with the value of the current line (curline%) (shown in bold below). As the Value property grows in size, it again causes dark squares to fill the progress bar:

```
'build an array to hold the text in the text box
ReDim strArray$(lineCount%) 'create array of proper size
curline% = 1
ln$ = ""   'use ln$ to build lines one character at a time
For i% = 1 To charsInFile%      'loop through text again
    letter$ = Mid(txtNote.Text, i%, 1)
    If letter$ = Chr$(13) Then 'if carriage return found
        ProgressBar1.Value = curline%  'show progress
        curline% = curline% + 1     'increment line count
        i% = i% + 1              'skip linefeed char
        ln$ = ""                'clear line and go to next
    Else
        ln$ = ln$ & letter$     'add letter to line
        strArray$(curline%) = ln$   'and put in array
    End If
Next i%
```

Finally, after the sort is complete, I hide the progress bar:

```
ProgressBar1.Visible = False
```

As you can see, the progress bar is a handy tool to have on your form when you're processing lengthy computations in a program. If you set the Min and Max properties to the appropriate range beforehand, you can easily control the progress bar within a For... Next statement or other looping structure.

# Managing Input Graphically with the Slider Control

If you like the look of pictorial bars in your application, you can also use an ActiveX control called the Slider to receive input and display the progress of a task. The Slider control is a user interface component containing a slider peg and optional tick marks. You can move the slider peg within the slider window by dragging the peg, clicking tick marks, or using the direction keys on the keyboard. I find the Slider control a useful input device for setting document margins in a word processor, controlling multimedia applications, scrolling in a window, and other tasks that require relative movements. You may also find the Slider control useful for entering numeric values or color settings.

## Running the RTFEdit2 Program

To practice using the Slider control, you'll load and run the RTFEdit2 program, an enhanced version of the RTF Editor you created in Lesson 15.

1. Open the RTFEdit2.vbp project located in your \LearnVb6\Less16 folder and run it.

2. On the program's File menu, click the Open command and open the file named picnic.rtf in the \LearnVb6\Less16 folder.

   Your form should look like the figure on the next page.

   The RTFEdit2 program contains two new features: a Slider control at the top of the form and a Status Bar control at the bottom of the form. This slider gives you a handy way to adjust the left margin of the text that is currently selected or contains the insertion point. In addition, you'll see a status bar with four panels that display the name of the open file, the selected font, the current time, and the current date.

3. Click the second line of text in the picnic.rtf file.

   The slider moves in one tab stop, reflecting the left margin of the current line.

4. Drag the slider to the right to increase the left margin.

   As you drag the slider, the text margin expands automatically. In addition, a tooltip (or pop-up text window) appears and indicates the size of the margin in twips, the default measurement scale for a Visual Basic form and its controls. (A twip is 1/1440 of an inch.) You can adjust the measurement unit by modifying the ScaleMode property for the form.

5. Practice setting margins with the slider until you get the hang of it.

   If you wish, you can select several lines and adjust the margin settings for the entire group in one action. Notice that each time you click a new line, the slider snaps to display the correct margin measurement.

6. When you're finished, click the Exit command on the RTFEdit2 File menu.

7. Click No when you are asked to save changes.

## Examining the Slider Control Source Code

Now that you've had a chance to see what the Slider control can do, take a minute to see how it's controlled by three event procedures.

1. Double-click the form to display the Form_Load event procedure. You'll see the following program code:

```
Private Sub Form_Load()
    'Set initial values for Slider control
    Slider1.Left = RichTextBox1.Left   'align to text box
    Slider1.Width = RichTextBox1.Width
    'note: all slider measurements in twips (form default)
    Slider1.Max = RichTextBox1.Width
    Slider1.TickFrequency = Slider1.Max * 0.1
    Slider1.LargeChange = Slider1.Max * 0.1
    Slider1.SmallChange = Slider1.Max * 0.01
End Sub
```

The Form_Load event procedure is the typical place to put statements that configure the slider for use. The first two statements use the Left and Width properties of the rich text box object to align the slider object with the text box. Although I aligned the control approximately when I created it above the rich text box, the Left and Width properties allow me to do this precisely, using the same settings as those of the rich text box.

Next, I set the slider's Max property to the width of the rich text box. You can also set the Max property with the Properties windows at design time, but I found it convenient to precisely link the maximum range of the slider object to the size of the word processing window. (If the window changes size, so will the slider.) The setting for the Min property, the initial setting for the slider, is zero.

Finally, I've configured the TickFrequency, LargeChange, and SmallChange properties in the Form_Load event procedure. TickFrequency sets the frequency of tick marks on the slider in relation to its range (in other words, the difference between the Min and Max value). For example, if the range were 1000, and the TickFrequency property were set to 100, there would be 10 tick marks. The LargeChange property sets the number of ticks the slider will move when you click to the left or right of the slider, or press Page Up or Page Down, respectively. The SmallChange property sets the number of ticks the slider will move when you press the Right or Left arrow key.

2. Use the Object list box in the Code window to display the Slider1_Scroll event procedure.

The Slider1_Scroll event procedure links the activity in the slider object to the margin formatting in the rich text box. Each time the user scrolls with the slider, Visual Basic calls this event procedure. Using the Value property of the slider object, this routine copies the value of the current slider position to the SelIndent property of the rich text box object, which sets the left margin of the selected text.

```
Private Sub Slider1_Scroll()
    RichTextBox1.SelIndent = Slider1.Value
End Sub
```

This statement works because I set the Max property of the slider object to the width of the rich text box object when I started the program. If the two objects were sized differently, the measurement scales in the slider's Value property would not match the dimensions of the rich text box.

3. Use the Object list box in the Code window to display the RichTextBox1_SelChange event procedure.

Visual Basic executes this event procedure when the current selection is changed in a rich text box object or when the insertion point has moved. Because I want the slider to move appropriately when different paragraphs are selected in the document, I've added program code to the event procedure that updates the slider position based on the margin formatting of the current selection:

```
Private Sub RichTextBox1_SelChange()
    ...
    'if there is one indent style in the selection, display
    'it on the slider bar (multiple styles return Null)
    If Not IsNull(RichTextBox1.SelIndent) Then
        Slider1.Value = RichTextBox1.SelIndent
    End If
End Sub
```

Note the IsNull function in this procedure, which checks to see if the SelIndent property of the rich text box object contains a Null (or empty) value. SelIndent returns Null when the current selection contains two different margin styles, which results in a runtime error when assigned to the Value property of the slider object. To stop this from happening, I verify that the measurement held in SelIndent isn't Null before I assign it to the slider. Your applications should also include this basic bulletproofing.

You've just learned how to use the Slider control to indent the margins in an RTF document. Before you move on, however, take a look at the data displayed by the Status Bar control in the RTFEdit2 application.

# Displaying Application Information with the Status Bar Control

A *status bar* is a collection of rectangular boxes or *panels* along the bottom of a Windows application. A typical example is the status bar in Microsoft Word, which displays the current page and section number, the position of the cursor, the status of several toggle switches, an AutoCorrect feature, and several other useful items.

You can add a status bar to your Visual Basic application by using the Status Bar ActiveX control, which is part of the Windows Common Control (mscomctl.ocx). When you place a status bar object on your form, it immediately snaps to the bottom of the form. You can then configure the general characteristics of the object with the Properties window, and you can add and remove panels in the status bar by right-clicking the status bar object, clicking the Properties command, and specifying settings in the Panels tab of the Property Pages dialog box, as shown in the illustration on the following page. You can include up to 16 panels of information in each status bar.

## Running the RTFEdit2 Program

Run the RTFEdit2 program again to see how the status bar works in the RTF editor.

*Start button*

1. Click the Start button on the toolbar to run the RTFEdit2 program again.

   If you closed the program or just started the lesson in this section, load the RTFEdit2 program from the \LearnVb6\Less16 folder now and run it.

   Notice that the current time and date appear on the status bar at the bottom of the screen. Point to the time and date with the mouse, and a tooltip will appear that describes what each box does.

2. Open the picnic.rtf file in the \LearnVb6\Less16 folder.

   The name picnic.rtf appears in the leftmost status box.

3. Click the last line in the document.

   MS Sans Serif, the name of the current font, appears in the second status box.

   Your form should look like the illustration at the top of the next page.

4. Select the third line, and then click the Font command on the Format menu.

5. When the Font dialog box appears, change the font to Times New Roman or another font in your system. Click OK.

   The font changes in your document, and the font name in the status bar changes to match.

6. On the File menu, click the Exit command to quit that program.

Now you'll take a look at the property pages that create the status bar.

### Examining the status bar property pages

A property page is a group of settings that work collectively to configure an aspect of a control's behavior. In Visual Basic, you can use property pages to customize several ActiveX controls. Follow these steps to see how I used property pages to create the panels on the RTFEdit2 status bar.

1. Click the status bar on the form with the right mouse button.

2. Click the Properties command on the pop-up menu.

   The Property Pages dialog box for the status box object appears.

3. Click the Panels tab.

   The Panels tab contains several settings for each panel in the status bar. To add a new panel to the status bar, click the Insert Panel button. To remove a panel, click the Remove Panel button. As a group, the panels that you create in the status bar are called the *Panels collection*. You can reference each panel individually by using the Panels collection and the index of a particular panel. For example, to place the filename *myfile.txt* in the first panel in the status bar, you would use the following program code:

```
StatusBar1.Panels(1).Text = "myfile.txt"
```

Likewise, you could assign the value held in another object to the status bar. For example, this program code places the filename (without path) that is stored in the common dialog object's FileTitle property into the first panel in the status bar:

```
StatusBar1.Panels(1).Text = CommonDialog1.FileTitle
```

4. Click the Alignment drop-down list box in the Panels tab.

   You'll see a list of text alignment choices in the list box, including left, center, and right. This setting controls how the text is displayed in the panel you're configuring.

5. Click the Style drop-down list box in the Panels tab.

   You'll see a list of formatting entries in the list box, which controls the type of information that is displayed by the status bar panel. The sbrText entry (the default) means that you will enter the contents of the panel manually with the Text property, either through the Text text box in the Panel tab or through the Text property in your program code (see step 3 above). The remaining style entries are automatic settings—if you choose one, Visual Basic automatically displays the value that you've selected when it displays the status bar. The style entries have the following meanings:

| Style | Displays the following information |
|-------|-----------------------------------|
| SbrText | User-defined text in Text property |
| SbrCaps | Status of Caps Lock key |
| SbrNum | Status of Num Lock key |
| SbrIns | Status of Insert key |
| SbrScrl | Status of Scroll Lock key |
| SbrTime | Current time from the system clock |
| SbrDate | Current date from the system clock |
| SbrKana | Status of Kana Lock key (Japanese operating systems only) |

6. Click the right Panel Index arrow in the Panel tab twice to advance to the third panel in the status bar (Time).

   I configured this panel so that it would display the current time on the status bar. (Note the sbrTime value in the Style setting.)

7. Click the right Panel Index arrow again to advance to the fourth panel in the status bar (Date).

   This panel uses the sbrDate setting to display the current date on the status bar.

   I've also manually set two other settings for each panel with property pages: ToolTip Text, which contains the tooltip text displayed when the user holds the mouse over the panel, and Minimum Width, which sets the starting width of the panel in twips. A minimum setting lets you align your panels on the form in design mode, while still allowing for growth if the user chooses to enlarge the form. Alternatively, I could have picked the sbrContents option in the AutoSize drop-down list box, which would have resized the panels dynamically based on their content.

8. Take a moment to explore the remaining settings and tabs in the Property Pages dialog box, and then click Cancel.

Now you're ready to look at the event procedures that control the status bar at runtime.

### Examining the status bar program code

Unlike many ActiveX controls, the status bar doesn't usually require much supporting code. Your task is typically to display one or two pieces of information on the status bar with the Text property. Let's see how this works in the RTFEdit2 program, where a status bar displays the current filename, font, time, and date.

1. Open the mnuSaveAsItem_Click event procedure.

   As you may recall from Lesson 15, this event procedure saves the current document as an RTF file by using a Save As dialog box and the SaveFile method of the rich text box object. To display the new filename in the first panel of the status bar object, I added the following line of code below the SaveFile method:

   ```
   StatusBar1.Panels(1).Text = CommonDialog1.FileTitle
   ```

   This statement copies the name in the FileTitle property (a filename without the path) to the Text property of the first panel in the status bar. To specify a different panel, you would simply change the numeric index.

---

 **IP** To handle the two other mechanisms for saving files in this program, I also added the preceding line of code to the mnuCloseItem and mnuExitItem event procedures.

---

2. Open the RichTextBox1_SelChange event procedure.

   As I noted earlier in this chapter, the RichTextBox1_SelChange event procedure runs when the current selection is changed in the rich text box object or when the user has moved the insertion point.

Because the second panel in my status bar needs to display the font used in the current selection, I've added an If...Then...Else decision structure to this event procedure to check for a new font name and copy it to the second panel:

```
Private Sub RichTextBox1_SelChange()
    'if there is one font in the selection, then display
    'it on the status bar (multiple fonts return Null)
    If IsNull(RichTextBox1.SelFontName) Then
        StatusBar1.Panels(2).Text = ""
    Else
        StatusBar1.Panels(2).Text = RichTextBox1.SelFontName
    End If
    ...
End Sub
```

Again, I use the IsNull function to check to see if SelFontName property contains a Null value. SelFontName returns Null when the current selection contains two different font names. Because this would result in a runtime error, I check for Null before I assign the value and simply clear the second panel if multiple names are found.

The status panels that display the time and date information in the program work automatically. You don't need to add any program code to run them.

## Displaying Caps Lock and Num Lock Status

Take a minute now to experiment with a few other automatic formatting styles on the status bar. As I mentioned earlier in the lesson, you can use the Panel tab in the Property Pages dialog box to configure your panels to monitor several useful keyboard toggle states, including Caps Lock, Num Lock, Insert, and Scroll Lock.

1. Right-click the status bar object, and then click the Properties command.

   The Property Pages dialog box appears.

2. Click the Panels tab.

3. Click the right Panel Index arrow twice to move to index 3 (Time).

4. Click the Style drop-down list box, and then click the sbrCaps style (Caps Lock).

5. Click the right Panel Index arrow to display the settings for the fourth panel (Date).

6. Click the Style drop-down list box, and then click the sbrNum style (Num Lock).

7. Click OK to close the Property Pages dialog box.

   With just a few mouse clicks, you've added Caps Lock and Num Lock information to the status bar. Now you'll run the program to see how they work.

*Start button*

8. Click Start on the toolbar to run the RTFEdit2 program.

9. Press the Caps Lock and Num Lock keys several times to check their toggle operation. The following figure illustrates how the keys will appear on your status bar.

# Displaying HTML Documents with Internet Explorer

In this lesson you'll learn how to display HTML documents in your applications by using the Internet Explorer object, which is a programmable component with properties, methods, and events that are available to every computer system that features a copy of the Microsoft Internet Explorer software. As you investigate the Internet Explorer object model, you'll learn how to add the Internet Explorer object to your Visual Basic projects and how to use Internet Explorer properties, methods, and events to display HTML documents. As you'll soon see, Internet Explorer features a useful object model that is similar in many ways to the objects exposed by Microsoft Office applications. With Internet Explorer, you can display complex HTML documents and World Wide Web pages without writing the browser software yourself.

# Getting Started with the Internet Explorer Object

Internet Explorer is a general-purpose browser application that displays HTML documents located on the Internet or on your hard disk. Microsoft designed the Internet Explorer so that you could use it as an individual application (started from the Microsoft Windows Start menu) or as a component object in a program of your own creation. Accordingly, Internet Explorer exposes its features as a collection of properties, methods, and events in a recognizable object model. You can investigate this object model by using the Visual Basic Object Browser and putting its features to work in your programs.

The *Internet Explorer object* isn't an ActiveX control included in the Visual Basic Working Model. Instead, it's an object library that resides on all systems with an installed copy of Internet Explorer. (In other words, the Internet Explorer needs to be present in the system registry.) Because Microsoft uses the Internet Explorer to display Help files in many of its applications (including Microsoft Office), you'll find the Internet Explorer object library on most systems that contain Microsoft software.

> **MPORTANT** The version of Internet Explorer described in this lesson is 5.0 (the version shipped with Microsoft Office 2000). Core properties, methods, and events in the Internet Explorer object have not changed significantly between versions. However, be sure to check which version of Internet Explorer you're using before you start this lesson. If you have a version other than 4.0 or 5.0, use the Object Browser to verify that it contains the properties, methods, and events that you plan to use. Like the object libraries in Microsoft Office applications, the Internet Explorer object model is updated from time to time. Undoubtedly, future versions will be a little different (and richer in features).

## Adding the Microsoft Internet
## Controls Reference to Your Application

The first step in using the Internet Explorer object is adding a reference to the object library in your application. You accomplish this by using the References command on the Visual Basic Project menu, as shown in the following exercise. Practice adding a reference now, if you like, or simply note the steps for later use. (The program I include in this lesson already includes this reference, but you should practice adding it now if you want to investigate the object model later in this section.)

### Including the Internet Explorer object in your project

1. Start Visual Basic, and open a new, standard project.

2. On the Project menu, click the References command.

3. Scroll to the Microsoft Internet Controls (shdocvw.dll) reference, and then click the check box to the left of the reference name.

   Your dialog box will look similar to this:

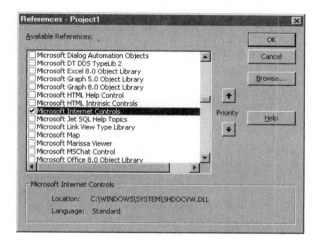

4. Click OK to add the reference to your project.

   Visual Basic adds the Internet Explorer object library to your project.

## Investigating the Internet Explorer Object Model

Before you use the Internet Explorer object in a program, take a moment to examine its properties, methods, and events with the Visual Basic Object Browser. The Internet Explorer object is stored in a class named InternetExplorer, which is a member of the SHDocVw library (the Microsoft Internet Controls reference you just added to your project). Within the InternetExplorer class are the properties, methods, and events that you can use to display HTML documents in your programs. As you learned in Lesson 14, the Object Browser is your best source of information for an object library that isn't shipped with Visual Basic. The Internet Explorer object library is a good case in point.

### Using the Object Browser

*Object Browser button*

1. Click the Object Browser button on the toolbar to display the Visual Basic Object Browser.

   The Object Browser utility appears in a window.

---

 **IP** F2 is the keyboard shortcut for displaying the Object Browser. You can also open the Object Browser by clicking the Object Browser command on the View menu.

---

2. In the Project/Library drop-down list box, click the SHDocVw library.

   The Classes and Members list boxes display the elements of the SHDocVw library (the objects associated with Microsoft Internet Controls).

3. Scroll down in the Classes list box and click the InternetExplorer class.

   Your Object Browser will look similar to the following illustration:

The properties, methods, and events of the InternetExplorer class appear in the Members list box on the right. You can click any of these members to see the syntax (and a short description) of each of the items that control how the Internet Explorer works. Try clicking a few of the properties, methods, and events now.

4. Click the Navigate method in the Members list box.

   You'll see the following syntax description:

   The Navigate method opens the URL specified, which can be either an Internet address or an HTML document someplace on your system. The Flags argument specifies whether to add this URL to the Internet Explorer's history list or disk cache. The TargetFrame Name, PostData, and Headers arguments describe how the HTML document should be opened and identified in the browser window. (The Flags, TargetFrameName, PostData, and Headers arguments are all optional.) Although it may appear complex, the Navigate method is very easy to use. In many cases, it's all you'll need to view an HTML document from within your application.

5. Click the LocationURL property in the Members list box.

The LocationURL property contains the pathname of the HTML document that is currently open in the Internet Explorer browser. If you want to keep track of each Web site a user visits in a computing session, you can use the Navigate method to copy the string in the LocationURL property to a text box or combo box after each successful connection to a Web page.

6. Click the NavigateComplete2 event in the Members list box.

The Internet Explorer object issues the NavigateComplete2 event when the Navigate method has been completed successfully and a new HTML document has been loaded into the browser window. We'll use this event later in this lesson to create a history list of visited Web sites.

 **TIP** When Microsoft makes improvements to the Internet Explorer object model, it often creates updated versions of the existing properties, methods, and events with new (incremented) numbers appended to their names. By looking at the syntax and description entries for these new members, you can often determine what new arguments or features they support. This explains why you see Navigate and Navigate2 methods in the Internet Explorer 4.0 and 5.0 object libraries.

7. Take a moment to explore other properties, methods, and events that look interesting with the Object Browser.

8. When you're finished exploring the object model, click the Close button to quit the Object Browser.

## Displaying HTML Documents

Displaying HTML documents with the Internet Explorer object requires just a few lines of program code in a Visual Basic application. First, you create an object variable in your application that represents the Internet Explorer object. Then you open the Internet Explorer application by setting the Visible property of that object variable to True. Next, you load an HTML document into the browser by issuing the Navigate method with a valid URL or local pathname as an argument. Here's what the process looks like with program code:

```
Set Explorer = New SHDocVw.InternetExplorer
Explorer.Visible = True
Explorer.Navigate "http://www.microsoft.com/"
```

In this example, I created an object variable named Explorer to represent the InternetExplorer class in the shdocvw.dll object library. If you want to use this object variable in every event procedure in your form, you should declare it as a global variable with the Public keyword in a standard module or in the Declarations section of your form.

To see how the Internet Explorer object works in a program, you'll run the ShowHTML demonstration that I created for this lesson. ShowHTML uses a combo box to present a list of favorite Web sites to the user, and uses the Internet Explorer's Navigate method to display whichever HTML document the user selects.

## Running the ShowHTML Program

*Start button*

1. Open the ShowHTML.vbp project in the \LearnVb6\Less17 folder.

2. Click the Start button on the toolbar to run the program.

   Your form will look like the following:

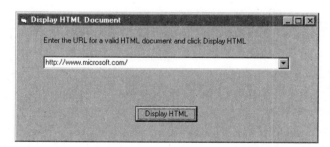

3. Click the Down arrow in the combo box on the form to display a list of favorite Web sites for Visual Basic programmers.

You'll see the following list of URLs:

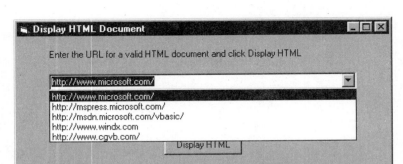

As you've probably noticed in your Internet browser, a combo box can be a handy control for presenting URLs to the user. In my Web applications, I usually try to display five or six URLs for users to choose from when they start their Web applications and allow them to add their own favorites when they visit additional sites. The Internet addresses I've included here will connect you to a few sites that I think are of general interest to Visual Basic programmers. Feel free to use them, but note that one or two of the URLs may not be valid a year or two from now. (These things change rapidly.)

The following table lists the Web sites I present in the program:

| Internet address | Description |
| --- | --- |
| *http://www.microsoft.com/* | Microsoft Corporation home page |
| *http://mspress.microsoft.com/* | Microsoft Press home page (with links for Visual Basic books) |
| *http://msdn.microsoft.com/vbasic/* | Microsoft Visual Basic Programming home page |
| *http://www.windx.com/* | Fawcette Publications' resources for VB programming |
| *http://www.cgvb.com/* | Carl and Gary's VB home page (a unique, non-Microsoft site) |

4. Click the Microsoft Visual Basic Programming home page (*http://msdn.microsoft.com/vbasic/*) in the combo box.

5. Click the Display HTML button.

   Visual Basic opens Internet Explorer and loads the Microsoft Visual Basic URL into the browser. If you're not currently online, Internet Explorer prompts you for your internet service provider (ISP) member ID and password with a sign-in dialog box and connects you to the Internet. (If you connect to the Internet through a corporate network, you may have a different logon process.) After a moment, you'll see the Microsoft Visual Basic home page, which will look similar to the following illustration. (Your HTML document will contain more recent information.)

6. Maximize the Internet Explorer window if it's not already full-size, and then click one or two links of interest to you.

   The Microsoft Visual Basic Programming home page is an excellent resource for late-breaking news about programming tools, tips, conferences, books, and other information about Visual Basic.

7. After you have finished reviewing the page, close the Internet Explorer window. If you're asked if you want to disconnect from the Internet, click No to remain connected.

8. Display the ShowHTML form again.

   The ShowHTML program is still running, although it may have settled beneath a few other open applications by this point. If you don't see it, press Alt+Tab to display a list of currently open applications, and then click Display HTML Document to bring the application to the forefront.

9. Pick another Web site from the combo box, and then click Display HTML to open it.

   After you've had a look at my selections, open a few of your own favorite sites with the program.

10. Place the cursor in the combo box on the ShowHTML form, remove the current URL, and enter a URL of your own choosing. Then click Display HTML to open it.

    In addition, you can use this tool to display HTML documents on your hard disk, if you wish.

11. After you've displayed three or four HTML documents, click the Close button on the ShowHTML program's title bar, and then close any open Internet Explorer windows on the task bar.

Now you'll take a look at the program code in the ShowHTML application that utilizes the Internet Explorer object.

## Examining the Internet Explorer Code in ShowHTML

1. Open the Declarations sections of the form in the Code window.

   You'll see the following program code:

   ```
   'Declare a variable for the current URL
   Public Explorer As SHDocVw.InternetExplorer
   ```

   The ShowHTML program begins by declaring a public object variable named Explorer that will facilitate the program's connection to the Internet Explorer object library. The declaration references the InternetExplorer class in the shdocvw.dll file, which must be included in your project by using the References command on the Project menu.

2. Open the Command1_Click event procedure in the Code window.

You'll see the following program code:

```
Private Sub Command1_Click()
    On Error GoTo errorhandler
    Set Explorer = New SHDocVw.InternetExplorer
    Explorer.Visible = True
    Explorer.Navigate Combo1.Text
    Exit Sub
errorhandler:
    MsgBox "Error displaying file", , Err.Description
End Sub
```

The Command1_Click event procedure runs when the user clicks the Display HTML button on the form. With this event, the user either is satisfied with the default entry *(http://www.microsoft. com/)* and wants to display it, or has specified another HTML document in the program's combo box to display. Accordingly, the event procedure sets an error handler to manage unexpected connection errors, and then creates a new Internet Explorer object. Next, it makes the Internet Explorer window visible and opens a document in the browser that corresponds to the user's selection in the combo box (a value currently held in the combo box object's Text property). At this point, the ShowHTML application runs in the background, while the user's attention is shifted to the now open Internet Explorer window, which manages the connection to the Internet (if necessary) and allows the user to view the selected Web site and click any existing hyperlinks on the page.

3. Open the Form_Load event procedure in the Code window.

You'll see the following program code:

```
Private Sub Form_Load()
'Add a few useful Web sites to combo box at startup
    'Microsoft Corp. home page
    Combo1.AddItem "http://www.microsoft.com/"
    'Microsoft Press home page
    Combo1.AddItem "http://mspress.microsoft.com/"
    'Microsoft Visual Basic Programming home page
    Combo1.AddItem "http://msdn.microsoft.com/vbasic/"
    'Fawcette Publication's resources for VB programming
    Combo1.AddItem "http://www.windx.com"
```

```
                    'Carl and Gary's VB home page (non-Microsoft)
                    Combo1.AddItem "http://www.cgvb.com/"
              End Sub
```

When the ShowHTML program loads, the user is presented with a list
of several "favorite" Web sites automatically. These URLs are presented
in a combo box that I configured initially in the Form_Load event procedure by using the AddItem method. Feel free to add your own favorite
URLs to this list by including additional AddItem statements—the combo
box object includes scroll bars when necessary and can accommodate
many entries.

# Responding to Internet Explorer Events

In this lesson you've manipulated the properties and methods of the
Internet Explorer object to display HTML documents in a window. You
can also take greater control of your browsing activities by responding to
events that occur in the Internet Explorer object. As you may recall from
previous lessons, each Visual Basic control has the ability to produce
status announcements, or *events,* in the regular course of its operation.
These events can include anything from a simple mouse movement in the
ImageBox control (the Drag event) to notification that a downloading
activity is complete (the ResponseComplete event in the Internet Transfer
control). The Internet Explorer object also produces events that you can
respond to programmatically with event procedures. These include
NavigateComplete2, DownloadBegin, DownloadComplete, TitleChange,
DocumentComplete, and OnQuit.

If you want to use Internet Explorer events in your program, you first
need to modify the statement in your program code that declares the
Internet Explorer object variable. Events produced by external ActiveX
components are not automatically listed in the Object drop-down list box
of the Code window. However, you can include these events by using the
WithEvents keyword when you make your object declaration. In the
ShowHTML program developed in this lesson, you edit the declaration
section of your form as follows:

```
'Declare a variable for the current URL
Public WithEvents Explorer As SHDocVw.InternetExplorer
```

After you use the WithEvents keyword, the Explorer object appears automatically in the Object drop-down list box in the Code window. When you select the Explorer object, its events appear in the Procedure drop-down list box. You can then select each event that you want to control and build an event procedure for it. You'll see how this works in the ShowHTML program.

## Using the NavigateComplete2 Event

In this exercise you'll write an event procedure that adds the URL for the current Web site in the Internet Explorer to the combo box object in the ShowHTML program.

1. Save the ShowHTML form as **MyHtmlHist.frm,** and then save the ShowHTML project as **MyHtmlHist.vbp.**

2. Display the Code window and scroll to the Declarations section of the program, which is located at the top of the program listing.

3. Add the WithEvents keyword to the Internet Explorer object declaration after the Public keyword.

   Your object declaration should look like this:

   ```
   Public WithEvents Explorer As SHDocVw.InternetExplorer
   ```

4. Click the Object drop-down list box in the Code window and click the Explorer object.

5. Click the Procedure drop-down list box in the Code window and click the NavigateComplete2 event.

   The parameters for the Explorer_NavigateComplete2 event procedure appear in the Code window.

6. Type the following statement in the event procedure:

   ```
   Combo1.AddItem Explorer.LocationURL
   ```

   Your procedure should now look like this:

   ```
   Private Sub Explorer_NavigateComplete2(ByVal pDisp _
           As Object, URL As Variant)
       Combo1.AddItem Explorer.LocationURL
   End Sub
   ```

The NavigateComplete2 event occurs when the Internet Explorer object has successfully loaded the specified document into the browser. This event only occurs when the document has been loaded successfully—an invalid Web page or URL won't trigger the event. As a result, watching for the NavigateComplete2 event is a useful way to keep track of the Web documents you've recently loaded. If you use the LocationURL property of the Explorer object, you can build your own history list of HTML documents. In this example, I've simply added the URL for the document to the combo box on the form, so you can easily revisit the site with a mere mouse click. However, you also could store this information permanently by writing the URL to a file or a database.

7. Click the Save button on the toolbar to save your changes.

*Start button*

8. Click the Start button on the toolbar to run the program.

9. Click one of the Web sites listed in the combo box and click the Display HTML button.

10. After the connection is established, click some of the hyperlinks on the site to jump to a few new URLs.

11. Click the Display HTML Document program icon on the taskbar, and then click the combo box again.

The new sites you visited will appear at the bottom of the list, as shown in the following illustration:

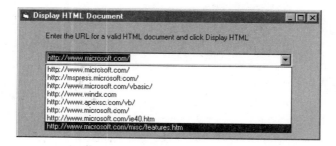

Experiment with the NavigateCompleted2 event by visiting a few more Web sites and adding them to the combo box.

12. When you're finished, close the Internet Explorer windows you have open. Then click the Close button on the HtmlHist application's title bar.

You're finished working with HTML in this lesson. Nice job!

# 18

# Managing Data with the FlexGrid Control

In Lessons 18 and 19, you'll continue your exploration of database programming by focusing on several essential database tools and techniques in Microsoft Visual Basic 6. In Lesson 13, you learned how to use the Data control to display database fields on a form and how to add, delete, and search for records with program code. In this lesson and the following one, you'll learn how to display database information with the FlexGrid control and how to work with a new database technology called ActiveX Data Objects (ADO).

In this lesson you'll practice using the FlexGrid ActiveX control to create a spreadsheet, or *grid,* on a Visual Basic form. The *FlexGrid ActiveX control* can be used to display grids with any type of tabular data: text, numbers, dates—even graphics. However, in this lesson you'll focus on using FlexGrid to display the fields and records of two Microsoft Access databases: Students.mdb and Biblio.mdb. The FlexGrid control translates the fields and records of a database table into columns and rows on a spreadsheet, respectively. You can perform many typical spreadsheet operations with FlexGrid, including selecting cells, resizing columns, aligning headings, and formatting text. You'll start by filling a simple FlexGrid control with text, selecting text, and setting a few formatting options. Next, you'll move on to binding the FlexGrid control to a database, displaying database tables, sorting records, and searching globally for user-defined text strings.

# Using FlexGrid as a General-Purpose Spreadsheet

FlexGrid is an ActiveX control included with the Visual Basic Working Model. (It's also included in Visual Basic Professional Edition and Visual Basic Enterprise Edition.) Before you can use FlexGrid in a project, you need to add it to your project's toolbox by selecting the Microsoft FlexGrid 6.0 control (msflxgrd.ocx) with the Components command on the Project menu. The FlexGrid control provides many of the traditional organizational benefits of a spreadsheet grid. You can use it to create invoices, calculate taxes, manage accounting ledgers, track parts lists and inventories, and so on. In addition, Microsoft designed FlexGrid to be a *bound control* capable of displaying database information from a Data control that is also located on the form. If you want to display database information quickly in its original table format, FlexGrid is the tool for you.

 **IP** Visual Basic also includes a companion spreadsheet control named the *Hierarchical FlexGrid ActiveX control* (mshflxgd.ocx). This control is used in the same way as the FlexGrid control and exposes the same core set of properties, methods, and events. However, the Hierarchical FlexGrid control can only be bound to the ActiveX Data Objects (ADO) control, not to the intrinsic Data control in the Visual Basic toolbox. The adjective "hierarchical" means that the control can display *hierarchical recordsets*—recordsets created from more than one table in a database.

## Understanding Rows and Columns

The spreadsheet grid produced by the FlexGrid control is a form containing a table with horizontal rows and vertical columns. By default, the top row and the left-most column are reserved for row and column titles and are displayed with a shaded background. You use the Rows property to set the number of rows in the table, and the Cols property to set the number of columns. The following illustration shows a form containing a FlexGrid table with eight rows and five columns:

The tabular data in a FlexGrid control is manipulated like a two-dimensional array. The first dimension of the table is a row number, and the second dimension of the table is a column number. For example, the cell in the upper-left corner of the grid is referenced by the address 0, 0 (row 0, column 0).

To place a value in a FlexGrid cell, you set the TextMatrix property and specify a cell location and a value. You may specify any numeric or string data type. For example, to place the word "Bob" in cell 3, 1 (row 3, column 1), you would type the following program statement:

```
MSFlexGrid1.TextMatrix(3, 1) = "Bob"
```

To assign the number 1500 to cell 2, 1 (row 2, column 1), you would use the following syntax:

```
MSFlexGrid1.TextMatrix(2, 1) = 1500
```

## Inserting Graphics into Cells

You can also add graphics to FlexGrid cells with the Set statement, the CellPicture property, and the LoadPicture function. The valid graphics types are icon (.ico), bitmap (.bmp), and Windows metafile (.wmf).

For example, the following program statement displays the Coins.wmf metafile in the selected cell on the grid:

```
Set MSFlexGrid1.CellPicture = _
    LoadPicture("c:\learnvb6\less02\coins.wmf")
```

When you add a graphic to a cell, the FlexGrid control doesn't resize the cell automatically to display it. However, you can manually adjust the height and width of a cell by using the RowHeight and ColWidth properties and specifying a measurement in twips for each. For example, the following statements widen the first row and the first column of the grid to 2000 twips. The numbers in parentheses represent the current row and column, respectively.

```
MSFlexGrid1.RowHeight(1) = 2000
MSFlexGrid1.ColWidth(1) = 2000
```

Placing these statements directly above the Set statement that loads your graphic into the CellPicture property will enlarge the cell sufficiently to display the entire graphic.

 **IP** When you resize one cell in the grid, you resize that cell's entire row and entire column.

## Selecting Cells

As with most spreadsheets, you need to select cells in the FlexGrid control before you can format them. In the FlexGrid control, you can select individual cells or a *range* (a contiguous block) of cells with program code. To select an individual cell, simply set the Row property to the row you want to select and set the Col property to the column you want to select. The selected cell will be at the intersection of the row and the column you specified. For example, to select cell 1, 1 on the grid, use the following program statements:

```
MSFlexGrid1.Row = 1
MSFlexGrid1.Col = 1
```

To select a range of cells, you need to specify a starting and ending point for the selection. The starting point is the cell you last selected with the Row and Col properties (row 1, column 1 above). The ending point of the selection is identified by the RowSel and ColSel properties. For example, the following program statements select a contiguous block of eight cells (cell 2, 2 to cell 5, 3) on the FlexGrid control:

```
MSFlexGrid1.Row = 2
MSFlexGrid1.Col = 2
MSFlexGrid1.RowSel = 5
MSFlexGrid1.ColSel = 3
```

On your form, the selection just described will look like the following figure:

Cell 2, 2 (row 2, column 2)

Cell 5, 3 (row 5, column 3)

Finally, if you plan to format a range of cells, you need to include the following program statement after you make the selection:

```
MSFlexGrid1.FillStyle = flexFillRepeat
```

The flexFillRepeat value allows the FlexGrid control to format more than one selected cell at a time. (The default value, flexFillSingle, allows only one cell to be formatted at a time.) After this statement, you're ready to begin formatting selected cells individually or in ranges.

---

 **IP** You can also involve the user in the selection process if you want. For example, you could allow the user to select a group of cells on the FlexGrid control and then click a button to change the text style of the selected cells to bold. You can control how the grid is accessed by users at runtime by setting the SelectionMode property to one of three options: flexSelectionFree (regular selection), flexSelectionByRow (selection by rows only), or flexSelectionByColumn (selection by column only).

---

## Formatting Cells

The FlexGrid control provides many of the standard cell formatting features that you'll find in a commercial spreadsheet application. These include properties for bold, italic, and underline formatting; text alignment in columns; font name and size; and foreground and background colors. The following table lists the most important formatting options available to you. You'll practice setting many of these properties later in this lesson.

| Property | Example |
| --- | --- |
| CellFontBold | MSFlexGrid1.CellFontBold = True |
| CellFontItalic | MSFlexGrid1.CellFontItalic = True |
| CellFontUnderline | MSFlexGrid1.CellFontUnderline = True |
| CellAlignment | MSFlexGrid1.CellAlignment = flexAlignRightCenter |
| CellFontName | MSFlexGrid1.CellFontName = "Courier New" |
| CellFontSize | MSFlexGrid1.CellFontSize = 14 |
| CellForeColor | MSFlexGrid1.CellForeColor = "1" |
| CellBackColor | MSFlexGrid1.CellBackColor = "500" |

## Adding New Rows

When you use the FlexGrid control to create invoices, accounting journal entries, and other tabular items, you'll find it useful to add new rows to the bottom of the spreadsheet. You can accomplish this with the AddItem method. The AddItem method works for the FlexControl just as it does for the ListBox and ComboBox controls. You specify the item you want to add, separating the information in each column with a tab character (the vbTab constant). For example, to add a new row to the bottom of a FlexGrid control with part information (beginning in the second column), use the following code:

```
Dim Row As String
Row = vbTab & "Soccer ball" & vbTab & "W17-233" & vbTab & "34.95"
MSFlexGrid1.AddItem Row
```

As shown in the figure on the next page, such a statement would create a new row with part information for a soccer ball.

## Using a FlexGrid Control to Track Sales Data

Now that you've acquired some knowledge of the properties and methods of the FlexGrid control, you'll practice using it to create a two-quarter sales table that tracks sales by region.

1. Start Visual Basic and open a new, standard project.

2. Enlarge the Project Container and Form windows so that you have plenty of room on your form to display a spreadsheet with several rows and columns.

3. On the Project menu, click the Components command, and then click the Controls tab.

   The ActiveX controls that have been registered in your system registry appear in the Components dialog box.

4. Place a check mark next to the Microsoft FlexGrid Control 6.0 entry, and then click OK.

   Visual Basic adds the FlexGrid control to your toolbox.

*FlexGrid control*

5. Click the FlexGrid control in the toolbox, and then create a large flex grid object on your form.

6. Double-click the CommandButton control in the toolbox.

   A default-sized command button object appears on your form.

7. Drag the command button object below the flex grid object.

8. Use the Properties window to change the Caption property of the command button object to "Add Rows".

9. Use the Properties window to change the Cols property of the MSFlexGrid1 object to 4.

The Cols property contains the number of columns that will appear in your flex grid object. (You can change this value at runtime with program code.) Your form will look similar to the following:

## Writing the FlexGrid Program Code

In this exercise you'll write the program code that creates a sales table in the flex grid object.

1. Double-click the form to open the Form_Load event procedure in the Code window.

2. Type the following program code:

```
With MSFlexGrid1      'use shorthand "With" notation
    'Create headings for Columns 1 and 2
    .TextMatrix(0, 1) = "Q1 1999"
    .TextMatrix(0, 2) = "Q2 1999"
    'Select headings
    .Row = 0
    .Col = 1
    .RowSel = 0
    .ColSel = 2
```

```
        'Format headings with bold and align on center
        .FillStyle = flexFillRepeat 'fill entire selection
        .CellFontBold = True
        .CellAlignment = flexAlignCenterCenter
        'Add three entries for first row
        .TextMatrix(1, 0) = "International"  'title column (0)
        .TextMatrix(1, 1) = "55000"              'col 1
        .TextMatrix(1, 2) = "83000"              'col 2
End With
```

The program statements in this event procedure are executed when Visual Basic starts the program and loads the first form into memory. These statements demonstrate several techniques for entering and managing information in a flex grid object: placing text in individual cells, selecting a cell range, formatting the range in bold type, and aligning the text in each cell in the range on center.

Of particular interest here is the With statement (introduced in Lesson 14), which allows you to forgo the drudgery of typing in the MSFlexGrid1 object name each time you want to access one of its properties or methods. Remember that each time you use a With statement in this way, as a shorthand notation, you must conclude the routine that follows it with an End With statement.

3. Next, click the Object drop-down list box in the Code window, and then select the Command1 object.

4. In the Command1_Click event procedure, type the following program code:

```
With MSFlexGrid1
    'Add four entries to table with each click
    .AddItem "North" & vbTab & "45,000" & vbTab & "53,000"
    .AddItem "South" & vbTab & "20,000" & vbTab & "25,000"
    .AddItem "East" & vbTab & "38,000" & vbTab & "77,300"
    .AddItem "West" & vbTab & "102,000" & vbTab & "87,500"
End With
```

The program statements in this event procedure are executed when the user clicks the Add Rows button on the form. The AddItem method creates a new row in the flex grid object and fills the first three columns with data. The vbTab constant marks the beginning of a new column in the table.

5. On the File menu, click the Save Project As command. Save your form as **MySaleGrid.frm** and your project as **MySaleGrid.vbp.**

### Running the MySaleGrid program

Now you'll run the program to see how the FlexGrid control displays tabular data.

*Start button*

1. Click the Start button on the toolbar.

   The program loads and displays the flex grid object with two column headings and one row of data. (These entries and formatting selections were defined by the Form_Load event procedure.)

2. Click the Add Rows button.

   Visual Basic adds four rows of sales data to the table. (These cells were created by the AddItem method in the Command1_Click event procedure.) Your form will look like the following illustration:

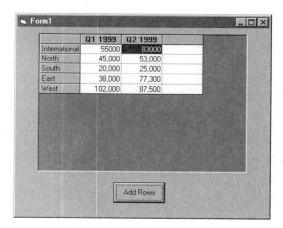

3. Click the Add Rows button two more times.

   Visual Basic adds eight more rows to the table. Scroll bars appear on the right side of the table to let you access the rows that are no longer visible.

4. Continue adding rows if you like and use the scroll bars to access them. When you're finished, click the Close button on the form's title bar.

The program terminates.

# Using FlexGrid to Display Database Records

As you've probably noticed, adding table entries one at a time to a FlexGrid control can be a little cumbersome. However, connecting the FlexGrid control to a properly configured Data control on your form makes the powerful text management capabilities of FlexGrid really apparent. Like other bound controls, the Data control is connected to the FlexGrid control by a property setting. In this case, you set the FlexGrid's DataSource property to the name of the Data control on your form. When you establish this connection, the flex grid object fills with database records automatically.

In the following exercise, you'll open and run the DataGrid program, which demonstrates how you can display database records on a form by using the FlexGrid control. The DataGrid program displays database records as a table and provides access to them with scroll bars. In addition, the program demonstrates two operations that are especially handy with large databases: a sort function that sorts database records by column and a search function that searches an entire database for keywords and highlights them. The DataGrid program is an extension of the Courses.vbp project developed in Lesson 13, which lets the user add, delete, and find records in a Microsoft Access database called Students.mdb. In the DataGrid program, you also have the options of displaying your database table as a grid and creating new views with the sort and search functions.

## Running the DataGrid Program

1. Open the DataGrid.vbp project in the C:\LearnVb6\Less18 folder.

If you are asked to save any changes to the MySaleGrid project, click Yes.

*Start button*

2. Click the Start button to run the DataGrid program.

Visual Basic loads the DataGrid form, which is similar to the DelRec.frm user interface you created in Lesson 13. The new Grid View button on the form is used to open a second form containing a flex grid object.

3. Click the Grid View button.

Visual Basic opens the second form (GridView.frm) and uses the flex grid object to display the Students table in the Students.mdb database. Your form will look like the following figure:

The flex grid object automatically loads database records from the Students.mdb database in this program—no program code is used to copy the individual rows from the database.

4. Move the mouse pointer to the top row of the flex grid object, between the Address and City headers.

The mouse pointer changes into a resizing pointer. When the FlexGrid control's AllowUserResizing property is set to 1 - flexResizeColumns, the user can change the width of the columns in the spreadsheet.

5. Use the resizing pointer to increase the width of the Address column.

The column increases in size and displays more data. In most cases you'll want to give your users this viewing convenience.

Now try using the sort and search features.

6. Click the Sort button on the Grid View form.

The flex grid object sorts the rows in the spreadsheet alphabetically by comparing each cell in the LastName column. (I chose this column as the sorting key in the program code, as you'll see later.) As in the figure below, it's easy to see the results of the sort because the first column (StudentID) still preserves the original creation order of the entries (although they're now jumbled about).

**TIP** The true, internal order of the Students.mdb database hasn't changed with this sorting operation—only the contents of the flex grid spreadsheet have changed. The link between the Data control and the FlexGrid control is one-way, so the changes you make in the flex grid object don't update the database.

7. Click the Find Text button on the Grid View form.

   Visual Basic searches the spreadsheet for the text in the find text box (currently "Seattle," a default value I put in the text box). After a moment, each cell that contains the Seattle text is highlighted with bold formatting.

   If you watch closely when you click the Find Text button, you might see a progress bar object appear briefly at the bottom of the screen to track the search progress. I added this to give users visual feedback during long searches (those involving thousands of records), but because this database is so small, it comes and goes pretty fast. You'll see this progress bar again later in this lesson when you search for text in the giant Biblio.mdb database.

8. Click the text box on the form, delete the current contents (Seattle), type **an**, and click the Find Text button.

   This time Visual Basic highlights four cells that contain the text string "an". Because I'm using the InStr function, I am also able to detect partial hits for my search. (In other words, this search will highlight words that contain the letters "an," such as Nancy.)

9. Click the Close button on the Grid View form, and then click the Quit button on the Data Browser form.

The program closes, and the development environment returns.

## Advanced Sort and Search Operations

The DataGrid program can sort and search the entire contents of a database table because of several handy features of the FlexGrid control and a few concise event procedures. Sorting is handled by the FlexGrid's Sort property, which sorts a table based on one or more key columns and a directional sorting argument. Searching is handled in a straightforward manner by two nested For...Next loops and an InStr function that compares each cell to the search string. You'll see how these event procedures work in the following exercise.

### Exploring the DataGrid program code

1. Open the Form2 Code window and display the cmdSort_Click event procedure.

You'll see the following program code:

```
Private Sub cmdSort_Click()
    'Set column 2 (LastName) as the sort key
    MSFlexGrid1.Col = 2
    'Sort grid in ascending order
    MSFlexGrid1.Sort = 1
End Sub
```

This simple event procedure uses two program statements to sort the entire contents of the database in the flex grid object. The first statement sets the second column as the comparison key for the sort. I chose the LastName field because it's traditionally used to order lists, but any column in the database table could be chosen. The sort itself is executed by the Sort property, which takes an integer argument from 0 to 9 that indicates the direction of the sort. I chose argument 1 (generic ascending), which means that the control sorts the cells in alphabetical order and tries to guess if the cell contains a number or a string before the sort begins. Other popular options include 2 (generic descending), 3 (numeric ascending), and 4 (numeric descending). In numeric sorts, strings are converted to numbers (their ASCII equivalents) before the sort begins.

2. Open the cmdFindText_Click event procedure in the Code window.

   You'll see the following program code:

```
Private Sub cmdFindTxt_Click()
    'Select entire grid and remove bold formatting
    '(to remove the results of previous finds)
    MSFlexGrid1.FillStyle = flexFillRepeat
    MSFlexGrid1.Col = 0
    MSFlexGrid1.Row = 0
    MSFlexGrid1.ColSel = MSFlexGrid1.Cols - 1
    MSFlexGrid1.RowSel = MSFlexGrid1.Rows - 1
    MSFlexGrid1.CellFontBold = False

    'Initialize ProgressBar to track search
    ProgressBar1.Min = 0
    ProgressBar1.Max = MSFlexGrid1.Rows - 1
    ProgressBar1.Visible = True

    'Search the grid cell by cell for find text
    MSFlexGrid1.FillStyle = flexFillSingle
    For i = 0 To MSFlexGrid1.Cols - 1
        For j = 1 To MSFlexGrid1.Rows - 1
        'Display current row location on ProgressBar
        ProgressBar1.Value = j
            'If current cell matches find text box
            If InStr(MSFlexGrid1.TextMatrix(j, i), _
            Text1.Text) Then
                '...select cell and format bold
                MSFlexGrid1.Col = i
                MSFlexGrid1.Row = j
                MSFlexGrid1.CellFontBold = True
            End If
        Next j
    Next i
    ProgressBar1.Visible = False 'hide ProgressBar
End Sub
```

The cmdFindText_Click event procedure runs when the user clicks the Find Text button on Form2. The purpose of the routine is to compare each cell in the flex grid object with the search text in the Text1 text box and to change the cell formatting of any matching cells to bold. The event procedure first clears any existing bold formatting from the flex grid object by selecting the entire spreadsheet and changing its CellFontBold property to False. Then the procedure initializes the progress bar object to display graphical output at the bottom of the screen while the search continues (the progress bar is filled once for each column in the table).

The flex grid search itself is accomplished by two For…Next loops: one loop to step through each row in the table and one loop to step through each column. The loop then uses the TextMatrix property and the InStr function to compare the current loop position (j, i) with the find text string (Text1.Text). If a match is found, the CellFontBold property sets the text formatting in the cell to bold.

3. Close the Code window.

You've finished looking at the DataGrid program code.

### DataGrid Property Settings

Before you leave the DataGrid program, take note of a few important property settings for the objects on Form2 (GridView.frm). They demonstrate the close connection between the flex grid object and the data object. (I set these properties at design time with the Properties window.)

- **Flex grid object** The FixedCols property is set to 0 to suppress the heading column on the spreadsheet. (The Students data table doesn't use it.) The first row and column of the flex grid is gray-shaded by default, but you can remove the shading by setting the FixedCols or FixedRows property to 0.

- **Data object** The DatabaseName property of this object is set to C:\LearnVb6\Less03\Students.mdb, and the RecordSource property is set to Students. The Visible property is set to False to hide the user interface to the control. This project has two Data controls that point to the same database (which is totally legitimate in Visual Basic). You can also have the Data controls point to different databases, as you'll see in the next exercise.

# Searching the Biblio.mdb Database

The DataGrid program provided a useful demonstration of the concepts in this lesson. Before you move on to the next lesson, I thought you might like to see how the FlexGrid control works with really big databases. When you write your own database applications, it's always a good idea to "stress test" your database tools before you put them to work on complex, mission-critical data sources.

Try revising the DataGrid program now to work with the Biblio.mdb database, an Access database included with the Visual Basic Working Model that contains over 10,000 records and several complex tables. To demonstrate how you can access two different databases from one project, you'll leave the data object on Form1 connected to the Students.mdb database, but you'll change the data object connection on Form2 to Biblio.mdb.

## Using the FlexGrid Control to Display Biblio.mdb Records

1. Display Form2 in the DataGrid.vbp project and select the data object on the form.

   (The DataGrid project should still be loaded in the development environment. If it's not, load it now from the C:\LearnVb6\Less18 folder.)

2. In the Properties window, change the DatabaseName property of the Data1 object to the Biblio.mdb database.

---

 **IP**  The Biblio.mdb database isn't located in the \LearnVb6\Less18 folder—you'll have to locate it on disk. If you installed the Visual Basic Working Model with the default settings, Biblio.mdb will be located in the C:\Program Files\Microsoft Visual Studio\Vb98 folder.

---

3. In the Properties window, click the RecordSource property of the Data1 object, and then click the Titles record.

   The Titles record contains a large collection of books about computer programming.

4. Double-click the Sort button on Form2 to open the cmdSort_Click event procedure in the Code window.

5. In the line that assigns the Col property to set the key column for the sort, change the 2 to a **0**.

   You want to use the first column in the table (Titles) as the key for the sort. The program statement should look like this:

   ```
   MSFlexGrid1.Col = 0
   ```

   Now you'll run the program.

*Start button*

6. Click the Start button on the toolbar.

   Visual Basic displays the first form in your program, which opens the Students.mdb database and fills several bound text boxes with data.

7. Click the Grid View button.

   Visual Basic loads the Biblio.mdb database in the flex grid object and displays it. (This may take a few moments—Biblio is large!)

8. Use the resizing pointer to widen the first column of the flex grid object.

   Your form will look similar to the following figure:

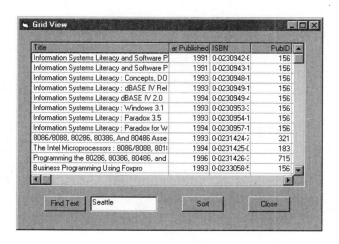

9. Click the Sort button to sort the table using the first column for the comparison.

   After a moment, the database is sorted alphabetically. Your form looks like this:

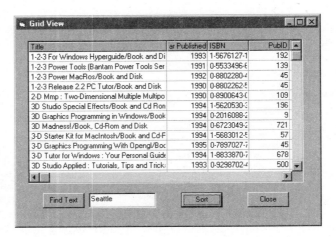

10. Now delete the text in the text box, type **Book**, and click the Find Text button.

    The search begins, and you can see several cells in the first column with bold formatting. The progress bar at the bottom of the screen gives you graphical feedback for the lengthy operation, which involves checking over 80,000 cells. (The progress bar fills once per column.) After several moments (depending on the speed of your computer), the flex grid will complete its global search task and the scroll bars will be available for use. Your form will look like the figure on the top of the following page.

11. Take a few moments scrolling through the database—you've just scanned a lot of text!

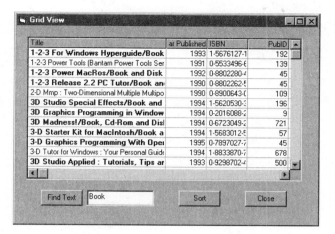

12. When you're finished, click the Close button on Form2, and then click the Quit button on Form1. (Closing the Grid View form will also take a few moments.)

# 19

# Exploring ActiveX Data Objects (ADO)

In this lesson you'll get your feet wet with an exciting new database technology from Microsoft called *ActiveX Data Objects (ADO).* You'll learn how to install and use the ADO ActiveX control, how to display database fields and records on your form with bound controls, and how to write program code that manages ADO transactions. These skills will help you manage stand-alone Microsoft Access databases, corporate intranet databases, and distributed database objects on the World Wide Web. You'll also be ready to exploit the Microsoft Data Environment Designer, an advanced database tool included with Visual Basic 6.0 Professional and Enterprise Editions.

This lesson requires that you either have Access 97 or Access 2000 installed on your system, or have installed drivers from a third-party database application that is compatible with ADO. The first part of this lesson steps you through the process of creating a Data Source Name, which you must build on your computer before you run the sample projects included in the \Less19 folder on your hard drive. If you don't create a Data Source Name for your database, you'll see the error message, "Data source name not found and no default driver specified" when you run the samples.

# Inside ADO

ADO is Microsoft's newest technology for working with information in relational and nonrelational databases. (Relational database management systems manipulate information in tables, but not all data sources follow this model.) ADO doesn't completely replace the existing database technology—Data Access Objects (DAO)—that you've been working with in this book, but it does extend DAO programming into new areas. ADO is based on Microsoft's latest data access paradigm, called OLE DB, which has been specifically designed to provide access to a wide range of business data sources, including traditional relational database tables, email systems, graphics formats, Internet resources, and so on. ADO requires less memory than DAO, so it's more suitable for networked computer systems that experience heavy traffic and high transaction rates.

Microsoft recommends that Visual Basic programmers use ADO when they create new database applications in Visual Basic and has included several features specifically designed to support ADO in Visual Basic 6. However, ADO is an emerging technology that you should explore only after you've gained a firm understanding of the fundamental database programming concepts discussed already in this book: using the intrinsic Data control, displaying data with bound controls, managing fields and records with event procedures, using a FlexGrid control to display and sort records, and so forth. When you upgrade to ADO, you'll be looking at database information in an entirely new way.

# Using the ADO ActiveX Control

The easiest way to experiment with ADO is to use the new ADO ActiveX control to display the fields and records in an Access database on a form. Following the ADO paradigm, the ADO control does not include a DatabaseName property that lets you connect directly to a database file on your computer. Instead, the ADO control contains a ConnectionString property that lets you connect to an ActiveX data source on your computer. A series of dialog boxes help you make this connection, and you can customize the process by building new ActiveX data objects from existing data sources with the Data Environment Designer. (You'll learn how to do this later in the lesson.)

Once you understand the practical differences between ADO and DAO connections, you'll find the ADO control to be quite similar to the intrinsic Data control. In this section you'll learn how to add the ADO control to your toolbox, how to set the ConnectionString property, and how to display database records on your form with a few bound controls. You'll also master the fundamentals of ADO program code.

## Three Database-Programming Paradigms

Microsoft has offered three different database-programming paradigms to Visual Basic programmers over the years, and each is fully supported in Visual Basic 6. Master these acronyms for small talk at your next cocktail party!

- **DAO** The Data Access Objects (DAO) paradigm was the first object-oriented interface that allowed programmers to manipulate the Microsoft Jet database engine. The Jet database engine is a technology used to access the fields and records in Access tables and other data sources. DAO is still popular and effective for single-system database applications and small-size to medium-size workgroup networks.

- **RDO** The Remote Data Objects (RDO) paradigm is an object-oriented interface to Open Database Connectivity (ODBC) sources. RDO is the object model used by most database developers who work intensively with Microsoft SQL Server, Oracle, and other large relational databases.

- **ADO** The ActiveX Data Objects (ADO) paradigm has been designed as the successor to DAO and RDO, and it has a similar object model. In ADO, programmable objects represent all the local and remote data sources available to your computer. You can access these data objects in Visual Basic by using the new ADO control, by binding data objects to intrinsic and ActiveX controls, by creating DHTML applications, and by using the new Data Environment Designer. (Note: the Data Environment Designer isn't included with the Visual Basic Working Model.)

## Installing the ADO Control

The ADO control is an ActiveX control that you need to add to your toolbox before you can use it in a program. You'll install the ADO control in this exercise.

1. Start Visual Basic and open a new, standard project.

2. On the Project menu, click the Components command, and then click the Controls tab.

3. Scroll down the list to the Microsoft ADO Data Control 6.0 item, and then click the check box next to it.

4. Click OK to add the control to your toolbox.

   Visual Basic adds the ADO control, as shown in the following illustration:

ADO Data control

Now you'll create an ADO object on your form to display a few records from the Students.mdb database.

## Creating an ADO Object and Bound Controls

*ADO Data control*

1. Click the ADO control in the toolbox, and then create a small, rectangular ADO object on your form.

    When you release the mouse button, Visual Basic creates an ADO object. Your form will look like this:

Like the Data control you used in Lessons 3 and 13, the ADO control creates a database navigation control with four arrows. At runtime, when the object is visible and connected to a suitable database, you can click the first left arrow to move to the first record in the database, and the last right arrow to move to the last record in the database. The inner arrows allow you to move to the previous and next database records, respectively.

---

 **IP**   You can change the title text displayed in the ADO data object by selecting the ADO object, opening the Properties window, and modifying the Caption property.

---

Now you'll add two text box controls to the form to display the LastName and PhoneNumber fields in the Students.mdb database.

*TextBox control*

2. Click the TextBox control in the toolbox, and create a text box object below the ADO object. After you create the first object, click the TextBox control again and create another one beside it.

Your form will look like this:

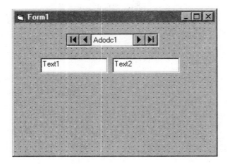

## Creating a Data Source Name

If you were using the Data control now, you'd simply set the DatabaseName property of the Data control to the pathname of a valid database on your system to link to the database. However, the designers of ADO have asked you to take one more preliminary step in the name of future flexibility. You need to describe the database record you want to link to by creating an ActiveX Data Object. You have three options when you create data objects: you can create an OLE DB file; you can create an ODBC Data Source Name (DSN) file; or you can build an OLE DB connection string. The Data Environment Designer is designed specifically to help you create ActiveX Data Objects. (You'll try this later in the lesson.) However, you can also create the necessary files by using the ADO control's ConnectionString property.

In the following exercise, you'll establish a connection to the Students.mdb database with the ADO control's ConnectionString property. To facilitate the connection and provide the necessary ActiveX data objects, you'll create an ODBC Data Source Name file.

 **IP**  You only need to create a Data Source Name (.dsn) file once for each data source you plan to use. After that, you can use the file over and over again to reference the same data tables.

### Setting the ConnectionString property

1. Click the ADO object on your form, open the Properties window, and click the button in the ConnectionString property field.

   A Property Pages dialog box appears, as shown in the following illustration:

2. Click the second option button in the list (Use ODBC Data Source Name).

   You'll create a Data Source Name file that references the Students.mdb database. You'll be able to use this file now and in the future.

3. Click the New button to the right of the Use ODBC Data Source Name option button.

   The illustration at the top of the next page shows the dialog box (the first in a series).

   This dialog box asks how you intend to share the database you're accessing in this Visual Basic program. The top selection (File Data Source) signifies that your database will be made available to users on other computers (through a network or the Internet). This option allows you considerable flexibility, but it isn't necessary for single-system database applications.

The second option (User Data Source) means that the database resides on the physical machine you're working on now and that it will be used only by you (a person with your username). You'll choose the second option in this lesson, because you're creating a simple demonstration for yourself only.

The third option (System Data Source) means that the database resides on the physical machine you're working on and should be made generally available to other people who use your computer and are logged in under different usernames. (A popular work arrangement on some Microsoft Windows workstations.)

4. Click the second option button (User Data Source), and then click the Next button.

As shown in the figure at the top of the next page, you'll be prompted for the database driver you want to use when making the connection to your database. A number of formats are supported.

5. Microsoft Access Driver (the option you want) is selected by default, so click the Next button to continue.

Visual Basic summarizes the selections you've made and asks you to click the Finish button to continue configuring your Data Source Name file.

6. Click the Finish button.

A new dialog box appears named ODBC Microsoft Access Setup. This dialog box lets you name your Data Source Name file, select the database you'll be connecting to, and customize your connection.

7. Type **Student Records** in the Data Source Name text box.

Student Records is the name you'll use later when you're prompted for a DSN file in the Property Pages dialog box.

8. Click the Select button, browse to the C:\LearnVb6\Less03 folder, click the Students.mdb database, and click OK.

Your dialog box will look like the following figure:

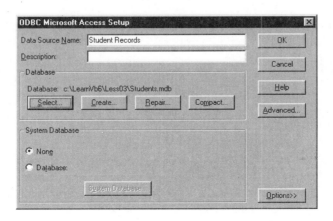

9. Click OK to close the dialog box.

   The Property Pages dialog box reappears. You just created a new DSN file, so your only remaining task is to select the DSN from the drop-down list box below the Use ODBC Data Source Name option button.

10. Click the ODBC Data Source Name drop-down list box, and then click the Student Records item.

11. Click OK in the Property Pages dialog box to finalize your connection.

    The Property Pages dialog box closes, and the entry DSN=Student Records appears in the Properties window next to the ConnectionString property.

That wasn't so bad, was it? Although creating a Data Source Name file takes a few extra steps, the process allows you substantial latitude in customizing how each database connection is configured and established. When you start managing complex databases with Visual Basic, you'll appreciate the flexibility and consistency that Data Source Names provide.

Now you'll put your database connection to work by binding database fields from the ADO object to your two text boxes.

## Binding ADO Data to Text Box Objects

1. With the ADO object (adodc1) still selected in the Properties window, scroll down to the RecordSource property, and click the button to the right of the RecordSource property name.

   You'll see the Property Pages dialog box again, and this time the RecordSource tab is visible. In ADO programming, you have access to more than just database tables in your database connections. You can also reference stored procedure objects and text objects in your data sources. In ADO, the ActiveX objects you use are called *commands*. In this exercise, you'll select the Table command type, which gives you access to the tables in the Students.mdb database and a few other table objects provided by ADO.

2. Click the Command Type drop-down list box, and then select 2 - adCmdTable.

   Using the DSN file, Visual Basic opens the Students.mdb database and loads the table names in the Table Or Stored Procedure Name drop-down list box.

3. Click the Table Or Stored Procedure Name drop-down list box, scroll down the list, and select the Students table.

   Your Property Pages dialog box will look like this:

4. Click OK to finalize your RecordSource selection.

   The table name Students appears in the Properties window next to the RecordSource property.

5. Click the Text1 object in the Properties window. Set its DataSource property to Adodc1 and its DataField property to LastName.

6. Click the Text2 object in the Properties window. Set its DataSource property to Adodc1 and its DataField property to PhoneNumber.

   As you learned in earlier lessons, linking intrinsic toolbox controls or ActiveX controls to a data object on a form in this way is called *binding* the data to controls.

Now you'll run the program you've created.

## Running the ADO Control Demo

*Start button*

1. Click the Start button on the toolbar.

   The text boxes fill with data from the first record in the Students.mdb database. Your form looks like this:

2. Click the inner-right arrow (Next) in the ADO object a few times.

   Each time you click the Next arrow, the LastName and PhoneNumber fields for a new record appear on the form.

3. Click the inner-left arrow (Previous) in the ADO object.

   The fields for the previous record appear on the form.

4. Click the outer-right arrow (Last) in the ADO object.

   The ADO object displays the fields for the last record in the database.

5. Click the outer-left arrow (First) in the ADO object.

   The fields for the first record appear again.

6. When you're finished experimenting with the ADO object, click the Close button on the Form1 title bar.

   The development environment reappears.

7. On the File menu, click the Save Project As command. Save your form under the name **MyAdoCtrl.frm** and your project under the name **MyAdoCtrl.vbp**.

Now that you've explored the basics of using ActiveX data objects, it's time to investigate a meatier topic—writing ADO program code.

# Writing ADO Program Code

Event procedures that manage ActiveX data objects are the core of a database application that exploits the ADO paradigm. The methods, properties, and events exposed by ActiveX data objects by means of ADO control are similar in many ways to the methods, properties, and events you processed with the Data control in Lesson 13. For example, you manipulate information in both paradigms through recordsets, which hold the current database information you're manipulating.

In the following exercise, you'll enter ADO program code into a skeleton program I wrote called AdoData. The AdoData program is a modification of the AdoCtrl program you built earlier in this lesson. In its revised form, AdoData allows the user to browse through database records with new Next and Previous command buttons, and it allows you to double-click a field name in a list box and copy all the records in the database that match that field to a text file. (For example, you can copy all the LastName fields to a text file with one double-click.) I've created the complete user interface for you in the project—you just need to enter the program code.

## Creating the MyAdoData Program

*Open button*

1. Click the Open button on the Visual Basic toolbar.

   If you're prompted to save your changes, save them to the MyAdoCtrl project.

2. Open the AdoForm.vbp project located in the C:\LearnVb6\Less19 folder.

3. On the File menu, click the Save AdoForm.frm As command, type **MyAdoData**, and press Enter.

   Saving the form and project under a new name preserves the original files in case you want to try the exercise again later.

4. On the File menu, click the Save Project As command, type **MyAdoData**, and press Enter.

   Your form will look like the following:

   The form still has an ADO object and two text boxes, but I've added a new list box object and two label objects.

5. Double-click the Next command button on the form to open the Command1_Click event procedure in the Code window, and then

enter the following program code between the Sub and End Sub statements:

```
'If not already at last record, move to next
If Not Adodc1.Recordset.EOF Then
    Adodc1.Recordset.MoveNext
End If
```

This simple routine checks the EOF property and advances the ADO object to the next record with the MoveNext method if the current record isn't the last record in the database. By checking the EOF (end of file) property before the move, you avoid the runtime error that would occur if the ADO control tried to move past the last record.

The ADO control is represented in this routine by the Adodc1 object, which is connected to the Students table in the Students.mdb database. As a member of the Adodc1 object, the Recordset property holds the Students table in memory and provides access to its data and commands. This recordset isn't the actual data in your table, but a copy of the data that your application works with at runtime. A recordset may be an exact copy of a table, or it may be the result of a query or other selection activity.

6. Open the Command2_Click event procedure in the Code window and type the following program code between the Sub and End Sub statements:

```
'If not already at first record, move to previous
If Not Adodc1.Recordset.BOF Then
    Adodc1.Recordset.MovePrevious
End If
```

This event procedure programs the Previous button to move back one record when the user clicks it. If the BOF (beginning of file) property evaluates to True, the routine skips the MovePrevious method, because attempting to move to the previous record when the first record is visible would cause a runtime error.

7. Open the Form_Load event procedure in the Code window, and type the following code between the Sub and End Sub statements:

```
'Populate list box with field names
For i = 1 To Adodc1.Recordset.Fields.Count - 1
    List1.AddItem Adodc1.Recordset.Fields(i).Name
Next i
'Display total number of records
Label1.Caption = "Total records: " & _
    Adodc1.Recordset.RecordCount
```

The Form_Load event procedure performs two tasks. It adds each field name in the Students table to the list box object (List1), and it displays the total number of records in the database with the first label object (Label1). Both tasks are accomplished by a careful use of the ADO object's properties.

I use the Fields collection to get both a count of the fields and the names of individual items. You can access the fields in a table by using an index with the Fields object name. For example, Fields(2) represents the second field in the table. With a For...Next loop that runs once for each field in the database, I copy the name of each field into the list box object so that the user can select it later by double-clicking it.

I use the RecordCount property to display the total number of records on the form. This value lets users know how many records will be written to disk if they choose to double-click field names in the list box object. To keep this value manageable, I have limited the Students.mdb database to seven records. (The user may want to think twice before writing the 10,000 fields from the Biblio.mdb database to a text file!)

8. Open the List1_DblClick event procedure in the Code window.

9. Type the following program statements between the Sub and End Sub statements:

```
'Create constant to hold text file name
Const myFile = "c:\learnvb6\less19\names.txt"
'Open file for Append (to support multiple fields)
Open myFile For Append As #1
```

```
Print #1, String$(30, "-")   'print dashed line
Adodc1.Recordset.MoveFirst   'move to first record
x = List1.ListIndex + 1      'get item clicked
'For each record in database, write field to disk
For i = 1 To Adodc1.Recordset.RecordCount
    Print #1, Adodc1.Recordset.Fields(x).Value
    Adodc1.Recordset.MoveNext
Next i
'Print success message and close file
MsgBox Adodc1.Recordset.Fields(x).Name & _
    " field written to " & myFile
Close #1
Adodc1.Recordset.MoveFirst
```

*Save button*

10. Click the Save button on the Visual Basic toolbar to save your changes.

The List1_DblClick event procedure handles the actual saving process by creating a text file on disk called Names.txt. First the routine declares a constant to hold the pathname to the file. Then it opens the file in Append mode so that more than one field can be stored in the file without overwriting the previous transaction. I use the MoveFirst method to move the recordset to the first record in the table. Then I determine the field that the user double-clicked in the list box by adding 1 to the ListIndex property and assigning it to the $x$ variable. ListIndex is a useful property that contains the number of the item selected in a list; I increment this number because I need to compensate for the fact that list boxes start with an index value of zero (0).

The actual field value is written to disk with the following program statement:

```
Print #1, Adodc1.Recordset.Fields(x).Value
```

As you learned earlier, the Name property of the Fields collection contains the name of the selected field. This time, I'm using the Value property to access the actual text stored in the field itself. The Print statement writes this value to the text file on its own line. This operation is repeated for each matching field in the database.

Now you'll run the program to see how the ADO code works.

## Running the AdoData Program

*Start button*

1. Click the Start button on the toolbar.

   The ADO object opens the Students.mdb database and displays its fields in two text boxes and a list box. The current record count (7) is also displayed, as shown in the figure below:

2. Click the Next button to display the next record in the database.

3. The Next button displays the next record, just as the inner-right arrow did on the ADO control.

4. Click the Previous button to display the first record again.

   The Previous button works just as the inner-left arrow does on the ADO control. Now try double-clicking the list box to write a few fields to disk.

5. Double-click the LastName field in the list box.

   The ADO object opens the Names.txt file in the C:\LearnVb6 \Less19 folder and copies seven last names from the Students.mdb database to this file. After the copy operation is completed, you see the following message box:

6. Click OK, and then double-click the Address field in the list box.

   The addresses are written to disk, and a message box again notifies you about the transaction.

7. Click OK, and then click the Close button on the form's title bar.

   You're done running the MyAdoData program.

8. If you like, open the Names.txt file in the C:\LearnVb6\Less19 folder on your hard disk and examine the text file you created with the LastName and Address fields.

   In Microsoft Word, the file looks like this:

Congratulations! You've taken several important steps in learning to work with ADO recordsets and event procedures.

**IP** To learn more about the ADO object model, open the Object Browser and examine the properties, methods, and events exposed by the MSAdodcLib library.

# Additional Resources for Visual Basic Programming

Congratulations! You've completed the *Learn Visual Basic Now* programming course. Skim through the lessons you've completed and assess the journey you've taken. Learning to write effective Visual Basic applications requires many skills. Among them are: a thorough understanding of intrinsic toolbox controls and ActiveX components; the ability to set and manipulate an object's methods, properties, and events; the capacity to write clean, reusable program code; and the vision to design an effective user interface. Each lesson in this course has emphasized these principles. You'll find that you can immediately apply the skills you've learned in the simple examples presented here to more sophisticated Visual Basic applications in the real world.

The secret to becoming a professional Visual Basic developer is writing programs that push your knowledge of Visual Basic to its limits and require you to learn more. As you seek to expand your programming skills, I recommend that you consult the following resources:

- For information about using Visual Basic for Applications to manage documents, streamline word-processing tasks, and collect information on the Internet, purchase *Microsoft Word 97/Visual Basic Step by Step* (Microsoft Press, 1997), by Michael Halvorson and Chris Kinata, ISBN 1-57231-388-9.

- To learn intermediate and advanced Visual Basic techniques in the context of a multimedia programming course featuring videos, animation, demonstrations, and step by step tutorials, try *Mastering Microsoft Visual Basic 6* (Microsoft Corporation, 1998).

- If you like to learn by using sample code and running real-world applications, I recommend *Microsoft Visual Basic 6.0 Developer's Workshop, Fifth Edition* (Microsoft Press, 1998), by John Clark Craig and Jeff Webb, ISBN 1-57231-883-X.

- For advanced information about professional programming techniques and using Windows API functions, try *Hardcore Visual Basic (5.0), Second Edition* (Microsoft Press, 1997), by Bruce McKinney, ISBN 1-57231-422-2.

- For an eclectic collection of articles and professional techniques from a group of humorous Visual Basic consultants, try *Advanced Microsoft Visual Basic (6.0), Second Edition* (Microsoft Press, 1998), by The Mandelbrot Set, ISBN 1-57231-893-7.

- For a comprehensive discussion of professional data access techniques using Visual Basic, see *Hitchhiker's Guide to Visual Basic and SQL Server, Sixth Edition* (Microsoft Press, 1998), by William R. Vaughn, ISBN 1-57231-848-1.

In addition to the printed and CD-ROM learning resources I've listed, I recommend that you check the Microsoft Visual Basic corporate Web site periodically for breaking news about Visual Basic technology. This site will give you up-to-date information about the entire Visual Basic product line and will let you know how new operating systems, applications, and programming tools affect Visual Basic development. You can also learn about certification training, conferences, software updates, new ActiveX controls, training materials, and other Microsoft products. Connect to:

*http://msdn.microsoft.com/vbasic/*

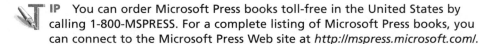 **IP** You can order Microsoft Press books toll-free in the United States by calling 1-800-MSPRESS. For a complete listing of Microsoft Press books, you can connect to the Microsoft Press Web site at *http://mspress.microsoft.com/*.

# M

# S

# About the Author

**Michael Halvorson** worked for Microsoft Corporation from 1985 to 1993, where he was employed as a technical editor, an acquisitions editor, and a localization manager. He is a graduate of Lydia Jane Hawk Elementary School in Olympia, Washington, where he played outfield on the school baseball team. Michael's first full-length book report at Lydia Hawk, *South Dakota: The Sunshine State*, received an A+ in Mr. Mauer's fifth grade homeroom class.

Michael is currently a doctoral candidate in History at the University of Washington in Seattle, Washington, and the author or co-author of ten computer books, including *Microsoft Visual Basic 6.0 Professional Step by Step*, *Microsoft Word 97/ Visual Basic Step by Step*, and *Running Microsoft Office 2000*, all published by Microsoft Press. You can send Michael electronic mail at *Mike_Halvorson@msn.com*.

The manuscript for this book was prepared and submitted to Microsoft Press in electronic form. Text files were prepared using Microsoft Word 97 for Windows 95. Pages were composed by nSight, Inc. using Adobe PageMaker 6.52 for Windows, with text in Melior and display type in Frutiger Condensed. Composed pages were delivered to the printer as electronic prepress files.

*Cover Designer*
The Leonhardt Group

*Principal Compositors*
Angela Montoya, Tara Murray

*Principal Proofreader*
Elissa Leclerc

*Copy Editor*
Joseph Gustaitis

*Indexer*
Rebecca Plunkett

# Visual Basic
## design and development
### to the *extreme.*

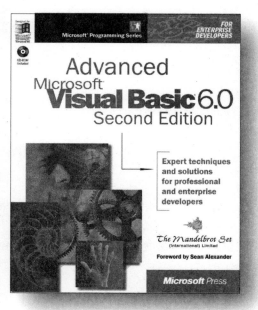

With the release of Microsoft® Visual Basic® 6.0, the Visual Basic product family has added functionality at the very highest level of the developer workspace—fully supporting the next evolution of distributed enterprise development. And for intermediate and advanced Visual Basic programmers looking to push this tool to its new limits, the experts at the renowned Mandelbrot Set (International) Limited have once again delivered the definitive, upper-strata Visual Basic reference.

**U.S.A.**     **$59.99**
U.K.          £55.49 [V.A.T. included]
Canada        $86.99
ISBN 1-57231-893-7

**mspress.microsoft.com**

# Unlock the power of Microsoft Visual Basic 6.0

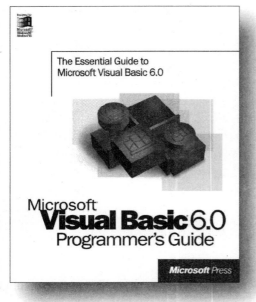

The Essential Guide to Microsoft Visual Basic 6.0

Microsoft **Visual Basic** 6.0 Programmer's Guide

*Microsoft* Press

| | |
|---|---|
| **U.S.A.** | **$39.99** |
| U.K. | £36.99 |
| Canada | $57.99 |
| ISBN 1-57231-863-5 | |

**C**reate applications for standalone desktops, networked PCs, the Internet, and the components market with the MICROSOFT® VISUAL BASIC® 6.0 PROGRAMMER'S GUIDE. Delivered direct from the Microsoft Visual Basic development team, this authoritative reference is designed to help optimize your work with Microsoft's rapid development system for Windows.® Exploit the new features and capabilities in version 6.0 using the expert guidance and official documentation packed into this guide—available in convenient print form exclusively from Microsoft Press.

**Microsoft**®

mspress.microsoft.com

# The
# *comprehensive*
## *official* resource
Microsoft® **for**
# *Visual Basic 6.0.*

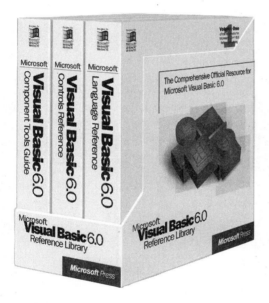

| U.S.A. | **$79.99** |
| U.K. | £74.99 |
| Canada | $115.99 |
| ISBN 1-57231-864-3 | |

**T**he three-volume MICROSOFT® VISUAL BASIC® 6.0 REFERENCE LIBRARY is the official print documentation for version 6.0 of Visual Basic—one of the world's most popular and prolific programming languages. This portable, easy-reference library includes:

- **MICROSOFT VISUAL BASIC 6.0 LANGUAGE REFERENCE**

  A–Z compilation of Visual Basic objects, functions, statements, methods, properties, and events

- **MICROSOFT VISUAL BASIC 6.0 CONTROLS REFERENCE**

  A complete alphabetic listing of the ActiveX® controls within Visual Basic, along with relevant properties, events, and methods

- **MICROSOFT VISUAL BASIC 6.0 COMPONENT TOOLS GUIDE**

  Covers every tool from add-ins and Dynamic Link Libraries (DLLs) to ActiveX components

Must-have tools for the Visual Basic programmer!

## *Microsoft*®
**mspress.microsoft.com**

# Your low-cost,
## one-stop solution for
# learning Visual C++ 6.0

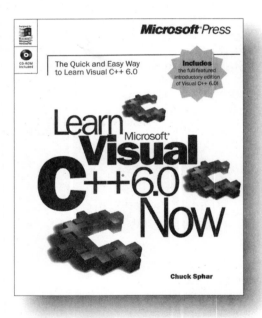

Learn programming with the Microsoft Windows® operating system the smart way with LEARN MICROSOFT® VISUAL C++® 6.0 NOW. If you have previous programming experience, you can quickly move your skills to the Visual C++ development system with this comprehensive introduction to version 6.0. Learn how to use the Microsoft Foundation Classes (MFC) to build Win32®-based applications. You'll hone your MFC programming skills through a series of hands-on lessons and sample programs. The more you work with the code, the greater your fluency!

| | |
|---|---|
| **U.S.A.** | **$49.99** |
| U.K. | £46.99 [V.A.T. included] |
| Canada | $74.99 |
| ISBN 1-57231-965-8 | |

**Microsoft**®

mspress.microsoft.com

# MICROSOFT LICENSE AGREEMENT
Book Companion CD

**IMPORTANT—READ CAREFULLY:** This Microsoft End-User License Agreement ("EULA") is a legal agreement between you (either an individual or an entity) and Microsoft Corporation for the Microsoft product identified above, which includes computer software and may include associated media, printed materials, and "online" or electronic documentation ("SOFTWARE PROD-UCT"). Any component included within the SOFTWARE PRODUCT that is accompanied by a separate End-User License Agreement shall be governed by such agreement and not the terms set forth below. By installing, copying, or otherwise using the SOFTWARE PRODUCT, you agree to be bound by the terms of this EULA. If you do not agree to the terms of this EULA, you are not authorized to install, copy, or otherwise use the SOFTWARE PRODUCT; you may, however, return the SOFTWARE PROD-UCT, along with all printed materials and other items that form a part of the Microsoft product that includes the SOFTWARE PRODUCT, to the place you obtained them for a full refund.

## SOFTWARE PRODUCT LICENSE

The SOFTWARE PRODUCT is protected by United States copyright laws and international copyright treaties, as well as other intellectual property laws and treaties. The SOFTWARE PRODUCT is licensed, not sold.

1. **GRANT OF LICENSE.** This EULA grants you the following rights:

   a. **Software Product.** You may install and use one copy of the SOFTWARE PRODUCT on a single computer. The primary user of the computer on which the SOFTWARE PRODUCT is installed may make a second copy for his or her exclusive use on a portable computer.

   b. **Storage/Network Use.** You may also store or install a copy of the SOFTWARE PRODUCT on a storage device, such as a network server, used only to install or run the SOFTWARE PRODUCT on your other computers over an internal network; however, you must acquire and dedicate a license for each separate computer on which the SOFTWARE PRODUCT is installed or run from the storage device. A license for the SOFTWARE PRODUCT may not be shared or used concurrently on different computers.

   c. **License Pak.** If you have acquired this EULA in a Microsoft License Pak, you may make the number of additional copies of the computer software portion of the SOFTWARE PRODUCT authorized on the printed copy of this EULA, and you may use each copy in the manner specified above. You are also entitled to make a corresponding number of secondary copies for portable computer use as specified above.

   d. **Sample Code.** Solely with respect to portions, if any, of the SOFTWARE PRODUCT that are identified within the SOFT-WARE PRODUCT as sample code (the "SAMPLE CODE"):

      i. **Use and Modification.** Microsoft grants you the right to use and modify the source code version of the SAMPLE CODE, *provided* you comply with subsection (d)(iii) below. You may not distribute the SAMPLE CODE, or any modified version of the SAMPLE CODE, in source code form.

      ii. **Redistributable Files.** Provided you comply with subsection (d)(iii) below, Microsoft grants you a nonexclusive, royalty-free right to reproduce and distribute the object code version of the SAMPLE CODE and of any modified SAMPLE CODE, other than SAMPLE CODE, or any modified version thereof, designated as not redistributable in the Readme file that forms a part of the SOFTWARE PRODUCT (the "Non-Redistributable Sample Code"). All SAMPLE CODE other than the Non-Redistributable Sample Code is collectively referred to as the "REDISTRIBUTABLES."

      iii. **Redistribution Requirements.** If you redistribute the REDISTRIBUTABLES, you agree to: (i) distribute the REDISTRIBUTABLES in object code form only in conjunction with and as a part of your software application product; (ii) not use Microsoft's name, logo, or trademarks to market your software application product; (iii) include a valid copyright notice on your software application product; (iv) indemnify, hold harmless, and defend Microsoft from and against any claims or lawsuits, including attorney's fees, that arise or result from the use or distribution of your software application product; and (v) not permit further distribution of the REDISTRIBUTABLES by your end user. Contact Microsoft for the applicable royalties due and other licensing terms for all other uses and/or distribution of the REDISTRIBUTABLES.

2. **DESCRIPTION OF OTHER RIGHTS AND LIMITATIONS.**

   - **Limitations on Reverse Engineering, Decompilation, and Disassembly.** You may not reverse engineer, decompile, or disassemble the SOFTWARE PRODUCT, except and only to the extent that such activity is expressly permitted by applicable law notwithstanding this limitation.

   - **Separation of Components.** The SOFTWARE PRODUCT is licensed as a single product. Its component parts may not be separated for use on more than one computer.

   - **Rental.** You may not rent, lease, or lend the SOFTWARE PRODUCT.

   - **Support Services.** Microsoft may, but is not obligated to, provide you with support services related to the SOFTWARE PRODUCT ("Support Services"). Use of Support Services is governed by the Microsoft policies and programs described in the user manual, in "online" documentation, and/or other Microsoft-provided materials. Any supplemental software code provided to you as part of the Support Services shall be considered part of the SOFTWARE PRODUCT and subject to the terms and conditions of this EULA. With respect to technical information you provide to Microsoft as part of the Support Services, Microsoft may use such information for its business purposes, including for product support and development. Microsoft will not utilize such technical information in a form that personally identifies you.

- **Software Transfer.** You may permanently transfer all of your rights under this EULA, provided you retain no copies, you transfer all of the SOFTWARE PRODUCT (including all component parts, the media and printed materials, any upgrades, this EULA, and, if applicable, the Certificate of Authenticity), **and** the recipient agrees to the terms of this EULA.

- **Termination.** Without prejudice to any other rights, Microsoft may terminate this EULA if you fail to comply with the terms and conditions of this EULA. In such event, you must destroy all copies of the SOFTWARE PRODUCT and all of its component parts.

3. **COPYRIGHT.** All title and copyrights in and to the SOFTWARE PRODUCT (including but not limited to any images, photographs, animations, video, audio, music, text, SAMPLE CODE, REDISTRIBUTABLES, and "applets" incorporated into the SOFTWARE PRODUCT) and any copies of the SOFTWARE PRODUCT are owned by Microsoft or its suppliers. The SOFTWARE PRODUCT is protected by copyright laws and international treaty provisions. Therefore, you must treat the SOFTWARE PRODUCT like any other copyrighted material **except** that you may install the SOFTWARE PRODUCT on a single computer provided you keep the original solely for backup or archival purposes. You may not copy the printed materials accompanying the SOFTWARE PRODUCT.

4. **U.S. GOVERNMENT RESTRICTED RIGHTS.** The SOFTWARE PRODUCT and documentation are provided with RESTRICTED RIGHTS. Use, duplication, or disclosure by the Government is subject to restrictions as set forth in subparagraph (c)(1)(ii) of the Rights in Technical Data and Computer Software clause at DFARS 252.227-7013 or subparagraphs (c)(1) and (2) of the Commercial Computer Software—Restricted Rights at 48 CFR 52.227-19, as applicable. Manufacturer is Microsoft Corporation/One Microsoft Way/Redmond, WA 98052-6399.

5. **EXPORT RESTRICTIONS.** You agree that you will not export or re-export the SOFTWARE PRODUCT, any part thereof, or any process or service that is the direct product of the SOFTWARE PRODUCT (the foregoing collectively referred to as the "Restricted Components"), to any country, person, entity, or end user subject to U.S. export restrictions. You specifically agree not to export or re-export any of the Restricted Components (i) to any country to which the U.S. has embargoed or restricted the export of goods or services, which currently include, but are not necessarily limited to, Cuba, Iran, Iraq, Libya, North Korea, Sudan, and Syria, or to any national of any such country, wherever located, who intends to transmit or transport the Restricted Components back to such country; (ii) to any end user who you know or have reason to know will utilize the Restricted Components in the design, development, or production of nuclear, chemical, or biological weapons; or (iii) to any end user who has been prohibited from participating in U.S. export transactions by any federal agency of the U.S. government. You warrant and represent that neither the BXA nor any other U.S. federal agency has suspended, revoked, or denied your export privileges.

---

## DISCLAIMER OF WARRANTY

**NO WARRANTIES OR CONDITIONS.** MICROSOFT EXPRESSLY DISCLAIMS ANY WARRANTY OR CONDITION FOR THE SOFTWARE PRODUCT. THE SOFTWARE PRODUCT AND ANY RELATED DOCUMENTATION ARE PROVIDED "AS IS" WITHOUT WARRANTY OR CONDITION OF ANY KIND, EITHER EXPRESS OR IMPLIED, INCLUDING, WITHOUT LIMITATION, THE IMPLIED WARRANTIES OF MERCHANTABILITY, FITNESS FOR A PARTICULAR PURPOSE, OR NONINFRINGEMENT. THE ENTIRE RISK ARISING OUT OF USE OR PERFORMANCE OF THE SOFTWARE PRODUCT REMAINS WITH YOU.

**LIMITATION OF LIABILITY.** TO THE MAXIMUM EXTENT PERMITTED BY APPLICABLE LAW, IN NO EVENT SHALL MICROSOFT OR ITS SUPPLIERS BE LIABLE FOR ANY SPECIAL, INCIDENTAL, INDIRECT, OR CONSEQUENTIAL DAMAGES WHATSOEVER (INCLUDING, WITHOUT LIMITATION, DAMAGES FOR LOSS OF BUSINESS PROFITS, BUSINESS INTERRUPTION, LOSS OF BUSINESS INFORMATION, OR ANY OTHER PECUNIARY LOSS) ARISING OUT OF THE USE OF OR INABILITY TO USE THE SOFTWARE PRODUCT OR THE PROVISION OF OR FAILURE TO PROVIDE SUPPORT SERVICES, EVEN IF MICROSOFT HAS BEEN ADVISED OF THE POSSIBILITY OF SUCH DAMAGES. IN ANY CASE, MICROSOFT'S ENTIRE LIABILITY UNDER ANY PROVISION OF THIS EULA SHALL BE LIMITED TO THE GREATER OF THE AMOUNT ACTUALLY PAID BY YOU FOR THE SOFTWARE PRODUCT OR US$5.00; PROVIDED, HOWEVER, IF YOU HAVE ENTERED INTO A MICROSOFT SUPPORT SERVICES AGREEMENT, MICROSOFT'S ENTIRE LIABILITY REGARDING SUPPORT SERVICES SHALL BE GOVERNED BY THE TERMS OF THAT AGREEMENT. BECAUSE SOME STATES AND JURISDICTIONS DO NOT ALLOW THE EXCLUSION OR LIMITATION OF LIABILITY, THE ABOVE LIMITATION MAY NOT APPLY TO YOU.

---

## MISCELLANEOUS

This EULA is governed by the laws of the State of Washington USA, except and only to the extent that applicable law mandates governing law of a different jurisdiction.

Should you have any questions concerning this EULA, or if you desire to contact Microsoft for any reason, please contact the Microsoft subsidiary serving your country, or write: Microsoft Sales Information Center/One Microsoft Way/Redmond, WA 98052-6399.